AF324177

ONLINE TEACHING
in K–12

Models, Methods, and Best Practices
for Teachers and Administrators

Edited by

Sarah Bryans-Bongey & Kevin J. Graziano

Information Today, Inc.

Medford, New Jersey

First Printing, 2016

***Online Teaching in K–12: Models, Methods, and Best Practices
for Teachers and Administrators***

The contents of Chapter 11 were developed under a grant from the U.S. Department of Education (#H327U110011). However, said contents do not necessarily reflect the policies and opinions of the DOE or of any other Federal Government department and no government endorsement should be assumed.

Library of Congress Cataloging-in-Publication Data

Names: Bryans-Bongey, Sarah, 1956- editor of compilation. | Graziano, Kevin J. editor of compilation.
Title: Online teaching in K-12 : models, methods, and best practices for teachers and administrators / Sarah Bryans-Bongey and Kevin Graziano.
Description: Medford, New Jersey : Information today, 2016. | Includes bibliographical references and index.
Identifiers: LCCN 2016002982 | ISBN 9781573875271
Subjects: LCSH: Web-based instruction. | Internet in education. | Computer-assisted instruction. | Distance education.
Classification: LCC LB1044.87 .O55 2016 | DDC 371.33/44678—dc23
LC record available at http://lccn.loc.gov/2016002982

Printed and bound in the United States of America

President and CEO: Thomas H. Hogan, Sr.
Editor-in-Chief and Publisher: John B. Bryans
Project Editor: Randall McClure
Production Manager: Tiffany Chamenko
Marketing Coordinator: Rob Colding
Indexer: Nan Badgett

Interior Design by Amnet Systems
Cover Design by Denise M. Erickson

infotoday.com

Contents

PART 1   FOUNDATIONS

PART 3   IMPLEMENTATION STRATEGIES

TABLES AND FIGURES

Tables

Figures

Foreword

Norman Vaughan

The number of K–12 students participating in online courses and programs continues to increase in the United States (Hanover Research 2013). The *Keeping Pace with K–12 Digital Learning: An Annual Review of Policy and Practice Report for 2014* indicates that 30 U.S. states now have fully online schools, and 316,320 students across the country attended these schools in SY 2013–2014, which represents an annual year-to-year increase of 6.2 percent (Watson et al. 2014, p. 5). With this steady rise in the number of K–12 online students, concerns have been raised about the quality of this educational experience. What theoretical and conceptual frameworks should be used to guide a successful online learning experience for K–12 students? How can an ever-increasing diversity of K–12 students be meaningfully engaged and supported in this educational environment? What are the best practices and educational strategies for implementing an online K–12 course or program?

The book *Online Teaching in K–12: Models, Methods, and Best Practices for Teachers and Administrators* addresses these questions and issues head-on. With regards to theoretical frameworks, this book begins with a Foundations section that clearly describes the collaborative-constructivist learning theory that forms the bedrock of a successful online educational experience. From this perspective, a student, in collaboration with a community of learners, takes responsibility to construct and confirm his/her own knowledge (Vaughan et al. 2013). Based on this approach to learning, the book then provides three conceptual frameworks for designing, facilitating, and directing an online course. These include the community of inquiry (CoI), technological pedagogical content knowledge (TPACK), and substitution, augmentation, modification, and redefinition (SAMR) models.

The CoI theoretical framework (Garrison 2011; Garrison et al. 2001) has been instrumental in helping researchers create and sustain collaborative learning communities in the online setting. This is the first framework developed specifically for the online instructional environment, and there is a growing body of research attesting to its value in guiding the design and implementation of blended and fully online courses that engage and retain students.

Punya Mishra and Matthew J. Koehler's (2007) TPACK model was specifically created as a *blueprint* for integrating technology in K–12 education using a constructivist approach. Another conceptual framework that was developed for K–12 education based on a constructivist approach to learning is the SAMR model (Puentedura 2015). This framework has the potential to act as a catalyst for transforming an online K–12 educational experience by redefining and creating educational tasks and experiences through the use of computer-based technologies.

The second part of the book addresses the question and concern of how to meaningfully engage and support diverse student learning needs in an online course or program. In the K–12 context, this support begins by developing a strong collaborative partnership with parents of online students. It also involves the application of universal design for learning (UDL) principles. The concept of UDL is related to the idea of universal design (UD), which is an architectural concept involving design of physical accessibility for all. Assistive technologies (ATs) such as voice-to-text computer applications can be used to effectively support a UDL approach in an online K–12 course or program.

The third part of the book focuses on implementation strategies that move online K–12 courses and programs from simply delivering content to enabling students to develop metacognitive strategies in order to *learn how to learn*. Mitchell Kapor (2015) states that "getting information off the Internet is like taking a drink from a fire hydrant." The challenge for online teachers is to focus on educational strategies that effectively make use of this global storehouse of digital content to support student learning. Strategies that are based on a constructivist approach to learning and involve inquiry and project-based activities can help students learn how to solve problems and become critical consumers of internet-based resources. For example, the Stanford mobile inquiry-based learning environment (SMILE; Seol et al. 2011) makes use of mobile devices for collaboration and creativity by tailoring digital content and problem-solving activities to local issues and customs. In addition, assessment strategies should be designed that focus on assessment *for learning* rather than *of learning*. Assessment in a K–12 online context can take on a triad approach where students are receiving feedback from not only teachers, but also external experts, their peers, and, most importantly, themselves (Vaughan 2015).

Online Teaching in K–12: Models, Methods, and Best Practices for Teachers and Administrators will serve as a key resource for teachers, schools, districts, and states desiring to design, facilitate, and direct online courses and programs that engage and empower K–12 students.

References

Garrison, D. Randy. *E-Learning in the 21st Century: A Framework for Research and Practice.* 2nd ed. London: Routledge, 2011.

Garrison, D. Randy, Terry Anderson, and Walter Archer. "Critical Thinking, Cognitive Presence, and Computer Conferencing in Distance Education." *American Journal of Distance Education* 15, no. 1 (2001): 17-23.

Hanover Research. "Future Trends in K to 12 Education," 2013. https://ts.madison .k12.wi.us/files/techsvc/Future%20Trends%20in%20K–12 %20Education.pdf.

Kapor, Mitchell. BrainyQuote.com, 2005. http://www.brainyquote.com/quotes/quotes /m/mitchellka163583.html.

Mishra, Punya, and Matthew J. Koehler. "Technological, Pedagogical Content Knowledge (TPACK): Confronting the Wicked Problems of Teaching with Technology." In *Society for Information Technology & Teacher Education International Conference* 2007, no. 1 (2007): 2214-26.

Puentedura, Ruben R. "SAMR: Approaches to Implementation," 2015. http://hippasus .com/rrpweblog/archives/2015/04/SAMR_ApproachesToImplementation.pdf.

Seol, Sunmi, Aaron Sharp, and Paul Kim. "Stanford Mobile Inquiry-Based Learning Environment (SMILE): Using Mobile Phones to Promote Student Inquires in the Elementary Classroom." In *Proceedings of the 2011 World Congress in Computer Science, Computer Engineering, and Applied Computing*, 2011.

Vaughan, Norman D. "Student Assessment in a Blended Learning Environment: A Triad Approach. In *Assessment in Online and Blended Learning Environments*, ed. S. Koc, P. Wachira, and X. Liu. Charlotte, NC: Information Age Publishing, 2015.

Vaughan, Norman D., Marti Cleveland-Innes, and D. Randy Garrison. *Teaching in Blended Learning Environments: Creating and Sustaining Communities of Inquiry.* Athabasca, Alberta, Canada: Athabasca University Press, 2013.

Watson, John, Larry Pape, Amy Murin, Butch Gemin, and Lauren Vashaw. *Keeping Pace with K–12 Digital Online Learning.* Durango, CO: Evergreen Education Group, 2014.

Acknowledgments

In bringing together the insights and experiences of more than two dozen experts and practitioners, *Online Teaching in K–12* represents a significant contribution to the field of online teaching in K–12. We are grateful to all our contributing authors, including foreword author Norman Vaughan, for sharing their expertise. The book would not have been possible without them.

We would also like to thank Information Today, Inc., and specifically Editor-in-Chief and Publisher John B. Bryans, who provided outstanding guidance and support throughout the project.

Our thanks also go to Randall McClure and Pat Greenwood for their excellent attention to detail during the editorial process.

Finally, we would like to thank our families, colleagues, and students for inspiring our work.

Introduction

The landscape of K–12 education has changed dramatically in recent decades. Our education system today is seeking to adapt and respond to the demands of a shifting economy as well as the changing structure and demographics of the U.S. family. Emerging technologies are the norm, and the demands to prepare citizens for college and careers continue to be emphasized in the context of standards-based learning.

While we know many students will need to fill roles and careers that do not yet exist, we also know that citizens of all ages will need to constantly learn and retrain themselves for new opportunities and careers that reflect our changing world. This suggests that not only do schools need to prepare students for jobs and college admission and tests as we know them, but that they also need to develop and reinforce skills in collaborating, problem solving, evaluating information, adapting, and innovating. While some of our online learners may initially seem more adept at these roles than others, practical online experiences are essential for students' long-term success in school and after graduation.

Online programs first became popular in higher education, continuing education, and professional development settings. However, blended and fully online courses and programs have now taken hold in K–12 education. Teachers and administrators who may have extensive education and background in face-to-face (f2f) classrooms and schools are now expected to lead and succeed in this new environment. Meanwhile, teacher preparation programs are realizing that online pedagogy comes with its own set of challenges and opportunities. For K–12 teachers to excel in an online setting, there is a learning curve in which new skills are emphasized, and it is not enough to be an outstanding teacher in the f2f classroom alone.

The emergence of professional learning communities and organizations gives testimony to the fact that online programs provide significant opportunities in K–12 education. The Online Learning Consortium (OLC) started out as the Sloan Consortium (Sloan-C) in 1992. Its grant programs and advocacy fueled the early development of blended and online learning in American higher education, and it is now a worldwide organization dedicated to providing access, advancing online learning, and supporting institutions, individuals, professional societies, and corporations.

Beginning in 2003, the North American Council for Online Learning (NACOL) drew worldwide attention that caused it to expand internationally. In 2008, NACOL evolved to become iNACOL—the International Association for K–12 Online Learning. iNACOL continues to be an active force in online education, as it is dedicated to supporting K–12 quality online and blended programs and practitioners at all grade levels. iNACOL not only brings together a professional community for teachers, but also unites a professional community for school counselors and school administrators.

Likewise, the International Society for Technology in Education (ISTE) hosts a popular and highly valued Online Learning Network dedicated to supporting a professional community of K–12 teachers. The rapid growth of online programs and their appeal to practitioners mean that organizations and other support structures and resources are needed. Professional K–12 teachers are seeking support that will allow them to develop and sustain exceptional online experiences to meet evolving needs of the 21st century learner. This book is dedicated to promoting that goal.

While one might be tempted to view K–12 online programs and schools as discrete and alternative forms of teaching and learning, it is more realistic to view such programs and schools as part of a larger and changing system that is redefining education today. K–12 online programs and schools have become drivers of change. Educational policy and philosophy are also in a state of transition as the changing landscape requires educational leaders to articulate concepts such as the greater role of education and the need to prepare students for collaboration and innovation as well as for success on proficiency tests. With a range of online programs and administrators expressing different goals and values of education, the manner in which online programs and schools continue to develop, grow, and evaluate their own effectiveness could have far-reaching implications on how public education and schools will evolve in the future.

Course quality, the level of personalization, communication options and processes, student interactions, and the types of learning experiences themselves can vary widely from one online program or course to the next, and such programs and courses can be driven by dramatically different and incompatible policies or philosophies of what an online course of study or online program can and should look like.

In their quests to design programs and experiences that are optimal for online learners, teachers and administrators may ask themselves the following questions: Do K–12 online students need or want personal interactions with peers and/or with adults? Are such interactions important, and do they serve a role in a democratic online classroom? What level of freedom should an online teacher have to teach the required content in a creative and authentic way? Is it possible for online teachers to be effective when they host their first class in the virtual environment of the learning management system (LMS)? What kind of preparation do teachers need to teach online? How can new online teachers gain a vision of what creative and effective online courses look like? Are teachers and administrators excited about the potential for a new online format and how it might be used to promote student success? If not, what could this mean for our students and our emerging educational system? How can administrators of online programs stay informed and support teachers, staff, students, and families? What are other experienced online teachers and researchers discovering? This multi-authored book, *Online Teaching in K–12,* explores and helps to answer these and many other questions.

Divided into three parts, the first part of this book covers essential foundations, and delves into technical, pedagogical, and practical elements that form the basis for any successful online course or program. The second part of this book recognizes the diverse needs and skills of students and shares strategies for engaging and supporting diverse learners. The third and final part of this book emphasizes implementation strategies for teacher-created content, project-based learning, assessments, free and open resources, and mobile devices that expand the horizons of online teaching and learning.

Through the collective insights and expertise presented in *Online Teaching in K–12,* new and experienced online teachers and administrators alike have access to a hands-on resource that can expand their knowledge and skills and improve their success in this emerging and challenging environment.

Audience and Purpose

Online Teaching in K–12 is designed for anyone who seeks a role as a well-informed contributor and leader in the changing landscape of K–12 education. Online and mobile approaches to learning and communication are revolutionizing the form and nature of our educational systems in f2f and nontraditional settings. Gaps in understanding the availability, limitations, and evolving potential for these approaches lead to loss of authority, influence, and advocacy. This book is for those teachers and administrators who want and need to be successful in the design, delivery, and sustainability of K–12 online courses and programs. With the widespread growth of online teaching and learning at all levels of K–12 education, those needing *to know* include policymakers, program managers, principals, teachers, parents, and faculty members in teacher preparation programs across the country. Here, we have gathered the knowledge and experience of an outstanding team of contributing authors in order to highlight models, methods, and best practices pivotal to quality online programs. Our intent is to present a single volume that will serve as an essential resource for a range of interested stakeholders.

How to Use This book

Online Teaching in K–12 can be used to support teachers and administrators with on-demand essentials, including key models and methods in online teaching and learning. It is also appropriate for use in professional development and teacher preparation programs, as its content includes practical information that can support and enhance the work of the busy professional seeking to get started with online formats or to take online teaching to the next level.

For leaders of K–12 educational policy as well as teachers and administrators in online programs and courses, this book shares expert knowledge, vision, and information designed to communicate capabilities of online programs and systems that may otherwise take time and experience for the uninitiated to discern. Without understanding the capacity of online infrastructures, programs, and methods, teachers and administrators coming into online education are at risk of confining themselves to that which is known, anticipated, or dictated as opposed to striving for the best of what is currently or potentially possible.

Readers may wish to read the chapters in the context of each part or to refer to them as specific questions or needs arise. The index provides a useful launching point from which to locate information on a specific topic of interest. In addition, readers will find a glossary of abbreviations and acronyms, and an *About the Contributors* section to learn about the various contributors. The chapters themselves include a wealth of practical strategies and examples, along with pointers to dozens of online resources including free and low-cost teaching, management, and communications tools.

About the Chapters

Written by experts and practitioners in the field, this book's chapters are organized within three parts: (1) Foundations, (2) Supporting Diverse Learners, and (3) Implementation Strategies. This thematic organization aside, each chapter stands on its own in providing expert consultation on the topic at hand.

The seven chapters that comprise Part 1 present foundational information relating to systems and environments, the teacher-learner experience, models and standards, and training programs that prepare teachers and schools for success in online teaching and learning. In Chapter 1, "The Online Course Environment: Learning Management Systems (LMSs)," Xavier Gomez shares need-to-know information on the LMS—the central software and system used to support online teaching and learning.

Building upon Gomez's discussion of the technical infrastructure comes Chapter 2, "The Online Teacher: Skills and Qualities to be Successful" by Steven C. Moskowitz. The author describes unique communication demands and the human angle of what teachers need to know to succeed in an online course. His research on the dispositions and strategies used by successful online teachers provides useful advice and support.

While Chapter 2 emphasizes the changing demands and expanded role of the online teacher, Chapter 3 by Sarah Bryans-Bongey provides a vision to help teachers meet those demands. Entitled "Building Community in K–12 Online Courses: The Community of Inquiry (CoI)," the chapter shares specific suggestions as to how online teachers can use cognitive and social approaches to engage, satisfy, and retain online students.

Whereas the CoI model was developed specifically for online and blended learning, the next three chapters share more general or long-standing learning theories in the context of K–12 online classrooms. Written by Michael Kosloski and Diane Carver, Chapter 4, "Online Constructivism: Tools and Techniques for Student Engagement and Learning," provides teachers with guidance on how to maximize active and compelling constructivist approaches in the K–12 online setting.

Chapter 5—"TPACK as Mediated Practice"—describes a technology integration framework that builds upon earlier work by educational psychologist Lee Shulman. Authors Rolin Moe and Linda Polin share practical examples that allow teachers to apply the technological pedagogical content knowledge (TPACK) framework in the online course environment.

Another model that continues to guide teachers in the best practice integration of technology is substitution, augmentation, modification, and redefinition (SAMR). This model is described by Chery Takkunen-Lucarelli in Chapter 6, "Captivating the Online Learner: Frameworks and Standards for Effective Technology Integration." Here, readers explore the SAMR model, discover key standards, and plan effective and engaging technology integration in online teaching and learning.

Chapter 7 is entitled "Online Student Teaching: From Planning to Implementation." Written by Lori Feher and Kevin J. Graziano, the chapter concludes the Foundations section by covering an essential human resource issue in K–12 online programs: the readiness and training of pre-service teachers to skillfully educate the online student. Feher and Graziano describe the overall status of online student teaching, and they share preliminary research on how one college is addressing this need.

Students in online programs represent diverse backgrounds, interests, and needs. Given the entirely new setting of the online environment, schools need to rethink traditional programs, services, and environments and find ways to support the new generation of K–12 online learners. Part 2, Supporting Diverse Learners, aims to survey resources and strategies that allow educators to support, engage, and motivate learners. Chapter 8, "Flipped Learning: Making the Connections and Finding the Balance," discusses the flipped classroom as a research-based gateway to online teaching and learning. Written by Kevin J. Graziano, the chapter helps f2f teachers understand and get started with online approaches through the use of flipped learning. Graziano shares significant data on the model's success, and explains how this web-enhanced approach can support a wide range of students.

Chapters 9 and 10 delve more deeply into the realm of online teaching and learning, and, as with Chapter 8, these chapters provide strategies that capitalize on web-based and asynchronous approaches as well as the use of multimedia to help students comprehend, revisit, or retain information.

In Chapter 9, "Virtual School-Home Communication," experienced K–12 online teacher Dianne Tetreault shares success strategies to establish and maintain communication between and among teachers, learners, parents, and coaches. As with the varied tools and approaches described in connection with Graziano's flipped classroom, Tetreault discusses the creative use of asynchronous, synchronous, and even social media communication tools to support the home–school connection for the online classroom.

Chapter 10, by Luis Pérez, Kendra Grant, and Elizabeth Dalton, is entitled "Universal Design for Learning (UDL) and Online Learning." The authors describe a multifaceted approach that involves varied representation of content, numerous options for student action and expression, and choices that encourage student engagement. By making the most of rich opportunities within the online environment and available multimedia web tools that can serve as a resource or an outlet for expression, the chapter describes an approach geared to bolstering the success of diverse learners.

While UDL aims to support a wide range of learners, it does not totally eliminate the need for support from special educators and/or the use of assistive technology (AT). Chapters 11 and 12 complete the second part of this book on support for diverse learners by covering those essential topics.

Chapter 11, by Richard Allen Carter, Jr., James D. Basham, and Mary Frances Rice, is entitled "Helping Special Education Teachers Transition to K–12 Online Learning." The chapter shares important information that can be used by special education teachers and principals seeking direct and indirect approaches to supporting the significant population of K–12 online students with special needs.

As is the case with the need for special education teachers, AT can be a key component in a K–12 student's ability to participate in an online program. In Chapter 12, "Assistive Technology in the 21st Century Online Classroom," Jacqueline Knight defines assistive technology and provides a wealth of information and resources relating to AT's unique use in the online setting.

Taken together, the chapters in Part 2 provide approaches to anticipate and address the needs of diverse learners. These chapters explore the use of flipped learning, AT, universal design, and promote the use of services, methods, and tools that are conducive to student learning and success.

In the third and final part of this book, Implementation Strategies, five chapters delve into implementation strategies that describe teacher-created content, student-centered and project-based learning, the curation of free and open educational resources, assessment challenges and solutions, and mobile learning approaches. Contributing authors round out earlier sections on foundations and diverse learners with a range of approaches for implementing online teaching and learning.

Chapter 13 covers "Teacher-Created Online Content: Two Teachers' Tech Tales." Here, Chris Rozitis, a secondary online teacher, and Heidi Weber, an elementary teacher, collaborate to share tried-and-true content strategies that are relevant to online teachers and learners across all grade levels. Their collective wisdom emphasizes strategies teachers can use to build content for students at all grade levels.

Next, Chapter 14 provides additional ideas and approaches to guide online teachers in their quest to help students learn. In "Student-Centered Digital Learning Through Project-Based Learning," Andrew Miller shares ideas, considerations, and procedures needed to create and facilitate an authentic project-based learning experience for students in the online environment.

Throughout various chapters of this book, authors have reflected and shared their own online teaching experiences, favorite websites, tools, and resources. Chapter 15, "Open and Free Educational Resources for K–12 Online and Face-to-Face Classrooms," provides readers with starting points that will allow them to locate useful multimedia resources that supplement and enrich the teaching and learning process. As experts in the creation of a specialized form of multimedia teaching tool, authors John Elwood Romig, Wendy Rodgers, Kat Alves, and Michael J. Kennedy also share research and how-to information needed for teachers to create and contribute their own content to the growing database of open educational resources (OERs).

Following on the heels of the three previous chapters that emphasize content creation, student-centered learning, and content curation, Chapter 16 provides important information on how such content and project-based approaches can be assessed in the online environment. Written by Kim Livengood and Lesley Casarez, "Tools and Strategies for Assessment in an Online Environment" discusses various types of assessments, free and low-cost tools for implementation, and industry standards that influence technology integration and online learning. By sharing tools to support the essential role of assessment, this chapter supports information provided elsewhere in this section on implementation strategies.

Chapter 17 imagines the possibilities of "Mobile Apps and Technology Integration for Virtual and Hybrid Learning Spaces." Author Gregory Shepherd explores exciting ways by which mobile learning (M-learning) can enhance and enrich the online course experience and sharing of ideas, information, and resources to allow teachers to implement M-learning. This final chapter of Part 3 on implementing the teaching and learning process recognizes that online learning does not simply take place in front of a computer. Exciting opportunities exist for students to research, collaborate, discover, document, learn, and even teach in the larger community and environment. The final chapters of this book as a whole are dedicated to helping teachers and administrators rethink the possible and tap the vast potential of the online format.

Why You Need This Book

Based on prolific growth of K–12 online programs, data suggest an immediate and widespread need to design and implement online courses and programs. *Online Teaching Methods in K–12* is intended for preservice teachers who are just learning about online teaching as well as for in-service teachers who may need to transform their classroom from an f2f to online or blended format and need ideas, resources, or assistance to get started. Those already working in online programs as teachers or administrators will also find value in this book.

The demand is expanding for online programs and courses that meet the needs of learners who may be in high school, middle school, or elementary school. This book is dedicated to supporting those with a vision and ambition to become expert teachers, facilitators, and leaders, including those who are being called upon to develop (or quickly adapt) to fully online formats. It provides practical and easy access to essential foundations, differentiation and support strategies, and effective approaches to implementing successful online programs and courses.

Written by 28 experts and practitioners, *Online Teaching in K–12: Models, Methods, and Best Practices for Teachers and Administrators* is here to support teachers and administrators with creative, research-based, and expert information on the wide-ranging aspects of online teaching and learning.

Teachers today are faced with a changing landscape and constant demands on their time and creativity. In face-to-face situations, it is often enough for an experienced teacher to rely on his or her background knowledge and ability to make a lesson engaging and effective. Likewise, principals and other school administrators can often move from one brick-and-mortar setting to the next with ease. However, the online setting requires an entirely new set of skills and experience and brings with it great opportunities along with challenges. We hope this book will support administrators and teachers in the quest to build, reinvent, and sustain dynamic and responsive schools of the 21st century.

PART 1

Foundations

The Online Course Environment: Learning Management Systems (LMSs)

Xavier Gomez

Abstract

A learning management system (LMS) is an essential component to online instruction and students' success online. At first glance, an LMS can be challenging, confounding the most web-savvy of teachers. Yet, despite the fact that LMSs are designed with the teacher in mind, understanding the powerful array of teaching tools and options requires an informative orientation. This chapter reviews major components found across most LMSs including module or lesson structure, content creation tools, quiz and assignment options, grading tools, discussion forums, and other communication functions. The versatility of each of these components can satisfy a variety of instructional needs. This chapter helps both new teachers and those with more experience understand and unlock the wide range of features that support the ability to teach, learn, and collaborate in a fully online environment.

Introduction

Mr. Martinez teaches a fifth grade dual language (English and Spanish) immersion class in the Mission District of San Francisco, California. Like most public school teachers, Mr. Martinez's reality as a teacher extends beyond the learning theories, teaching methods, assessment instruments, and all the practices he honed through his teacher accreditation courses.

In reality, Mr. Martinez's responsibilities extend beyond the simple and noble act of helping children to develop intellectually, succeed at their tasks, and eventually graduate to the sixth grade. Mr. Martinez is also accountable to a number of interests that depend on him to do his job and to keep them informed of every lesson assigned, milestone met, and standard achieved.

He is accountable to the parents or guardians of the students he teaches. He must maintain ongoing communication, advising parents of their child's performance, upcoming events, new lessons, and any other information relevant to the student's experience in the classroom. This, at times, may be a challenge given that the majority of his students are from working class immigrant Latino families—families who have varying degrees of financial resources and may be conditionally restricted from taking an active role in their children's education.

Given that some of the curriculum is based on the common core state standards, Mr. Martinez is also accountable to the California Department of Education, the San Francisco Unified School District, and even the administration of the school in which he teaches. So, in addition to providing his students with a safe and welcoming environment, Mr. Martinez must also ensure that their performance meets state-mandated performance standards, which by extension may become a measure of his own teaching effectiveness. In addition to being accountable to students, parents, and administrators, he must also be careful to observe student privacy and remain a safe distance from overstepping Family Educational Rights and Privacy Act (FERPA) guidelines.

Teachers have been teaching for years without the help of digital technology, so it is not as if Mr. Martinez could not do his job without the latest gadget or *edtech app*. For example, he could keep hard copies of all submitted student assignments to justify student grades when called upon to do so. He could print newsletters for his students hoping that they would not lose them on the way home and pass them on to their parents. He could keep detailed spreadsheets of student performance based on rubrics gleaned from Common Core resources as a measure of his instructional abilities. He could do all of these things in his afterschool administrative time if he wanted to, but the question is, does he *need* to? In the digital age, there seems to be an app for everything; and for a situation like this, there is definitely an "app for that," and it is called a *learning management system* (LMS).

Terminology

The term LMS has become the vernacular for any "software on which the online portion of any partially or fully virtual course is delivered, documented, and reported" (Quillen 2012, p. 2). From the perspective of LMS vendors, the type of system used requires more specific terminology. For example, according to Don McIntosh (2015) in his article "Vendors of Learning Management and eLearning Products," the specific terminology used to describe LMSs in education is *learning management system* (p. 3). However, in this chapter, I use the vernacular terminology and refer to education LMSs simply as LMSs. Additionally, although I use generic terms that describe specific LMS functionality, that functionality will have different names under different vendors. It is important to keep in mind that, despite the generic titles I use, the functionality is roughly the same.

LMS—a Tool Kit for the Online Learning Environment

As a teacher, you may not always have a choice in the LMS you use, as your administration will typically adopt one for the entire institution. However, if you do have that choice, you must consider that adopting the appropriate LMS depends on understanding what each one offers, the differences between systems, and how to select the right solution to meet your needs.

Despite many of the LMS product offerings that exist today, there are only about four serious contenders in K–12 and higher education: Blackboard, Desire2Learn, Moodle, and Instructure Canvas (McIntosh 2015, p. 4). Any of these LMSs will satisfy most instructional needs, from acting as simple file repositories to designing lessons aligned with regulatory standards and running advanced learning analytics. When choosing an LMS, understanding the functionality will help in making the most informed decision.

LMS functionality and the attendant features are structured according to the following categories:

- navigation
- content creation
- communication
- collaboration and social learning tools
- assessments

- grading
- user management
- administrative abilities

While learning about LMSs and researching the different products, it is helpful to keep in mind that every LMS provider strives to solve a specific set of instructional problems, and while one may not solve every problem, you will most likely find one that comes close to solving yours.

Navigating Your LMS

LMS navigation is fairly standard between products. If teachers are familiar with most online applications such as banking, shopping or ecommerce, or social networking portals, they will immediately recognize the LMS interface. Like most online applications, the first page that will appear upon logging in is the application dashboard.

Dashboards

As with any web application, dashboards vary from product to product, and their contents will differ depending on the user's role and permissions. For teachers, a dashboard may display a list of all the courses they are teaching. It may have notifications of tasks that need to be completed, emails to answer, and assignments to grade. For students, the dashboard could display looming assignment due dates, teacher announcements, or notifications that assignments have been reviewed and graded or discussion forum posts answered. In short, the dashboard is a high level overview of your online experience.

Global Navigation and Interface

When opening a course within your LMS, you will notice an interface that will be standard from course to course. Your course will be structured into major areas, some of which are customizable. Figure 1.1 outlines the LMS interface: the course navigation panel, global navigation menu, and the content area.

Course Navigation Panel

The course navigation panel is the central navigation for your course. Placement of the navigation panel varies between products. Some products have their navigation panels situated to the left of the screen, while others situate the course navigation panel at the top of the screen. Despite where the

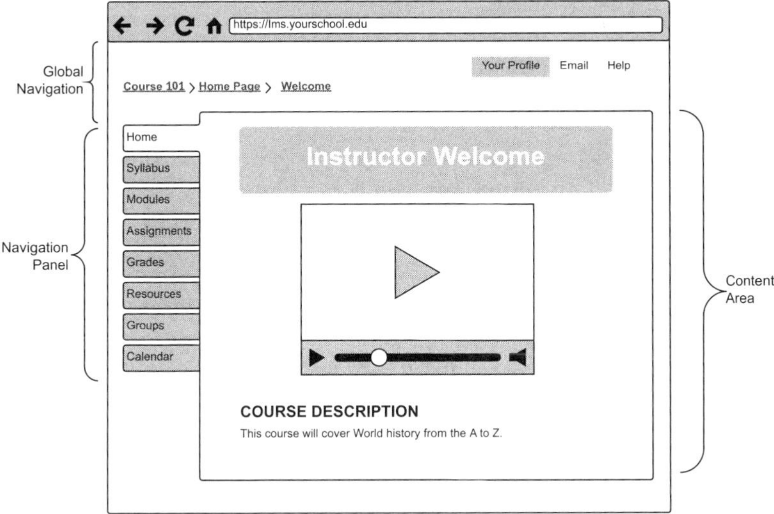

Figure 1.1   Wireframe of an LMS interface

course navigation panel sits, you use it to access common course elements such as the course home page, the syllabus, modules or lessons, assignments, quizzes, grades, course roster, collaboration spaces, and discussion forums.

Depending on the LMS, the navigation panel has some degree of customizability, which may present both benefits and pitfalls. One benefit of customizable navigation is that you have more control over the design of your course. A potential pitfall, however, is that the navigation panel could become unwieldy if you are not conservative with the amount of objects placed in the menu. Also, if students take several online courses, the navigation of online classes that allow such customization may tend to be less standard or predictable from one course to the next.

Content Area

Exactly as the name suggests, the content area is where your instructional materials appear. The content area works in tandem with the course navigation panel. Clicking a link in the navigation panel displays content in the content area. If you click the syllabus link, then the syllabus appears in the content area. If you click the discussions link, then a discussions list appears in the content area. If you click the modules or lessons link, then the module list appears in the content area. Think of the content areas as the container in which all of your instructional activities occur, as the content area is where you and your students spend most of your time designing and interacting in the course.

Global Navigation Menu

Global navigation refers to the immutable navigation links and menus that are hard-coded into the LMS architecture. In some instances, your institution's LMS administrator will customize the global navigation menu based on institutional requirements. Global navigation can include links to the dashboard, help files, or your own profile and account settings.

Get to Know Your LMS User Interface

LMSs are designed in such a way that they can dictate the student learning experience in a course. The LMS architecture forces a hierarchy of information that runs from left to right and from top to bottom. This is especially apparent when looking at module, assignment, and discussion lists. Before designing your course, familiarize yourself with the structure of the LMS and then design within the delivered functionality. Doing so allows your course to be consistent from lesson to lesson and module to module. Inconsistency within a course may be frustrating to students and may therefore impede the ease with which they access your instructional material and learn the content.

Lesson Design

Before we dive into the specifics of LMS functionality, let's pause for a moment to review lesson design within an LMS. First, let's start by making the assumption that if instruction could be formulated into a sequence of events, as described in *Principles of Instructional Design*, then a lesson would be designed according to the following nine steps:

1. gain attention
2. inform learners of objectives
3. stimulate recall of prior learning
4. present the content
5. provide learning guidance
6. elicit performance
7. provide feedback
8. assess performance
9. enhance retention and transfer (Gagné et al. 2005, p. 194–202)

So, how—you may ask—can this be achieved in an LMS? The answer is found in the module or unit functionality.

Consider that a module is like a container in which you can group various instructional items. Most likely, the items will be arranged linearly, much like Gagné et al.'s (2005) instructional events, and will flow from top to bottom. The type of instructional items and the sequence in which they are arranged in the module become the heart of lesson design as well as the architecture of the learning experience for your course. Later in the chapter, I go into further detail about the types of instructional objects or activities available through LMS functionality; however, a brief introduction is required to demonstrate LMS alignment with instructional best practices. A module designed with the *Nine Events of Instruction* in mind may be structured according to the matrix shown in Table 1.1.

Notice how *content page* in the right column is repeated several times throughout the module structure. As you can see, a single LMS function is flexible enough to provide solutions for various requirements

**Table 1.1   Matrix of Module Design Based on
*Nine Events of Instruction***

Module or Lesson Item or Event	Nine Events	LMS Functionality
Lesson introduction	Gain attention	Content page (rich-text editor)
Objectives statement	Inform learners of objectives	Content page (rich-text editor)
Review of previous lesson	Stimulate recall of prior learning	Content page (rich-text editor)
Present a lecture, reading or other content deliverable	Present the stimulus material	Content page with embedded or linked resources
Open an informal question and answer forum	Provide learning guidance	Discussion forum session
Post assignments	Elicit performance	Assignment, quiz, discussion,
Provide feedback on assignment	Provide feedback	email, chat, grade book
Provide assessment value	Assess performance	Grade book, rubric
Summarize key learning outcomes in the lesson	Enhance retention and transfer	Content page (rich-text editor)

in a lesson design. Again, the module or unit function is where you will design your lesson at a high level. However, before you can structure your course and lessons, you need to understand how to create content within the course.

Content Creation

As a teacher in the LMS environment, you are not just a content creator, you are a content curator. In an online course, content can be created, curated, and shared through the rich text editor, content or Wiki pages, Learning Tools Interoperability (LTI), and the LMS's file repository.

Rich-Text Editor

When creating content, whether it is a static page, an assignment, quiz, or discussion, you will always come across what is referred to as a *rich-text editor*. The rich-text editor allows you to write and format text-based content that can include anything from a lengthy text-based lecture, such as an essay, to simple instructional sets. The editor typically includes tools for formatting text similar to those found in word processor applications that allow you to customize character styles such as font family and type, font size and color along with line justification, line spacing, and background color. In some cases, the rich-text editor also has predefined styles for heading and paragraph text.

Additionally, most rich-text editors allow you to embed images, videos, audio files, tables, and hyperlinks. If you are hypertext markup language (HTML) savvy, then you will be happy to know that rich-text editors come with an HTML view that allows you to code your content on the back end, giving you more flexibility than what the formatting tools offer. Some teachers use this HTML mode if they want to incorporate a video or other content involving embedded code.

You can use rich-text editors to enhance your assignments as well. A discussion, for example, need not be a question and a set of instructions in plain text. You can create a more engaging discussion by embedding media and then asking students to discuss specific topics around the media piece. You can take a similar approach to creating quizzes, as some LMSs allow you to format the question area using the rich-text editor to create a more engaging experience for the student. Used correctly, the rich-text editor can help to create more dynamic and engaging content within the LMS.

Content Pages

Content page is a term that generally refers to a page created using a rich-text editor. Content pages can be customized to deliver any of the instructional objects discussed in the previous section, from text-based lectures to media-rich experiences. As shown in Table 1.1, a content page can serve many uses within the spectrum of course design. It is up to you as the course designer to determine how to use the content page and to determine how creative you would like to be within the confines of HTML code and embedded content.

When creating your content pages, I would like to caution you against copying content from other sources such as Microsoft Word documents and websites and pasting them into the content pages. Most likely, the code from those formats will be pasted in the document along with the text. Although you may not notice it initially, examining the page in HTML view will likely reveal reams of unsightly code. If you need to format the text, then the unwanted code will pose time-consuming complications. I have worked with many frustrated teachers who created pages this way and then spent several frustrating hours trying to remedy the problem. It is best to create the layout within the editor rather than copy from another source.

Learning Tools Interoperability (LTI)

LTI is a valuable asset to enhance the instructional ability of an LMS. It can be helpful to think of LTI tools as apps that you can add to your LMS, much like installing apps on your smartphone. For example, both YouTube LTI and Khan Academy LTI allow you to search their libraries and embed their videos directly into your course, without having to manually copy and paste the embedded code. LTIs expand the utility of the LMS and provide students with a richer interactive experience. LMSs typically provide a list of LTI tools that integrate with their product. When researching LTIs for your course, please review what is recommended by the LMS.

Third-Party Technologies

When designing your course, you may find yourself in situations in which there is no LMS tool or LTI that does exactly what you need. For example, collaboration tools in the LMS may not be flexible enough to provide real-time collaboration, whether through document editing or real-time interaction such as video conferencing. In situations like these, you may have to rely on popular, widely available technologies such as Google's host of collaboration tools. Google Docs' collaborative ability has made this product an ideal solution for educational activities. The presentation, word processing, and spreadsheet applications permit students to collaborate asynchronously as well as synchronously in content creation. Additionally, Google Drive's ability to store and share both Google Doc files and other file formats further underscores Google's value as an educational tool.

File Management

Like a cluttered desk, online courses can become an unwieldy repository of good intentions and great ideas. The file management and structuring capacity of the LMS is critical in organizing your instructional content. When creating your course, it is essential to properly organize all of your files within the course's file repository. A well-organized file repository will save you much time and energy when updating or redesigning your course.

If you are like most teachers, then chances are you have lesson plans, reading assignments, PDFs, images, media, and other file types that you have compiled over time. If you are linking or embedding files into your modules, then those files will be automatically placed into the file repository. In the file repository, you can then organize your files into folders and subfolders. When doing so, it is helpful to create a folder structure that is both meaningful and consistent. Let's presume, for example, that your course is composed of three subject areas, and, in turn, each subject area is composed of three lessons. In this situation, you should consider

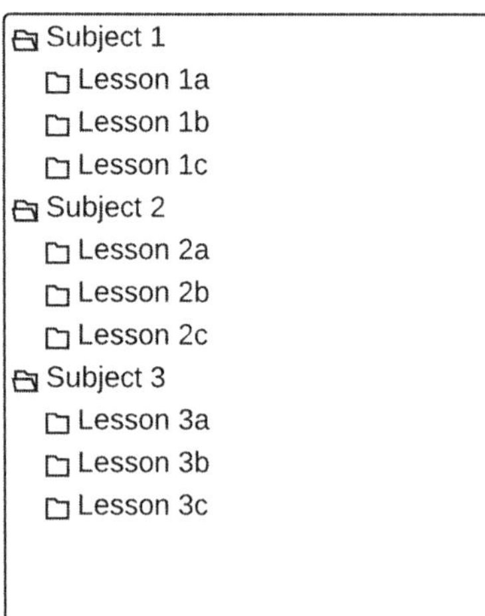

Figure 1.2 Example of an organized file structure

structuring your folders so as not to become overwhelmed when conducting a search or uploading a file. One possible approach would be to create three subject area folders, and within each folder create three lesson subfolders. Each of these lesson subfolders contains the instructional objects that pertain to that specific lesson and all of the attendant media and documents (see Figure 1.2). Again, a well-structured file system will save you time and energy in the future.

Communication

According to "The Rubric for Online Instruction" developed by Chico State University (2015), a hallmark of good online course design and best practice is a high level of *student-to-student* and *student-to-teacher* communication. Although communication may not be essential to learn a concept, ongoing dialog can enhance student motivation and engagement. LMSs strive to enhance the social dynamic by providing different avenues for communication such as announcements, email, and chat rooms.

Announcements

Posting announcements is an effective method for enhancing communication in your online course. Announcements are useful in that you can communicate changes in the course or assignment; for example, you can send reminders about upcoming due dates; or simply post information, links, and resources that are relevant to the topic at hand. Also, announcement settings can be customized so that, upon logging in, students will see the latest post and receive the most topical comment, link, or object. In addition, you can also customize your announcement settings to send email notifications (and in some cases mobile text messages) whenever you post an announcement to the course.

Email Communication Options

One of the most ubiquitous methods of online communication is, of course, email, which most LMSs include in their offering. It is important to note, however, that LMS-based email may not integrate with school or personal email accounts. In some cases, you can adjust the settings to forward messages to your external personal accounts. A final time-saving feature is that you will be able to email all students within a course, all students within a course section, and all students whom you are teaching if you are teaching more than one class.

Every institution will have some stance on email use. Whether established guidelines exist or not, the question of how to email, who to email, and when to email will inevitably arise. If your administration has established guidelines regarding emailing, then communicate those guidelines to your students and families. If, however, the email policy is established at the teacher's discretion, then make sure to communicate it to your students and parents at the beginning of your class. Setting clear expectations with regard to your availability and response times is highly recommended.

Chat

Some LMSs offer a chat feature, which can be useful as just-in-time communication for students and teachers. The chat function resembles third-party chat technology and should not require additional training. Typically, chat room functionality does not allow for the archiving of chats; therefore, the value they provide is through the facilitation of question and answer (Q&A) sessions and one-to-one real-time conversations.

Communication through an LMS will be new for many learners, and the rules of interaction should align with your own netiquette standards or those established by your school.

Collaboration and Social Learning Tools

In addition to communication, fostering a social environment online is also desirable such that it provides students with the opportunity for collaborative learning. Collaboration and social learning capabilities in LMSs come in the form of group sites, online discussions, peer reviews, conferencing tools, and (in some cases) Wiki pages. For the on-ground K–12 teacher, these functions may not seem useful at first, given that most interaction will take place in class; however, understanding their function and ability can present you with opportunities to creatively enhance your assignments.

Conferencing Tools

A conferencing tool is an environment in which participants can communicate online with each other in real-time. The conferencing tool is a technology that may include a chat room, presentation ability, file sharing ability, whiteboarding, desktop sharing, and in some cases audio and video interfacing. Conferencing tools are useful for group presentations and group meetings. If you have ever attended a webinar, then it is likely you have used a conferencing tool.

Group Sites

An important distinction between a group site and a conferencing tool is that a group site serves as the hub for group projects, wherein a conferencing tool can be accessed through the site for the purpose of collaboration. Group sites are structured in much the same way as a course in an LMS, such that they are composed of a side navigation panel, global navigation links, and a content area. It is important to note, however, that they do not have their own teacher administrative abilities. Group sites are managed by groups of students for the sole purpose of group projects and collaboration, which in turn are facilitated by the teacher for the purpose of assessment.

Wiki Pages

Wiki pages are collaborative pages that can be authored by one student and edited by another. Depending on the LMS, Wiki pages can be added as an assignment within the course, or they can be included as a function within a group site for the purpose of collaborative learning.

Third-Party Social Media Tools

We are all familiar with the social media giants Twitter, Facebook, and Instagram, along with the compulsion to share information amongst our own online communities. The unrivaled popularity of social media is a testament to the human inclination to communicate, connect, and be heard. This same inclination to reach out in the social sphere can be harnessed for instructional purposes to provide students with a place to share information and engage in a creative and collaborative space. If you are considering social media-based activities for your course, then determine first if there is an LTI available for the app. If there is not, then you can always rely on the content page function to link to or perhaps embed a Facebook group site or a Twitter or Instagram feed. Also, consider integrating social media activities into your assignments, discussions, and perhaps even quizzes.

As with communication, guidelines for collaboration need to be established. When writing instructions for group or collaborative projects, you can also establish or reiterate guidelines for interaction.

Assessments

The authors of *Principles of Instructional Design* define assessments as to "show whether or not … instruction has met its objectives" (Gagné et al. 2005, p. 264). By that definition, an assessment can be a quiz, short essay, book report, oral presentation, classroom observation, video presentation, podcast, slideshow, or any other means that measures a learned behavior.

LMSs cannot provide a function for every possible assessment under the sun; however, they have arrived at a couple of solutions. These solutions accommodate most types of assessments that measure learning along the spectrum of Bloom's taxonomy of learning outcomes as outlined in *A Taxonomy for Learning, Teaching and Assessing* (Anderson and Krathwohl 2001, p. 31): remember, understand, apply, analyze, evaluate, and create.

To do this, LMS assessments are offered through *assignments* that often include project-based approaches, discussion forums, quizzes, and, in some cases, journals. It is important to bear in mind, however, that as a teacher you will be able to customize any of the LMS functions to meet the specific requirements of your assessments.

Assignments

An assignment in an LMS is a function that allows students to submit work for grading and feedback. The assignment function is common across LMSs and carries many of the same attributes. Assignments provide a rich-text editor for typing responses, notes, and, if desired, essays and short answer questions. With most assignment functions, students are able to attach files of various format types for submission to the teacher. More recently, some vendors offer assignment functions that have the capability of recording audio and video directly into the LMS itself.

Again, as with most LMS functionality, the assignment function can be tailored to your instructional requirements. Typical grade settings include assignment type designation; point, percentage, or letter grade value; and time restrictions such as availability dates. With this kind of flexibility, you have creative leeway with your assessments.

Discussion Forums

Another type of assessment is the threaded discussion forum. Discussion forums are a common feature in most LMS offerings. Just like assignments, discussions can be graded or nongraded. In either case, what distinguishes a discussion from a chat is that discussion forums are threaded, can be completed asynchronously, and can be archived. Because they are threaded, students can reply to a teacher's post or to other student posts.

Threaded discussion forums can be useful in on-ground courses for several reasons. The first is that asynchronous online discussions may appeal to students who would like to participate in a discussion but might find speaking in a group to be challenging. Having the space to pause and reflect before participating also provides students the opportunity to adequately form their ideas and contribute well-articulated responses.

When reviewing an LMS, take a serious look at discussion forum functionality, including the availability of an option for separating discussants into small groups. Some LMSs have discussion forums that are as flexible as the assignment function. Students can move beyond responding to a post with just text; they can embed media, link to external resources, and record an audio or video into the body of the thread. Having this flexibility pushes the threaded discussion beyond what is traditionally considered a discussion forum interface.

The discussion forum on its own, however, will not encourage lively interactions between students. Discussion forums require at least two criteria in order to be effective. First, discussion questions should prompt the student to exercise analysis and evaluation skills as outlined in the cognitive process dimension of Bloom's revised taxonomy (Anderson and Krathwohl 2001, p. 31). Second, a threaded discussion forum can be more meaningful for students if the teacher facilitates the discussion, prompting students to respond to each other's questions and guide them through the process of analysis and dialog.

Quizzes and Test Banks

In addition to assignments and discussion forums, LMSs provide robust quizzing and test bank creation functionality. Quizzes can be composed of several question types, the most common being true/false, multiple choice, multiple selection, matching, fill-in-the-blank, short answer, and essay questions. Each question can be assigned a point, percentage, or letter grade value. LMSs also provide quiz setting customization that allows you to deliver the assessment according to your specific needs. For example, it is possible to set a time limit for a test and also to allow extended time on a test for a student with special needs. Other popular features include the ability to allow multiple attempts and the ability to embed images, video, and other content types within a test question.

Another helpful quiz function is that test banks can be created and used in subsequent instances. The questions will always be there to be reused, edited, or repurposed if needed. In some situations, test banks provided by textbook publishers can be uploaded into the LMS, saving the teacher the work of having to build one from scratch.

Surveys and Polls

Online teachers often worry that the ability to conduct formative evaluations is lost in the online environment. While it is true that changing your instruction based on student feedback requires a redesign effort on your part, you can still deliver a survey or a poll to gauge your students' level of comprehension. Although there are, indeed, survey LTIs that you could install, some LMSs provide you with a way to conduct a survey within the course or module. Surveys and polls are in enough demand as instructional tools that they warrant inclusion into LMS functionality. Lastly, keep in mind that although surveys are delivered online, they can still be effective in gathering formative feedback for the teacher in a hybrid or on-ground environment. When needed, surveys can be anonymous to encourage unbiased responses from your students.

Journals

Journaling is available in some LMSs, and it can be designated as a graded assignment or a nongraded activity. Like asynchronous threaded discussions, journals are valuable because they can provide students with the opportunity for critical reflection. For situations in which metacognitive strategies are employed, journaling can be a valuable tool. In this sense, journal assignments provide students with a benchmark of their knowledge about a given topic. If journaling is assigned periodically throughout the course, then students are able to track the development of their understanding and make adjustments if needed. In addition, teachers can provide encouragement, corrective feedback, and guidance based on the content of student journal assignments. Journals can also be used for consultation and private communication between teacher and student.

Performance Reports and Analytics

Many LMSs offer the ability to run performance reports on individual students. Performance reports can yield insight into student activity such as course log-on and log-off times, number of page views, discussion postings, assignment submissions, and summative grades. This information can be helpful in identifying students who are struggling at any point in the course.

Analytics differ from performance reports because they offer a statistical analysis of class performance overall. Analytics provide teachers with data to conduct effective evaluations of their own course and lesson design.

Depending on the type of analytics established in the course, analytics can help teachers evaluate performance in relation to course and lesson learning outcomes.

Grading

An LMS's built-in gradebook can be a valuable, timesaving tool for teachers. LMSs provide sophisticated grading schemes and gradebooks in order to assess student work in a methodical and expedient manner. Grading functionality typically includes gradebooks and rubrics. In many systems, it is possible to download all assignments for offline review. The ability to export gradebook data to and from a spreadsheet is another capability offered by leading LMSs.

Gradebook

As mentioned previously, all assignments can be linked to a gradebook. Depending on the LMS, gradebooks tend to have different functions, limitations, and opportunities. Gradebooks centralize student assignment submissions into a tool that facilitates grading and teacher feedback. In some cases, the LMS gradebook integrates into your school's student information system, saving you the work of having to copy grades from one system to the next. More advanced gradebook features allow the course facilitator to run reports on individual student performance as well as overall classroom performance based on a single assignment or assignment type.

Rubrics

Rubrics provide an objective set of criteria that help teachers communicate expectations and grade finished work quickly and fairly. The fact that they are electronic means the LMS does the work of tallying points, making these electronic rubrics a popular grading tool. However, rubrics can be a challenge for teachers—some find them convenient to use, while others find them cumbersome. In cases where a rubric lacks the subtlety to accurately assess a student's work, the teacher is able to adjust the point value and/or include personalized comments. For many teachers, especially those working in the public school system, using a rubric to assess student performance is a requirement. Let's take the common core state standards, for example. Teachers required to teach to Common Core Standards often create assignments to ensure that students meet those standards. Thankfully, rubrics are supplied to aid in lesson and assignment design. Within the LMS, teachers can recreate rubrics based on Common Core Standards and then apply them to assignments they have created.

Another benefit to the use of rubrics is that when reporting to administrators, and perhaps even auditors, embedding rubrics into your assignments can provide the proper transparency into your grading process and your course.

User Management

As part of LMS administrative capabilities, you or your system administrator will be able to assign user roles to anyone enrolled in the course. User roles are defined by permissions that determine the type of experience users have in your course. Although there can be many predefined roles, there are three major roles that are relevant to a teacher: the teacher role, the student role, and the observer role.

Teacher Role

Teacher roles almost always have complete control over their courses in an LMS. However, teacher permissions may be limited if the LMS administrator makes that determination based on organizational guidelines.

In situations in which the teacher is also the course designer, the teacher has permissions to create content within the course. They are able to design assessments, post discussion forum questions, create quizzes, manage the grading system, and add and delete enrollees, assigning them with specific roles. In addition, teachers are able to complete some administrative tasks such as duplicating courses, setting course preferences and specifications, and running reports and analytics.

Student Role

Student roles, for obvious reasons, are limited in scope of permission and ability. Students are able to see the content you create and publish under modules. They have access to the home page, the calendar, the syllabus, discussion forums, quizzes, their grades, and all assignments that are available for the course. They are not able to see other student grades, content and assignments that are not published, or the course's file repository. In short, they only see what the teacher allows through customized settings and the default limitations of the student role. Conversely, this means that the teacher needs to be vigilant in ensuring that essential course content is visible and available to the student on an as-needed basis.

Observer Role

An extremely valuable role in some LMSs is the observer role. In many cases, parents or guardians like to be kept informed of their child's performance and find it useful to be enrolled in the course for observation. According to FERPA guidelines published on their website, "[A] school must provide a parent with an opportunity to inspect and review his or her child's education records" (p. 1). An observer role, therefore, allows parents or guardians to review their child's performance without having to make periodic requests of the teacher. Naturally, this can be an effective time-saving tool for teachers who must regularly engage with parents to keep them apprised of their student's performance.

Profile and User Settings

Profile and user settings refer to an individual's profile customization. User settings are personalized settings and dictate how they experience the course. In addition, notification settings can be customized according to individual preferences. Announcements, emails, assignment due dates, and discussion forum posts can all trigger a notification. Of course, users can choose how they want to receive notifications, either through email, text, or not at all.

Administrative Abilities

Using an LMS comes with administrative responsibilities as well. Luckily, as a teacher, you never need to know about LMS accounts and subaccounts, authentication processes, language settings, roles and permissions (outside of teacher, student, observer roles), or integration with organizational legacy systems. However, there are some administrative tasks that could benefit a teacher working within tight deadlines and limited resources.

Course Exports, Copies, and Migrations

Novice LMS users often ask if their courses can be duplicated or repurposed to avoid having to rebuild them in the LMS. The answer, to their pleasure and gratitude, is *yes*. Most LMS products have the ability to export a course, create a copy of a course, or migrate a course. Essentially these options all do the same thing, which is to create a copy of your course; however, there are subtle differences in each task, which will prompt you to choose one over the other.

For example, if you want to save a compressed file of your entire course for later use, then you can export your course. This can be helpful especially when you are adopting another LMS. LMSs allow for the importation of courses created in other LMSs. If you do this, then please be aware that the course does not always import in the same way that it was built, so expect to spend some time rearranging your files and adjusting your course to get the desired result.

Copying a course creates an exact duplicate of the course. Based on the LMS, the duplicate course may or may not have copied student data such as assignment submissions, discussion forums, and so forth. When copying a course, be sure to verify what copies over and what does not. It would be a shame to deliver a course with old content or, worse, without the content you thought you had.

Finally, course migrations are only relevant when the course is associated with a specific semester or quarter, and a new shell is generated for subsequent iterations. In this case, your system administrator generates the new course shell. As far as the teacher is concerned, the process for migrating a course requires the same effort as copying a course. The difference here is that rather than simply duplicating a course, you are copying the content from one course shell into another—in other words, migrating content from an old shell into a new one. The LMS that you choose to work with will provide you more information to help you choose the best method for your needs.

To summarize, migrations are beneficial when you need to port over content from a course associated with a previous semester or quarter to a new one. If, however, you are creating your own shells and enrolling your students manually, then a simple course copy will be sufficient. Finally, if you are moving from one LMS to another, then the course export/import function is the option you should use.

Conclusion

So, how do the technologies described in this chapter help our teacher Mr. Martinez in the facilitation of his course and the attendant obligations expected of him? As you saw, LMSs are designed to provide instructional solutions in a digital environment such as lesson and assignment design, gradebook management, and the enhancement of communication and collaboration. Additionally, LMSs provide functionality that help Mr. Martinez satisfy FERPA obligations when enrolling parents as *observers* in the online course. Lastly, the delivery of his course material through the LMS provides him the opportunity to archive student performance measurements for grading and administrative reasons.

At this point, you too should be primed to begin the process of adopting an LMS or to design your course in one. Keep in mind that although different LMSs strive to solve the same problems, they often solve them in different ways. By having an understanding of their solutions, limitations, and opportunities, you will be able to optimize the LMS to meet the demands of your curriculum and the needs of your students.

References

Anderson, Lorin W., and David Krathwohl. *A Taxonomy for Learning, Teaching, and Assessing: A Revision of Bloom's Taxonomy of Educational Objectives*. Abridged ed. New York: Longman, 2001.

"Common Core State Standards." Resources (California Department of Education). Accessed July 15, 2015, http://www.cde.ca.gov/re/cc/.

San Francisco Unified School District. Accessed July 15, 2015, http://www.sfusd.edu/en/curriculum-standards/state-content-standards.html.

"FERPA General Guidance for Parents." FERPA for Parents. Accessed July 15, 2015, http://www2.ed.gov/policy/gen/guid/fpco/ferpa/parents.html.

Gagné, Robert M., Walter W. Wager, Katharine C. Golas, and John M. Keller. *Principles of Instructional Design*. 5th ed. Belmont, CA: Thomson/Wadsworth, 2005.

"Learning Tools Interoperability." IMS Global: Learning Tools Interoperability. Accessed July 15, 2015, http://www.imsglobal.org/toolsinteroperability2.cfm.

Martinez, Gerardo. "Assessing the LMS Needs of an Elementary School Teacher." Interview by author. April 26, 2015.

McIntosh, Don. "Vendors of Learning Management and E-Learning Products." Accessed July 15, 2015, http://www.trimeritus.com/vendors.pdf.

Quillen, Ian. "New Companies Seek Competitive Edge in LMS Market." *Education Week Digital Directions,* June 13, 2012. http://www.edweek.org/dd/articles/2012/06/13/03lms.h05.html.

"The Rubric for Online Instruction." Exemplary Online Instruction. Accessed July 15, 2015, http://www.csuchico.edu/eoi/the_rubric.shtml.

The Online Teacher: Skills and Qualities to be Successful

Steven C. Moskowitz

Abstract

The number of institutions offering online courses and programs has substantially increased in the past decade in both K–12 and higher education. As this growth continues, more and more individuals are gravitating toward online learning, as teachers, learners, or both. Teaching online, however, requires a different skillset compared to face-to-face (f2f) teaching. Communication and technology skills, content and subject area knowledge, as well as dedication, flexibility, and organization are important prerequisites to teaching online. This chapter takes a closer look at skills and qualities needed to be a successful online teacher. This chapter also offers guidance for teachers looking to teach, design, and implement online courses.

Introduction

Over the past decade, online education has grown dramatically in both higher education and in the K–12 setting. In a 2014 report, thirty U.S. states had fully online schools operating across the entire state. In the 2013–2014 school year, an estimated 315,000 students attended those statewide fully online schools (Watson et al. 2014, p. 5). The context for these online classes is varied, with course experiences ranging from self-paced to moderated or blended opportunities. Some of these courses may be set in a brick-and-mortar school environment while others stand alone or make up part of an overall program that is fully online.

The proliferation of online programs and courses can be challenging for teachers. Teachers are refining their approaches to online teaching through collaborative efforts with colleagues in the field or through affiliation with professional organizations such as the International Association for K–12 Online Learning (iNACOL), the Online Learning Consortium (OLC), and the International Society for Technology in Education (ISTE). There is also an emerging body of research on successful practices for online schools. While teaching in the online setting presents challenges, experienced teachers continue to learn through college- or school-based professional development opportunities, guide books, articles written by leaders in the field, and sometimes through trial and error. This chapter examines skills and qualities that are needed to be a successful online teacher, and it provides insights on how to attain those skills and qualities.

Online education has the potential to transform the landscape of the educational system in dramatic ways. Students have access to more types of digital learning than ever before. Digital learning options are available to many students and take on a wide range of formats, including online courses from multiple sources, dedicated schools built around aggressive digital instruction models, and many digital learning opportunities inside traditional school settings (Watson et al. 2014, p. 7). Perhaps more than its digital learning counterparts, online learning has the ability to personalize education and become an impetus for major transformation in education.

There are three main categories of online teaching and learning. They include the following: (1) fully online, (2) blended/hybrid, and (3) web-enhanced (Allen and Seaman 2011). In a fully online course, all of the content is delivered online. In a blended/hybrid course, 30 percent to 79 percent of the content is delivered online. In a web-enhanced or web-facilitated course, a learning management system (LMS) or other online resource is used to facilitate an f2f course (Archambault and Crippen 2009).

Research suggests that the online format is an effective alternative to the f2f course. In considering the professional development of K–12 math teachers, researchers at Boston College studied a teacher-training course that offered the same content in both f2f and online formats. Both formats of the course were delivered over the same eight-week period, and the researchers concluded that there was no measurable difference in the outcomes of the training (Russell et al. 2009).

In a qualitative study that elicited feedback from twenty-eight teachers of online courses for gifted students, Dana L. Thomson (2010, p. 702) concluded that online learning not only allows students to take advanced courses that would otherwise not be available or accessible to them, but also opens up opportunities for new modes of learning. Other studies have shown that increased teacher interaction with students in online courses increased academic performance and course completion rates (Hawkins et al. 2013).

In addition to convenience, flexibility, and other strengths of the online format, the course content and the learning environment itself can be tailored to meet students' specific needs. Virtual and blended learning programs support universal design for learning (UDL) and personalized approaches to teaching and learning, allowing students to learn at their own pace and through a variety of media and experiences. Some programs even allow parents to select customized educational environments for their children based on ability and interest (Marsh et al. 2009). Students can also take courses that are not currently offered at their school, allowing school districts to share resources with each other. Customization or *personalized learning* has led to the increase in cyber schools, as many parents are choosing this approach for their child's education.

Online Teaching

Online teaching is very different from on-ground teaching, and a much different skill set is needed. To connect with students one cannot see requires deliberate yet different strategies and approaches. For this reason, teachers are taking on different roles, as they become facilitators of online instruction. Their obligations often involve new skills such as course and content design, technical autonomy to navigate the LMS, and interpersonal and coaching skills that are often communicated through email messages, online journals, or other asynchronous means (Baran et al. 2011). Online teachers must anticipate student needs, challenges, and potential obstacles, frequently asking for feedback and input from students.

Online teachers must also "think very differently about themselves as teachers, recognize the challenges in the educational paradigm, engage in new kinds of activities, and reconsider the meaning of becoming an expert" (Conceição 2006, p. 19). A concern for new online teachers is the amount of time it takes to teach an online course. Joseph Cavanaugh (2005), who studied the time required to prepare and teach a traditional course and that required for the same course to be presented in an online format, concluded that teaching an online class takes significantly more time than an on-ground class. There were three major findings from Cavanaugh's (2006) study: (1) the number of students in online classes predicts the time spent by the instructor at a directly proportional rate, (2) online time on task is tied directly to the course rate, and (3) time demands for even small online courses exceed those for in-class courses. Similarly, 254 (78.2 percent) respondents (n=325) from Leanna Archambault and Jean Larson's (2015) case study on the needs of online teachers indicated that teachers provided instruction online between 80 percent and 100 percent of the time.

There are several reasons why teaching online takes more time than teaching on-ground. First, teachers may be responsible for providing the content for the class. Second, many times teachers rotate teaching a class, and they may not initially be familiar with the content. Third, it takes a few rotations of teaching online to learn how to pace instruction. Many online teachers login to their class at least five days a week to provide instruction, which does not include weekly tasks that include grading and posting announcements. Finally, online teaching is writing intensive and often involves many interactions with students on discussion boards, via email exchanges, online advising and tutoring, and feedback on assignments.

Most online teachers have been trained to teach in traditional classrooms (Archambault 2011), and most teacher preparation programs are still training teachers for a brick-and-mortar classroom environment. With the increase in online and virtual schools, teachers often struggle to succeed in this new environment. According to Leanna Archambault (2011), the challenges of preparing well-qualified teachers to teach online are significant and need to be addressed. Online teachers require strong writing and communication skills, time management skills, enhanced abilities to recognize different learning needs, and skills in adapting instructional methods to meet the diverse needs of students (Watson 2008).

What Other Skills Do Teachers Need in Order to Teach Online?

Teacher skills needed to teach online suggest that attributes of a successful online teacher are the same as those for a successful teacher in the f2f setting: good communication and classroom organization skills (McKenzie and Roblyer 2002), nurturing and engaging all students (Barrett 2010), and an ability to understand online classroom management (DiPietro et al. 2008). Greg Kearsley (2008) argues that online teachers should interact regularly with students, both individually and as a group via email, discussion postings, and, if feasible, live web conference sessions; provide timely feedback on all assignments, tests, and inquiries; create opportunities for collaboration among students; and design meaningful activities that engage and motivate students to participate fully in the course.

These skills are aligned with my own research on teachers' skills needed for effective online teaching. In 2013, I interviewed 17 online teachers, who taught f2f and on-ground in both K–12 and higher education, on the perceived skills and qualities necessary to teach successfully in an online environment (Moskowitz 2013). The term *teacher* is used throughout this discussion and represents both K–12 teachers and faculty from higher education.

When asked to rate their own technology skills on a three-point scale (novice, intermediate, and advanced), 35.3 percent of the teachers interviewed rated themselves as advanced and 64.7 percent of the teachers rated themselves beginner to intermediate, suggesting that not all online teachers are expert technology users. Four themes also emerged from the interview data: (1) online communication skills, (2) content and subject area knowledge, (3) prior online experience, and (4) technology skills.

Online Communication Skills

Communication skills are critical for every teacher, but they are particularly important for an online teacher. Online teaching requires a heightened awareness of how one communicates virtually, and it requires teachers to ask the right questions with the appropriate tone. With no students to see in front of them, teachers reported having to make significant adjustments in how they communicate with students and in identifying different ways to encourage students. It is essential that the teacher monitors her students for understanding and makes adjustments as needed regarding questioning, outreach, and other techniques to ensure a smooth continuum for student learning. Using the video and voice response capabilities of the LMS, it is also possible for teachers to add expression and tone to their online feedback.

Content and Subject Area Knowledge

In addition to effective online communication skills needed to be a successful online teacher, teachers stated that having a strong knowledge of course content was a critical element in their online teaching experience. Teachers noted that they were frequently asked to create or modify curricula. Being able to create or modify curricula and having an understanding of the LMS are important skills for being successful in online teaching.

Prior Online Experience

Teachers spoke about the importance of their prior experience in online learning environments, either as a learner or as a teacher. Such experiences gave them the foundation to teach their own courses and provided them with a student perspective to modify instruction as needed.

Technology Skills

Teachers reported that anyone who teaches online should have a firm grasp of the technology skills required to run the class. While teachers agreed that it is not necessary to be an expert in the use of technology, they acknowledged that they were often asked to solve problems or give direction to students in situations when the technology was not working properly. Teachers who taught for smaller, less-structured institutions were required to have a more sophisticated technology skill set due to the inability of the institution to provide support for technical and connectivity issues.

Teacher skills needed to teach online are often discussed at required training programs for new online faculty at most virtual schools, as many teachers have no prior online experience. Also, most institutions that offer online courses (K–12 schools, charter schools, and public or private colleges and universities) provide formal training on the LMS in use at the institution.

What Qualities Does It Take to be an Effective Online Teacher?

Teacher responses from the interviews I conducted also suggest there are five beneficial qualities needed to become an effective online teacher. They include the following: (1) dedication/motivation, (2) flexibility, (3) organization, (4) passion, and (5) patience.

Dedication/Motivation

An inherent element of online instruction is that teachers usually work alone, often unsupervised. Consequently, qualities important for effective online teachers include dedication and motivation. While brick-and-mortar teachers might share this quality, online teachers often need to go back to the virtual classroom at varied hours. Many online teachers work independently and may not have the same level of collegial interaction as their f2f counterparts.

Flexibility

Online learning is highly flexible and supports universal design for learning (UDL) approaches and ongoing access to course content. Online courses are available 24/7 and are not location bound, which means there is an expectation for the teacher to communicate on a more frequent basis with students. A teacher may also need to change her lesson design or supplement instruction in order to suit the individual needs of students. Unexpected things can and do happen in the online environment, including hardware and software malfunctions. Therefore, flexibility is an important characteristic of a successful online teacher.

It is essential that teachers seeking to make a successful transition from f2f to online teaching have the flexibility needed to address the opportunities and challenges of teaching online. Time is spread out very differently in online teaching, usually in smaller and more frequent blocks of time than brick-and-mortar teaching. This adjustment is difficult for many who are new to teaching online. Additionally, online teachers usually teach on their own, with minimal interaction from colleagues and supervisors. It may take several cycles of teaching the same classes for teachers to fully transition into online instruction.

Organization

Online teachers need to be highly organized. There are multiple routines and procedures that are important to the successful implementation of an online course, including monitoring discussions, grading assignments, composing weekly announcements and other forms of feedback, and managing content. Murray (2011) offers teachers several suggestions for organizing content in an online course. He argues online teachers should

- outline class sessions, so students know what the major tasks are in each lesson

- create sections for major steps in a lesson so that each major task is its own section

- make introductions clear, explain why the material is important, and clearly state the objectives

- reinforce the learning in each section with exercises

- summarize sections and activities and touch on the main points covered

The online teacher also has many housekeeping tasks that need to be performed on a regular and timely basis. Teachers must be constantly aware of deadlines, and they also need to be attuned to technical aspects of the course such as the need to release new online content or establish small group discussions. This awareness is important, as there are numerous elements within an online course, and students must be able to continue their course work—any issue or glitch in a course can prevent a student from moving forward, perhaps for several days, and can affect student instruction and motivation.

Passion

Teachers identified passion as an important quality needed to become an effective online teacher: passion for the content area and passion for motivating online students. Several teachers reported that it was difficult to connect with online students and they needed to make repeated efforts, especially to reach nontraditional students. This again is different in the online forum, as there is no regular scheduled f2f time.

It is recommended that teachers make connections with students as soon as possible when starting an online class. The sooner a teacher can begin structured activities and routines, the sooner she can begin to make connections with individual students and create an environment of trust and support. This can include simple things such as addressing students by first name in discussions, icebreaker activities, and mutual sharing of interests.

Patience

Patience was determined to be an important quality in online instruction. There are numerous variables in an online classroom, including organizational issues, technical problems, and retention issues, to name a few. Online teachers need to react and adjust to unexpected issues and situations, usually working in isolation. It is very easy to become frustrated as a teacher, and patience can make an important difference in the short- and long-term success of the online teacher and course. This quality is important for teacher-student interaction as well, as students often have many questions regarding the different aspects of an online course.

Establishing Clear Expectations and Support

Because students are not in the same physical space as the online teacher, it is common for them to be in situations where they need to monitor and regulate their own behavior and processes. For that reason, it is helpful (if not essential) for the online teacher to establish clear guidelines relating to student behavior and expectations. Such guidelines can relate to regular attendance expectations and timely homework submission as well as participation and interaction. In a traditional brick-and-mortar classroom, it is possible for one student to sit back and observe other students in a discussion, and perhaps not participate. This is very different in an online environment, where it is easy for the teacher to require and verify student participation in discussions and other activities.

Just as students enjoy the convenience of a course that is ubiquitously available for anytime anywhere access, the online teacher may feel pressured to respond anytime, day and night. Therefore, it is important for the teacher to clarify her anticipated response time to student emails, texts, or other forms of inquiry. The convenience and flexibility of online courses require that needed boundaries and guidelines are established and shared with students at the outset of the course.

Effective online teachers work to facilitate a strong sense of community, provide resources relating to success with the technological infrastructure, and provide the feedback and support that promotes self-efficacy and achievement en route to completing the course. Online teachers can also help students develop essential time-management and self-motivation skills by providing explicit strategies and by modeling, and reinforcing positive student behaviors. The need to encourage student autonomy and the importance of developing and sustaining relationships between students and teachers are also desirable qualities of an effective online teacher. (Roblyer and Marshall 2002; Beaudoin et al. 2009).

Conclusion

It is important to note that not every online teacher from the onset will have all of the skills and qualities mentioned in this chapter. A teacher may not initially have extensive experience teaching in the online setting. If you are a teacher who is looking to move into online instruction, consider the following:

- ensure that you have reliable technology and online access
- review your content and look to have a depth of knowledge in your content area
- work on your organizational skills, knowing how and where to locate resources online and offline

- improve your time management skills and establish distributed blocks of time at least five times a week to devote to online courses
- make use of electronic grading rubrics, video and voice feedback, web meetings, and other tools that streamline communication and grading
- join professional organizations devoted to online learning, including, but not limited to, iNACOL, OLC, ISTE, and the Consortium for School Networking (CoSN)
- meet regularly with colleagues who also teach online and share best practices, strategies, and lessons learned
- observe other online teachers teach

These are just some of the considerations relating to teaching online. As this medium continues to grow and more and more institutions expand their online offerings, effective and efficient online teaching and learning skills and qualities will be important and highly valued.

References

Allen, I. Elaine, and Jeff Seaman. *Going the Distance: Online Education in the United States, 2011*. Babson Park, MA: Babson Survey Research Group, 2011.

Archambault, Leanna. "The Practitioner's Perspective on Teacher Education: Preparing for the K–12 Online Classroom." *Journal of Technology and Teacher Education* 19, no. 1 (2011): 73-91.

Archambault, Leanna, and Kent Crippen. "K–12 Distance Educators at Work: Who's Teaching Online Across the United States." *Journal of Research on Technology in Education* 41, no. 4 (2009): 363-91.

Archambault, Leanna, and Jean Larson. "Pioneering the Digital Age of Instruction: Learning From and About K–12 Online Teachers." *Journal of Online Learning Research* 1, no. 1 (2015): 49-83.

Baran, Evrim, Ana-Paula Correia, and Ann Thompson. "Transforming Online Teaching Practice: Critical Analysis of the Literature on the Roles and Competencies of Online Teachers." *Distance Education* 32, no. 3 (2011): 421-39. doi:10.1080/01587919.2011.610293.

Barrett, Bob. "Virtual Teaching and Strategies: Transitioning From Teaching Traditional Classes to Online Classes." *Contemporary Issues in Education Research* 3, no. 12 (2010): 17-20.

Beaudoin, Michael F., Gila Kurtz, and Sigal Eden. "Experiences and Opinions of E-Learners: What Works, What are the Challenges, and What Competencies Ensure Successful Online Learning." *Interdisciplinary Journal of E-Learning & Learning Objects* 5, no. 1 (January 2009): 275-89.

Cavanaugh, Joseph. "Teaching Online—A Time Comparison." *Online Journal of Distance Learning Administration* 8, no. 1 (2005).

Conceição, Simone C. O. "Faculty Lived Experiences in the Online Environment." *Adult Education Quarterly* 57, no. 1 (2006): 26-45.

DiPietro, Meredith, Richard E. Ferdig, Erik W. Black, and Megan Preston. "Best Practices in Teaching K–12 Online—Lessons Learned From Michigan Virtual School Teachers." *Journal of Interactive Online Learning* 7, no. 1 (2008): 10-35.

Hawkins, Abigail, Charles R. Graham, Richard R. Sudweeks, and Michael K. Barbour "Academic Performance, Course Completion Rates, and Student Perception of the Quality and Frequency of Interaction in a Virtual High School." *Distance Education* 34, no. 1 (2013): 64-83.

Kearsley, Greg. "Preparing Engineering Faculty to Teach Online." *Educational Technology* 48, no. 5 (2008): 28-33.

Marsh, Rose M., Alison A. Carr-Chellman, and Beth R. Sockman. "Selecting Silicon: Why Parents Choose Cybercharter Schools." *TechTrends* 53, no. 4 (2009): 32-36.

McKenzie Barbara K., and M. D. Roblyer. "Distant but Not Out of Touch: What Makes an Effective Distance Learning Instructor?" *Learning & Leading with Technology* 27, no. 6 (2002): 186-214. http://hrd.sagepub.com/content/1/2/186.short.

Moskowitz, S. C. 2013. Transitioning to online teaching: An inquiry into qualities, skills, and support structures of online instructors. PhD diss., Manhattanville College, Ann Arbor. In ProQuest Dissertations and Theses, http://gateway.proquest.com/openurl?url_ver=Z39.88-2004&res_dat=xri:pqdiss&rft_val_fmt=info:ofi/fmt:kev:mtx:dissertation&rft_dat=xri:pqdiss:3608367.

Murray, Katherine. "Five Tips for Designing Effective Online Learning Modules." 2011. http://www.techrepublic.com/blog/five-apps/five-tips-for-designing-effective-online-learning-modules/.

Roblyer, M. D., and Jon C. Marshall. "Predicting Success of Virtual High School Students: Preliminary Results From an Educational Success Prediction Instrument." *Journal of Research on Technology in Education* 35, no. 2 (2002): 241.

Russell, Michael, Rebecca Carey, Glenn Kleiman, and Joanne Douglas Venable. "Face-to-Face and Online Professional Development for Mathematics Teachers: A Comparative Study." *Journal of Asynchronous Learning Networks* 13, no. 2 (2009): 71-87.

Thomson, Dana L. "Beyond the Classroom Walls: Teachers' and Students' Perspectives on How Online Learning Can Meet the Needs of Gifted Students." *Journal of Advanced Academics* 21, no. 4 (2010): 662-712.

Watson, John. "Online Learning: The National Landscape," 2008. www.Ciconline.org/Thresholdfall08.

Watson, John, Larry Pape, Amy Murin, Butch Gemin, and Lauren Vashaw. *Keeping Pace with K–12 Digital Online Learning.* Durango, CO: Evergreen Education Group, 2014.

Building Community in K–12 Online Courses: The Community of Inquiry (CoI)

Sarah Bryans-Bongey

Abstract

For all learners, foundational research suggests that learning has a social and interactive component and that the teacher plays an important role in student success. Research in online learning continues those ideas, with growing evidence as to the effectiveness of the community of inquiry (CoI) framework (Garrison et al. 2000). The CoI represents a process of creating an effective collaborative-constructivist learning experience through three interdependent elements—Social, Cognitive, and Teaching Presence. This chapter provides K–12 online teachers with an essential introduction to the CoI framework, including ways to implement and measure its success in specific online programs and courses.

Introduction

In the face of continued and anticipated growth, K–12 online programs, administrators, and teachers seek research-based approaches needed to design, facilitate, and direct teaching practices that are effective in online settings. Online programs and courses are usually offered in the password-protected and feature-rich environment of a learning management system (LMS), and this online course environment has continually evolved to offer more and more features and multimedia options, including online announcements, discussions, gradebook, multimedia integration, and voice recognition. A typical LMS also supports the easy inclusion of various outside sources such as Flickr images and YouTube videos as well as tools that can be purchased for integrated access such as VoiceThread, Khan Academy, web conferencing, StudyMate games, and test monitoring and proctoring services.

Yet, despite the many specialized features, teaching and learning online can be vastly different from face-to-face (f2f) instruction, and even a visually appealing, content-rich, and age-appropriate online course can seem lacking. This is true at all levels, and perhaps even more so for younger learners enrolled in fully online programs and courses. Many K–12 teachers are still learning what elements make online courses effective and how to design and teach them. One promising approach to effective online course design and delivery is the community of inquiry (CoI) framework, which was the first model developed to guide the design and research of fully online learning experiences. Developed by Garrison et al. (2000), the CoI framework represents a process of creating an effective collaborative-constructivist learning experience through three interdependent elements—*Social Presence*, *Cognitive Presence*, and *Teaching Presence*.

Promising Research

Research on the CoI framework indicates that courses constructed to address social, cognitive, and teaching elements described in the CoI are associated with higher levels of student satisfaction and improved perceptions regarding the quality and quantity of learning in an online course. When all three aspects of CoI are implemented in an online course (Social Presence, Cognitive Presence, and Teaching Presence), research indicates that higher retention and higher levels of student confidence and satisfaction are the result (Arbaugh et al. 2008).

So, what can program supervisors, specialists, instructional designers, and teachers do to develop and sustain this type of learning experience in the online K–12 course environment?

Research-Based Solutions

Guided by the CoI model (Garrison et al. 2000), this chapter explains the CoI framework and describes practical approaches for building a dynamic and synergistic environment addressing Social, Cognitive, and Teaching Presence. In considering the CoI, it is important to note that this model is more than an approach that simply adds social elements to an online course. While student interaction is an essential element,

Social Presence described by the CoI is intrinsically associated with a learning community that is orchestrated by a teacher and built around inquiry.

CoI research identifies engaging and successful course design and teaching strategies. To measure the existence of CoI approaches, researchers have applied and developed a survey instrument that has been used, tested, and refined since the time it was initially established in 2000. The CoI survey/assessment tool (Arbaugh et al. 2008) is reproduced in the Appendix of this chapter, beginning on page 52. At the conclusion of an online course, teachers and/or researchers distribute the survey to students to identify the existence or lack of each of the three key CoI elements. Shared with permission, the survey may also be useful as a resource to help guide the inclusion of CoI approaches.

Community of Inquiry (CoI)—Background

The CoI model was developed as part of a 1997–2001 grant-funded project from the Canadian Social Sciences and Humanities Council. It centered on fully online learning environments. At the time of the study, these environments were text-based and placed a heavy emphasis on promoting interaction through online discussion (Athabasca University 2015). The seminal paper by Garrison et al. (2000) entitled "Critical Inquiry in a Text-Based Environment: Computer Conferencing in Higher Education" has been cited more than 2,780 times since its publication according to a 2015 search conducted using Google Scholar, and the model has inspired design and research efforts that extend beyond higher education and continue to take hold in K–12 online teaching and learning.

Even as the CoI has been growing in popularity, a wealth of interactive online resources along with the evolution of the LMS have allowed for a more multifaceted approach to online course design. For example, some online courses have explored the CoI using virtual reality while others have adopted the use of audio, video, direct messaging, or other means of communicating in online course interactions (Ice et al. 2007; Nippard and Murphy 2007).

The CoI emphasizes both collaborative and constructivist approaches, and was developed to guide research. The model identifies three interacting elements of an online learning community:

- Social Presence emphasizes the importance of social-emotional aspects of online learning. This aspect of the model describes how the individual identifies herself as a part of the larger learning community within an online course. This often drives the climate of the course and whether or how students feel comfortable participating, interacting, and even questioning or challenging comments or actions by others in the course.

- Cognitive Presence is how participants in an online course interact and engage with the course content and others in the course. It describes a practical inquiry (PI) design (Garrison 1991) involving a typical sequence through which students experience cognitive presence. Learning is launched through a triggering event that activates the student's curiosity. It then causes the student to explore and seek answers and solutions, includes a phase in which the student integrates or connects ideas and is followed by a time of resolution or production.

- Teaching Presence describes approaches in which the teacher codesigns, organizes, facilitates, and directs the cognitive and social processes in collaboration with the students throughout the course. Teaching Presence also supports student involvement as content creators and teachers (as well as learners) in the process, and it has been connected with student satisfaction and success. Teaching Presence is dynamic and contextual, and interacts, drives, and is sometimes driven by the other two (cognitive and social) aspects of this model. Examples of such presence might include presentation of content, summarizing and reflecting upon a discussion assignment, or establishing an assignment or in-course activity. Certain projects and activities put the students themselves in a teaching role, thus further fostering the Teaching Presence envisioned by the CoI.

Figure 3.1 (adapted from coi.athabascau.ca) provides a visual explanation of these three dynamic and overlapping presences.

Research Base

The CoI model made its debut in 2000, and its initial implementation was at the college level. Although LMSs of the time lacked the advanced levels of multimedia and web tool integration available today, the model espoused constructivist-collaborative approaches, with teachers and students interacting via the asynchronous discussions, announcements, and journals available in online courses of the time. Since the CoI was initially introduced, researchers have successfully applied the model in the design, presentation, and research of instruction delivered through blended as well as fully online formats (Garrison and Vaughan 2008).

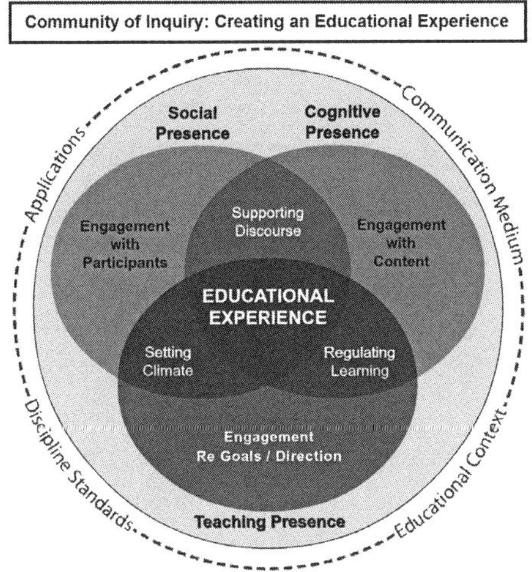

Figure 3.1   The CoI model

The CoI has been widely explored and adopted, and it is "the first learning model developed specifically and solely for online learning" (Meyer 2014, p. 16). Researchers and practitioners at the high school, college, and institutional settings use a student survey/instrument designed by Garrison et al. (2000). Researchers have also conducted extensive transcript analysis in the early years of applying this approach.

By implementing the CoI model, the teacher/practitioner can use a systematic model to address the holistic needs of the online learner. Specific domains to be considered include social, cognitive, and teaching/learning. Akyol and Garrison (2008) provide the following operational definitions for each of the three presences.

- Social Presence involves open communication, group cohesion, and participants exhibiting personal/affective engagement.

- Cognitive Presence involves a triggering event or hook, followed by exploration, integration, and resolution. These phases are what Garrison (1991) refers to as the PI model of cognitive engagement.

- Teaching Presence involves design and organization, facilitating discourse, and direct instruction in collaboration with students.

Approaches used to evaluate CoI include transcript analysis of actual statements and projects generated in an online course to identify the absence or the existence of the previously mentioned elements. Additionally, practitioners have used student self-reported data to quantify a course's level of consistency with the CoI model. See the Appendix to this chapter for a survey instrument you can use to measure attainment of the three CoI presences.

One fascinating aspect of the research has been how the different presences are dynamic and evolving throughout the duration of a specific online course. For example, while Teaching Presence may be manifested predominantly by the teacher in early phases of the course, a larger proportion of these responsibilities may be taken on by students in the CoI environment. The CoI framework is formed by the intersection of three main elements (Akyol and Garrison 2008, p. 4) making the three presences (Social, Cognitive, and Teaching) interdependent.

Research to date reveals that Teaching Presence has a positive impact on Cognitive Presence. Data also suggest that when Teaching Presence is high, students are more likely to identify themselves as satisfied with the course and their learning. It has also been seen that Social Presence and a sense of community affects Cognitive Presence. However, Cognitive Presence has not been widely researched in terms of its potential to promote Social Presence. Suggestions for pursuing this line of research might center on situations in which students self-select into one of several groups/topics based on personal interest. Social Presence seems to have its most notable impact on the climate of the course, with the potential to support a sense of belonging, openness, collaboration, and interaction.

The CoI model has been applied in secondary settings (Nippard and Murphy 2007) and has also gained recognition among K–12 teachers (Heafner et al. 2015). This application appears unique in that previously the model was used most frequently in the higher education setting. This model seems to have the potential to inform the design and teaching of K–12 online classes as even younger learners at elementary and middle school levels begin to participate in online schools.

The remainder of the chapter describes practical approaches for addressing the three overlapping and evolving aspects of the CoI model.

Implementing the CoI in the K–12 Fully Online or Hybrid Classroom

Observations and strategies shared here are based on practices described in the literature as well as the author's experience of course design and online teaching methods.

Social Presence

Social Presence is "the ability of participants to identify with the community, communicate purposefully in a trusting environment, and develop interpersonal relationships by way of projecting their individual personalities" (Garrison 2011, p. 134). Research indicates that there is a significant relationship between Social Presence and satisfaction with an online course experience (Akyol and Garrison 2008). To this end, the CoI model values settings in which online students get to know other class participants and develop a sense of belonging in the course. Social Presence is also intrinsically connected with Teaching Presence since it is the teacher who generally establishes ground rules and facilitates interactions among students.

The CoI survey is a student survey instrument designed to measure an online course's consistency with the CoI model (Garrison et al. 2000). Teachers can use the CoI survey in the Appendix to plan and implement approaches to evaluate an online course and/or to design and align course features that promote the three presences of the CoI model. This next section provides specific strategies to help the K–12 teacher implement Social Presence while upcoming content includes implementation strategies for Cognitive Presence and Teaching Presence.

One approach to implementing Social Presence relates to the teaching of netiquette (internet etiquette). As a new course begins, teachers often provide information on how students can behave in an appropriate, constructive, and mutually respectful manner. Videos, websites, self-tests, and other resources are offered with the goal of helping students know how to behave appropriately in an online community (Albion.com 2011). Establishing guidelines and expectations and promoting constructive and positive behavior among students can help build Social Presence and community.

The use of student introductions (often referred to as "icebreakers") is another strategy online teachers use to promote the Social Presence aspect of the CoI model. These icebreaker introductions are generally conducted as asynchronous discussions within the LMS, and they can be optimized to complement the subject matter being taught. For example, an English teacher might use the online discussion area to have students introduce themselves with an acrostic poem that uses the letters of their own name. For teachers preferring a more straightforward approach, icebreakers could simply involve the sharing of initial greetings and inviting students to submit pictures, videos, or other multimedia to enrich these introductions further.

In addition to asynchronous interactions that are possible through the online discussion board, synchronous class meetings can also be managed using a web conferencing tool or other options such as Google Hangouts, Zoom, or Skype. Offering various options for students to make connections with the teacher and with one another helps promote Social Presence in an online course.

Frequency of interaction as well as quality of interaction is an important aspect of developing cohesive online course community. Making discussions graded and required is important as it motivates students to participate and leads to a higher level of Social Presence and a greater sense of community in an online course (Rovai 2002). Clear expectations communicated through the use of a rubric can also help guide interactions among class participants.

Modeling appropriate interactions is a way the teacher can exemplify the desired in-course behavior when participating in discussions, web meetings, or other interactions. Ideas here include being involved, both publicly and behind the scenes, in discussions and working with individual students as needed to reinforce positive behaviors or suggest alternate approaches.

The International Society for Technology in Education (ISTE) and the International Association for K–12 Online Learning (iNACOL) both offer standards and guidelines that can assist with the development of Social Presence. ISTE's standard on digital citizenship calls for students to "understand human, cultural, and societal issues relating to technology and practice legal and ethical behavior" (ISTE 2007, p. 2). In its National Standards for Quality Online Courses, an extensive document from iNACOL (2011), it is suggested that a quality online course provides "opportunities for appropriate instructor-student and student-student interaction…." (p. 13). It is further suggested that "discussions are available for developing community" (p. 12).

At the K–12 level, some programs and teachers may make only occasional use of online discussions. Consider exploring their benefits in a gradual manner. Social Presence has been found to be essential to a CoI and has been shown to lead to higher levels of student retention and satisfaction in an online course (Boston et al. 2009). Advanced options of the LMS support the ability to include avatars, video, and voice. Additionally, secure third-party applications such as wikis, web meeting software, or other tools such as VoiceThread, Glogster, Prezi, and Google Slides can promote Social Presence through sight, sound, and opportunities for collaboration.

Cognitive Presence

Cognitive Presence is the extent to which learners are able to construct and confirm meaning through sustained reflection and discourse (Garrison et al. 2000).

This Cognitive Presence is associated with the cycle of PI (Garrison 1991). It starts with a triggering event designed to inspire authentic curiosity. From there, curiosity drives exploration, integration, and resolution.

The teacher seeking to address Cognitive Presence in an online course environment would develop creative and engaging ways to creative cognitive dissonance or trigger curiosity about the subject at hand. After the trigger or hook comes a time of exploration for answers. The practical strategy of presenting resources that support such exploration, including the curation of quality resources, can enrich the exploration phase. With so many free and open resources on the internet, it is possible to locate and incorporate age-appropriate resources in the online course environment. Teachers or instructional designers can team up with the school media specialist or librarian to locate quality resources. Alternatively, teachers can use their own subject matter expertise in conjunction with the Creative Commons Search Engine, Google Advanced Search, Flickr search function, TED Talks searchable archive, or other tools integrated within the LMS to in order to identify quality content. Other sources for materials to support the exploration phase include professional organizations, learning object (LO) repositories, and government sources. Additionally, Chapter 15 of this book describes approaches for locating open and free educational resources for the online classroom.

Providing a multimedia array of resources is likely to support the exploration phase of the PI model by intriguing and enticing a wide range of learners. The integration phase is where the learner starts to make connections between prior knowledge, what they are discovering in the course, and what they can imagine or create. This is a great time for online discussion, creation, and reflection, particularly through journaling, in order to capture thoughts and ideas as they emerge. Resolution—which is not necessarily a closed process as the name might imply—is a likely time to have students presenting or sharing. Here, the very act of presenting and sharing reinforces student accomplishment and enriches the experience and connection with and among other students in the course. If wikis, blogs, social media, or other publicly visible tools are used, authentic audiences may emerge from outside of the course itself.

A culminating or capstone experience of this nature can—in turn—expand the community's authenticity and reach. As in the previous section on implementing Social Presence, this section shares strategies to address the Cognitive Presence associated with the CoI model. Preliminary surveys to students might be used to identify areas of interest that can later be incorporated into the course curriculum. Course activities could be designed to offer choice and to support exploration through avenues that further overall learning and are also of specific interest to the learner.

When presenting collaborative projects, a suggested strategy is to offer students the opportunity to engage in an assignment or project based on interest in one of a selection of topics. The LMS often offers sign-up sheets, and the teacher can promote Cognitive Presence by allowing students to self-select according to the topic/s of greatest interest.

Providing students with options to explore content via a choice of media and resources is another way the teacher can support Cognitive Presence. This approach has some similarities to UDL, which promotes accessibility through the provision of many avenues for cognition, action, expression, and engagement (Center for Applied Special Technology [CAST] 2015).

Online documents or whiteboards such as Twydla or Padlet offer students an opportunity to brainstorm in a collaborative environment. These collaborative pages (including Google Docs and Google Slides) can be easily set up and embedded within the online course.

Another approach for developing Cognitive Presence is through the use of concept maps, such as MindMeister, Inspiration, Webspiration, Kidspiration, MindMup, or Popplet. These concept-mapping tools can be a great venue through which students can explore and articulate their questions and understanding. Furthermore, they can have relevance at numerous points in a lesson or course.

The use of discussion areas, journals, blogs, or wikis can help students share and view examples from others in their online course, which has the potential to further knowledge and help build empathy and appreciation for other people's ideas and perspectives. A tool that supports peer review among students is offered by most LMSs, and online discussions can also provide a forum where students can share and provide feedback on one another's work. Having students express their thoughts for review by an authentic audience can help promote pride of authorship and a level of reflection and engagement that is integral to the CoI.

In addressing Cognitive Presence, consider projects or activities in which students (individually or collaboratively) construct a presentation or other form of course content. A few examples of projects that can be created using (free) web-based tools include the following:

- website creation using Weebly, Google Sites, or Wix
- flyers or poster creation using Smores
- creative expression through avatars, videos, books, or cartoons using Voki, Animoto, Storybird, GoAnimate, or Pixton
- development of online presentations using Prezi
- creation of a wiki according to a specific theme using WikiSpaces
- collaboration and inquiry-based challenge set forth in a WebQuest

Reflections associated with the projects and responding to guided questions can further promote Cognitive Presence and an understanding of fundamental concepts.

Based on rubrics or other evaluation procedures (including participation in a guided peer review process), students can comprehend, apply, and articulate an understanding of *quality*, and can thus improve their own and one another's work as a result. Practical projects or experiences accompanied by explanations that can be generated in various forms (audio, video, and text) can help students make real-world connections between concept and application.

In promoting Cognitive Presence, the teacher's or course designer's knowledge of the students (through surveys, discussions, or other approaches) can support the creation of activities, experiences, and meanings that have practical significance and build upon prior knowledge of the students themselves. Free survey tools include Google Forms and SurveyMonkey. It is also possible to use survey or quiz tools that are built into the LMS. It has been noted that interactions in the course evolve through time, and as teachers become more familiar with their students' needs and interests, they likewise become better able to identify and present activities that are likely to be engaging and meaningful.

Teaching Presence

Teaching presence is the codesign, facilitation, and direction of cognitive and social processes in collaboration with students for the purpose of realizing personally meaningful and educationally worthwhile learning outcomes (Anderson et al. 2001). The use of the verb form of the word, *teaching*, is deliberate as the CoI's concept of teaching presence also acknowledges that students themselves may often learn through creating, curating, presenting, and teaching. Some of the implementation strategies found in this section on teaching presence encompass that philosophy.

Based on the CoI model, online K–12 teachers can consider one or more of the strategies provided for promoting teaching presence. As with the earlier sections on Social Presence and Cognitive Presence, a wealth of ideas are included. The CoI survey on page 52 was developed for online students.

Ongoing communication and a high level of teacher responsiveness is essential to teaching presence. This communication can take the form of prompt and thoughtful responses to emails, or phone calls as appropriate, or it can be a proactive approach related to the course design. For example, providing a basic outline or visual map of learning objectives, course content, and activities can be helpful to students as they embark on a new course of study. Tools for creating such a visual map might include MS Word Smart Art, or a concept-mapping tool such as MindMeister, Webspiration, or Inspiration.

Teachers can use web meeting software, Google Hangouts, Skype, or other free tools to host online office hours, class meetings, or opportunities for students to work in collaborative teams or project groups. Links to technical support, the provision of quick and easy-to-make Jing screen capture videos, and additional written instructions can also be used to clarify procedures. Some teachers offer an *Ask the Teacher* discussion area where all students can post questions and read, view, or hear the answers. These are all strategies for supporting students in their basic ability to interact, navigate, and succeed in the course.

To ensure that students are aware of key due dates and milestones, teachers should identify, communicate, and regularly use their preferred communication tools and LMS features. Examples of such tools or media include the syllabus, course calendar, announcements, course messages, and web meetings.

Researchers suggest providing "prompt but modest feedback, peer facilitation, protocols, and audio feedback" (deNoyelles et al. 2014, p. 159). Too much activity by the teacher may actually inhibit the process of students exploring and integrating ideas for themselves. It is still important, though, to monitor and intervene on an as-needed basis. At the end of the discussion, students should not be left with misconceptions or unresolved questions. Depending on the age group and complexity of the topic, students can even take turns crafting a summarizing/clarifying post or the teacher can post a written, audio, or video summary of the discussion.

In addressing teaching presence, the teacher should ensure that students demonstrate respect for one another's opinion while also feeling free to express an alternate viewpoint. The online teacher can and should coordinate, model and monitor interactions consistently. Using announcements, class meetings, video recordings, discussion posts, and other approaches can also really help keep students on track with their learning.

As the course progresses and students build foundational knowledge and curiosity about different aspects or topics, it is useful to craft assignments and projects that allow individual choice and options for independent expression of ideas. Such projects put the students themselves in the role of creator or teacher and might include the collaborative construction of a book or website. Tools like Animoto video or Pixton comic strips allow students to create an entirely new learning object and express their learning in new and individualized ways.

Teachers should also consider having students submit some type of homework in a small-group discussion area or present their work in a web meeting or other public forum. The act of submitting an assignment to a forum that is visible to peers can be helpful as it provides an opportunity for students to explore the work of others. This public submission can also be motivating because the student knows his or her project will be viewed by a larger audience as well as the teacher. Asking questions relating to student projects is another way the teacher can introduce new ideas or expanded lines of inquiry into discussions, presentations, and other projects. This can be done privately in assignment feedback or publically depending on teacher judgment.

In providing feedback on discussions, activities, and assignments, the use of online rubrics help teachers maintain objectivity and save time while ensuring that students have a clear understanding as to why they received the grade they did and what could have been done differently. Additional comments including encouragement and constructive suggestions will help students know what they did well and how they can improve in the future.

As part of the communication process, teachers can and should advise students of their availability and of any standard timing or expectations relating to the grading of work or responses to discussion questions or email. Learning and the construction of knowledge and understanding build as the course proceeds. Therefore, students need to know what they are doing right and what needs to be improved. It is important to provide prompt feedback and to let students know if delays are slowing the expected response time.

In the process of giving feedback, teachers should consider using a range of approaches. Typical LMSs offer many means for responding to students. Teachers can use rubrics, written comments, audio comments, and even video or voice comments. Also, teachers should consider using web conferencing to hold one-on-one meetings and host discussions of project ideas or to provide interim/formative feedback on major projects. Other ideas for establishing connections between student and teacher and from student to student include projects with interim deadlines in which the teacher or students in small groups provide feedback and support. Information from these feedback sessions can then help guide the adjustment and ultimate improvement of the finished work.

Finally, teachers can and should consider offering an incremental and formative process that allows students to discuss course topics or specific aspects of a project as that project unfolds. Taken together, these ideas combined with strategies for addressing Social Presence and Cognitive Presence within the CoI model offer a solid starting point for the online teacher seeking to implement the CoI.

Conclusion

Implementing the CoI framework is a promising approach that promotes student perseverance and success in an online course. Research conducted at the higher education level indicates that when social, cognitive, and teaching aspects of the CoI framework are in place, improved learning, retention, and satisfaction results.

Studies of the framework's effectiveness in K–12 online courses have been less frequent than those conducted in professional development and university settings, most likely due to the fact that the model emerged at a time when the online format was less prevalent in K–12 settings. However, data collected thus far suggest that—like their counterparts in higher education and institutional settings—these younger students are likely to enjoy, learn, and persevere through the combined presences of social, cognitive, and teaching elements (Nippard and Murphy 2007).

For school districts, program directors, principals, instructional designers, and teachers, adherence to the CoI involves a deliberate design and process. Adopting the CoI may require some programs to reconsider policies and existing designs. However, through the adoption and continued monitoring of the CoI, K–12 online programs stand to benefit greatly through higher rates of student satisfaction, perseverance, and retention associated with the CoI model.

In considering future implementation of the CoI in K–12 online courses, D. Randy Garrison (2015) confirmed that "the CoI framework is generic and K–12 is prime for application of this framework" (2015, p. 1). With both challenges and opportunities to propel them, K–12 online practitioners are poised to pursue this research for the betterment of students, teachers, and online programs as a whole. The strategies provided for promoting Social, Cognitive, and Teaching presence are consistent with the CoI evaluation criteria established by Garrison et al. (2000). In sum, the CoI framework offers research-based promise in the area of student satisfaction and retention. Consider implementing the CoI in your own online class and contribute to the growing body of research on the CoI in K–12 online teaching and learning.

References

Akyol, Z., and D. Randy Garrison. "The Development of a Community of Inquiry Over Time in an Online Course: Understanding the Progression and Integration of Social, Cognitive, and Teaching Presence." *Journal of Asynchronous Learning Networks* 12 (2008): 3-22.

Albion.com. "Netiquette Home Page." Last modified 2011, http://www.albion.com/netiquette/.

Anderson, Terry, Liam Rourke, D. Randy Garrison, and Walter Archer. "Assessing Teaching Presence in a Computer Conferencing Context." *Journal of Asynchronous Learning Networks* 5 (2001): 1-17.

Arbaugh, J. B., Martha Cleveland-Innes, Sebastian Diaz, D. Randy Garrison, Phillip Ice, Jennifer Richardson, and Karen Swan. "Developing a Community of Inquiry Instrument: Testing a Measure of the Community of Inquiry Framework Using a Multi-Institutional Sample." *Internet and Higher Education* 11 (2008): 133-36.

Athabasca University. "CoI Survey." Accessed June 12, 2015, https://coi.athabascau.ca/coi-model/coi-survey/.

— "The Community of Inquiry Research Site." Last modified June 15, 2015, https://coi.athabascau.ca/.

Boston, Wally, Sebastián R. Diaz, Angela M. Gibson, Phil Ice, Jennifer Richardson, and Karen Swan. "An Exploration of the Relationship Between Indicators of the Community of Inquiry Framework and Retention in Online Programs." *Online Learning Consortium,* 2009. onlinelearningconsortium.org/sites/default/files/v13n3_8boston.pdf

Center for Applied Special Technology (CAST). "Universal Design for Learning," 2015. http://www.cast.org/our-work/about-udl.html#.VbVdoEJViko.

deNoyelles, Aimee, Janet Zydney, and Baiyun Chen. "Strategies for Creating a Community of Inquiry Through Online Asynchronous Discussions." *MERLOT Journal of Online Learning and Teaching* 10 (2014): 153-65.

Garrison, D. Randy. "Community of Inquiry and K–12 Education," 2015. Email correspondence.

—. "Critical Thinking and Adult Education: A Conceptual Model for Developing Critical Thinking in Adult Learners." *International Journal of Lifelong Education* 10, no. 4 (1991), 287-303.

—. *E-Learning in the 21st Century: A Framework for Research and Practice.* 2nd ed. New York: Taylor and Francis, 2011.

Garrison, D. Randy, Terry Anderson, and Walter Archer. "Critical Inquiry in a Text-Based Environment: Computer Conferencing in Higher Education." *The Internet and Higher Education* 2 (2000): 87-105.

Garrison, D. Randy, and Norman Vaughan. *Blended Learning in Higher Education: Framework, Principles, and Guidelines.* San Francisco: Jossey-Bass, 2008.

Heafner, Tina. L., Richard Hartshorne, and Teresa M. Petty. (2015). *Exploring the Effectiveness of Online Education in K–12 Environments.* Hershey, PA: IGI Global.

Ice, Phil, Ben Arbaugh, Sebastian Diaz, D. Randy Garrison, Jennifer Richardson, Peter Shea, and Karen Swan. Community of Inquiry Framework: Validation and Instrument Development. Athabasca University. Elluminate Recording. Accessed June 11, 2015, http://www.irrodl.org/index.php/irrodl/article/viewArticle/573/1091.

International Society for Technology in Education. 2007. "Standards for Students," 2007. https://www.iste.org/docs/pdfs/20-14_ISTE_Standards-S_PDF.pdf.

Meyer, Katrina. 2014. "Student Engagement Online: What Works and Why," series ed. Kelly Ward, and Lisa E. Wolf-Wendel. *ASHE Higher Education Report* 40, no. 6.

Nippard, Eric, and Elizabeth Murphy. "Social Presence in the Web-Based Synchronous Secondary Classroom." *Canadian Journal of Learning and Technology* 33 (2007): 1.

Rovai, Alfred. "Sense of Community, Perceived Cognitive Learning, and Persistence in Asynchronous Learning Networks." *Internet & Higher Education* 5, no. 4 (2002): 319.

Watson, John, Larry Pape, Amy Murin, Butch Gemin, and Lauren Vashaw. *Keeping Pace With K–12 Digital Online Learning.* Grand Rapids, MI: Evergreen Education Group, 2014.

Appendix: CoI Survey

Five-point Likert-type scale:

1 = strongly disagree, 2 = disagree, 3 = neutral, 4 = agree, 5 = strongly agree

Teaching Presence
Design & Organization

1. The teacher clearly communicated important course topics.
2. The teacher clearly communicated important course goals.

3. The teacher provided clear instructions on how to participate in course learning activities.

4. The teacher clearly communicated important due dates/time frames for learning activities.

Facilitation

5. The teacher was helpful in identifying areas of agreement and disagreement on course topics that helped me to learn.

6. The teacher was helpful in guiding the class towards understanding course topics in a way that helped me clarify my thinking, including assignments and experiences that caused me to engage, produce, present and evaluate course content.

7. The teacher helped to keep course participants engaged and participating in productive dialogue.

8. The teacher helped keep the course participants on task in a way that helped me to learn.

9. The teacher encouraged course participants to explore new concepts in this course.

10. Teacher actions reinforced the development of a sense of community among course participants.

Direct Instruction

11. The teacher helped to focus discussion on relevant issues in a way that helped me to learn.

12. The teacher provided feedback that helped me understand my strengths and weaknesses.

13. The teacher provided feedback in a timely fashion.

Social Presence
Affective Expression

14. Getting to know other course participants gave me a sense of belonging in the course.

15. I was able to form distinct impressions of some course participants.

16. Online or web-based communication is an excellent medium for social interaction.

Open Communication

17. I felt comfortable conversing through the online medium.

18. I felt comfortable participating in the course discussions.

19. I felt comfortable interacting with other course participants.

Group Cohesion

20. I felt comfortable disagreeing with other course participants while still maintaining a sense of trust.

21. I felt that my point of view was acknowledged by other course participants.

22. Online discussions help me to develop a sense of collaboration.

Cognitive Presence
Triggering Event

23. Problems posed increased my interest in course issues.

24. Course activities piqued my curiosity.

25. I felt motivated to explore content related questions.

Exploration

26. I utilized a variety of information sources to explore problems posed in this course.

27. Brainstorming and finding relevant information helped me resolve content-related questions.

28. Online discussions were valuable in helping me appreciate different perspectives.

Integration

29. Combining new information helped me answer questions raised in course activities.

30. Learning activities helped me construct explanations/solutions.

31. Reflection on course content and discussions helped me understand fundamental concepts in this class.

Resolution

32. I can describe ways to test and apply the knowledge created in this course.

33. I have developed solutions to course problems that can be applied in practice.

34. I can apply the knowledge created in this course to my work or other non-class-related activities.

Online Constructivism: Tools and Techniques for Student Engagement and Learning

Michael Kosloski and Diane Carver

Abstract

Teachers strive to maximize learning effectiveness, and one way to improve student success is to help learners discover and construct their own meaning. In the effort to implement such constructivist approaches, online learning can provide teachers with challenges that are not typical in a traditional classroom. In and of themselves, the instructional strategies used in an online environment may be similar to the strategies used in a traditional classroom. However, the implementation of those strategies can vary greatly from one format to the other, and teachers need tools and techniques to ensure success. This chapter discusses the psychosocial learning environment and effective approaches that course designers and teachers should understand to maximize constructivism in an online classroom.

Introduction

Constructivism, or helping students to create new meaning out of instruction, is no small order. Add the complexities of online learning, and teachers need to deliberately and intentionally utilize strategies that help students to learn and synthesize concepts. In this chapter, two elements of online learning are examined. First, course designers and teachers must grasp the notion of the psychosocial learning environment of an online course before they can manipulate it for maximum effectiveness. Second, course designers and teachers must not only select instructional strategies that are conducive to higher level thinking, but must also implement those strategies and ensure they are conducive to an online environment. Once the psychosocial learning environment has been optimized, the teacher may then utilize learning strategies that help learners to construct new meaning.

Psychosocial Learning Environment

Online secondary education is growing in popularity around the world. Flexible scheduling and expanded learning opportunities make an online environment appealing for high school students with a variety of educational needs and personal circumstances. In addition to offering students more educational choices, online learning may help school districts provide opportunities that may not otherwise be available. In order to meet the ever-increasing demand of offering greater course selections with few (if any) additional resources, school districts around the country are looking at online education as an alternative or an addition to face-to-face (f2f) offerings. A systematic approach to designing and developing online courses may best assist instructional designers and teachers to optimize the learning environment, resulting in enhanced creation of new meaning for learners from the intended course content.

The psychosocial learning environment in an online course is represented by the communication and social context developed within the course and among its participants. Within any educational environment, there are certain factors related to student success and learning achievement. These factors include connectedness and support through teacher and classmate relationships, students' expectations for their learning, student autonomy, relevant learning activities, and academic motivation (Walker and Fraser 2005).

A learning environment can be described in terms of appeal, challenge, meaningfulness, academic self-efficacy, and independence. Gentry and Owen (2004) indicate that these constructs are central to effective learning. Education is also most effective when the information presented is challenging, relevant, meaningful, interesting, and sparks a student's imagination. Consideration of these factors in a learning environment represents "an important aspect of quality education" (p. 21).

According to Walker and Fraser (2005), the psychosocial learning environment can be divided into six categories, including:

- teacher support, which describes the level of support students receive from a teacher
- student interaction and collaboration, which describes interactions with other students
- personal relevance, which describes the relevance of the material taught in the courses
- authentic learning, which describes the reality of content covered in the class
- active learning, which describes how actively students manage their own learning
- student autonomy, which describes how much control students take for their own learning

Enjoyment, a likely result of the previous six factors, can predict student success in an online learning environment. As such, these categories should attract considerable attention during the online course design process.

Make no mistake; there is no substitute for human interaction. While online learning may not place students in physical proximity, there is a wealth of tools that can be utilized to help students engage, collaborate, and construct meaning in ways that a traditional classroom cannot replicate. The role of the teacher in online education has expanded from that of a traditional teacher in an f2f environment to one that facilitates teamwork and collaboration, engagement, communication, and relevance within an online setting (Hawkins et al. 2012). An increase in sense of community in an online environment is directly related to cognitive learning and results in greater student persistence toward learning objectives.

Studies of middle and high school students suggest that when students have positive perceptions of their communications and connections in school, it correlates to higher grades and graduation rates (Nasir et al. 2011). Positive student perceptions of the online psychosocial learning environment may lead to greater persistence and more motivation to pursue additional online courses.

Engaging students in an online course presents challenges that are unique to that environment, however. Encouraging collaboration, developing productive teams, helping students manage their own learning, and providing relevance through a facilitated approach requires additional efforts that may appear to be more obvious in the preparation of an f2f course. However, with the right approach to course development and implementation, these elements can be incorporated into any online environment. The following section describes how an online teacher can ensure each of the six categories previously discussed are addressed in ways that encourage and promote student success in an online learning environment.

Teacher Support

The importance of teacher support in an online learning environment can never be underestimated. Support for online learners is critical for student persistence, retention, and ultimately their success. Teacher support is evident when the teacher exhibits a sense of presence even without a physical presence. When online students feel their teacher is virtually present, they are more likely to exert the effort and persevere even when they face challenges and obstacles in their learning. An element of teacher support is how quickly and how thoughtfully he or she responds to student inquiries. Responses within 48 hours, and preferably less than 24 hours, show a student that the teacher is present and listening. When a student runs into a question or a roadblock, a timely response will allow him to continue working without losing interest or momentum (Bennett and Lockyer 2004). Well-thought-out responses further demonstrate to students that they and their work are valued. Teachers should ensure responses are thoughtful, clearly and appropriately worded, encouraging, constructive, informative, and helpful. Teacher responses must prompt the students to continue to produce and further refine their work and should not leave them feeling unclear as to the meaning of the feedback. Written messages must be clearly worded to avoid confusion and frustration, and they should provide students with enough information to learn and grow. These responses take time, effort, planning, and careful review on the part of the teacher. Timely, clear, and purposeful responses allow students to move quickly to the next step in their learning and encourage them to continue to seek teacher input.

In addition to fast and appropriate responses, a teacher must also exhibit a supportive, welcoming, and encouraging atmosphere within the course environment. Starting an online course with a letter of introduction that shares a personal message from the teacher helps students feel more relaxed and may encourage them to freely ask questions and participate in discussions. Allowing students to share personal anecdotes and information with the teacher and classmates also encourages a warm, open online environment promoting more natural interaction and collaboration.

Strategies to enhance teacher support include the following:

- have clear, consistent expectations for students
- be available to work with students synchronously during specified times each week
- provide regular feedback on assignments and assessments
- be open, honest, and relatable
- keep regular contact with students. Call if you have not seen regular attendance and progress
- notify students right away of all changes in the course, assignments, expectations, and policies
- use VoiceThread, TinyTake, or other video software to introduce new units and information through brief (2 to 3 minute) videos featuring you, the teacher
- use Jing, TinyTake, or Snapdraw to record screen captures to illustrate and annotate complex information

Teachers who utilize most or all of these strategies will create a more welcoming online classroom environment, thereby creating an atmosphere where students may be more willing to engage in the instruction.

Student Interaction and Collaboration

Interaction and collaboration within the content of an online course can help students feel connected to classmates and the subject matter, which tends to promote an increase in student effort, perseverance, and achievement. A sense of belonging within any educational environment is shown to help improve student persistence and retention (Rovai 2003). Regularly working with others and participating in group assignments encourage students to feel connected and to believe their contribution is important to their own and others' success. Holding students accountable by making them part of a team and encouraging interaction promotes a sense of importance as valuable team members and instills pride and commitment to learning.

Another way to provide support and encourage interaction and collaboration is to host webinars and synchronous, interactive, remote learning sessions where students can work together and contribute in real-time. Online learning management software such as Canvas even allows students to enter virtual breakout rooms where the teacher may monitor and engage with individual groups. These sessions help students relate to one another, build collaborative teams, and encourage effective communication efforts even during asynchronous times. Teachers should also create opportunities for students to collaborate through team projects and team expectations. Allowing students to evaluate their own and their teammates' contributions and participation in the team encourages students to contribute positively and regularly. For example, student presentations can be posted onto a private class YouTube room and learners can be required to evaluate presentations, thereby enhancing their own learning.

Strategies to enhance student interaction and collaboration include the following:

- select group participants based on student interests and learning goals
- create teams of manageable size to ensure all participants remain engaged
- provide clear expectations for group behaviors and participation
- provide clear expectations for each team assignment
- encourage team members to use interactive collaboration tools such as Google Drive and Blackboard Collaborate

These strategies can lead learners to heightened interest in the course material and process, resulting in greater a willingness to engage with the content, as well as other students.

Personal Relevance

Personal relevance in learning is the feeling that the course content is meaningful and contributes to students' lives. For example, a math teacher may wish to address binary networks, exponents, or algorithms and how they relate to the social media technologies that many students use every day, or a language arts teacher may prompt a virtual discussion related to how social media has changed the way humans communicate. Seeing relevance in any learning environment is essential to students' willingness to put forth effort toward their learning goals, and personal relevance within an online learning environment requires that students commit to the learning. A commitment to learning allows students to create personal learning goals and helps them understand the importance of the material from a personal perspective.

Strategies to enhance personal relevance include the following:

- incorporate social media into lessons and discussions
- use current news stories to begin unit-relevant discussions

- ask for and use student input for discussions, assignments, and assessments
- embed student discussion points in assessments

By integrating such strategies, students may better understand the relevance of course content as it relates to them, resulting in greater student engagement.

Authentic Learning

Authentic learning refers to the genuineness of the learning environment. An authentic learning environment incorporates real-life problems, genuine learning situations, and realistic opportunities. Even in a remote online environment, helping students see the authenticity of lessons provides incentive to work toward learning goals. Synchronous lessons hosting guest speakers, virtual field trips, and the sharing of personal experiences related to the content will develop students' sense of relevance and authenticity of the course content. Real-world problem-solving opportunities and the ability for students to apply their learning to real situations are also important aspects of developing effective online lessons that promote authenticity (Walker and Fraser 2005). For example, a social studies teacher may launch a class with a video of the President's most recent speech, identifying a specific problem that may relate to high school–age students.

Strategies for enhancing authentic learning include the following:

- incorporate problem-based learning (discussed in detail in the following section)
- use threaded discussions with timely topics
- involve the community in projects to provide help evaluate ideas for projects
- use interdisciplinary topics and assignments, such as a project that helps students connect computer programming with mathematics or biology with food science
- use analysis, synthesis, and evaluation-level questioning techniques

Understanding how to develop authentic lessons can positively influence students' acceptance of the content and their willingness to engage in that content.

Active Learning

Active learning is the extent to which students take charge of their own learning. Active learning incorporates relevance and authenticity insofar as those elements encourage students to be attentive to their learning and achieve their goals. Helping students create learning goals and allowing them to continually monitor their own progress supports active learning (Walker and Fraser 2005).

To help students remain active in their learning, be sure to keep grading updated to allow students to continually monitor their progress. Ensure that students know all course expectations, and provide students with frequent opportunities to compare their progress with those expectations. Encourage students to review their own work and their own progress, and provide them with a pacing calendar for assignments and performance goals. Ensuring students have this information easily accessible allows them to keep an appropriate pace and achieve their own and preset learning goals. One example of encouraging active learning is to have a weekly quiz that includes one simple question: "What is your grade as of today?" By doing so, students know that they will be required to monitor their own progress.

Strategies for enhancing active learning include the following:

- create a system whereby students can keep track of their own progress
- set expectations early and continually reinforce and remind
- personalize learning using student interests and ideas
- involve the community in the learning when feasible

By using active learning strategies, students are more likely to take control of their own learning, resulting in greater accountability for all learners. Students willing to be accountable for their own learning also tend to recall and address their own learning goals.

Student Autonomy

With updated and accessible information about pacing, goals, and progress at their fingertips, students can take more control of their learning. Independently taking control of their learning is student autonomy, and autonomy is a key factor in student success in an online environment. Self-directed activities can be intermixed with collaborative activities to help promote independence and autonomy that encourage students to make continued progress and not fall behind. For example, individuals may each be given a *piece* of a problem to solve, and then team members determine how to assemble the individual pieces together. When students feel they are in control of their own learning and their own success, their locus of control becomes internal, allowing students to be self-reliant and develop a sense of self-efficacy in their education (Gentry and Owen 2004).

Strategies for enhancing student autonomy include the following:

* provide students with resources and guidance on how to use them
* provide choices for student projects and assignments
* encourage creativity in problem solving by expecting students to freely explain their thought processes
* be available and encourage students to persevere when facing challenges and disappointment

Such learning strategies can create an environment in which students are more likely and willing to work autonomously when the situation calls for it, both as a team member and as an individual learner.

Enjoyment

Overall, when students enjoy the learning environment, they are more likely to experience success. A clear and concerted effort to create an environment that incorporates teacher support, student interaction and collaboration, personal relevance, authentic learning, active learning, and student autonomy can increase the likelihood that a student enjoys an online course. Enjoyment in a course typically leads to higher levels of student engagement, more robust participation in their own learning, and greater learning success by encouraging students to actively pursue their learning goals (Simpson and Du 2004).

Once the six categories previously mentioned have been developed and optimized, teachers may then implement strategies to aid students in constructing meaning. For example, until an online classroom has a conduit for collaboration, students may not have the same opportunities to learn from each other.

Online Constructivism Strategies

What is Constructivism?

Manipulating the psychosocial learning environment is but the first step in creating an online learning system conducive to constructivism. Recall that constructivism is the building or *construction* of new knowledge whereby learners use their senses to gather and organize information, then create new layers of knowledge by assimilating what is known (Mahoney 2004). While the term constructivism may be familiar to most teachers, implementing instructional strategies to promote constructivist learning in an online environment may be challenging.

According to Davidson-Shivers and Rasmussen (2006), an effective online environment should include four elements: (1) an orientation to learning that includes an introduction and directions on how to navigate the learning system; (2) instruction on the content, including delivery of the content itself, as well as an opportunity to practice with and apply the content via activities; (3) a measurement of the learning that has taken place; and (4) a summary and close to enhance and enrich learning. Constructivism utilizes higher order learning, and as a result, the online learning environment must first be as effective as possible before such higher order learning can take place. Therefore, implementing these four elements into the learning environment is essential to constructivist learning online. Once they have been satisfied, instructional strategies within the instruction may be employed to promote constructivist learning (Guizzardi 2006). An effective strategy that may be employed is problem-based learning, but others, including guided instruction, simulations and games, case studies, and capstone assignments, can also be effective.

Problem-Based Learning

A primary educational strategy used to promote the construction of new knowledge is problem-based learning. While problem-based learning may occur in many forms, ultimately it is more than just a *project*. It provides a structure for discovery, appeals to learners' instincts to investigate and create, and provides a method for learners to internalize knowledge and skills, allowing for a transferal of knowledge in other applications (Larmer and Mergendoller 2010). In short, it promotes active learning.

While there are several models on how to best implement problem-based learning, The Consortium for Entrepreneurship Education (2010) breaks problem-based learning down into particular elements:

- a relevant, driving question on which to focus
- learner communication and collaboration
- learner inquiry and research
- feedback and revision

Implementing each of these four elements into an online lesson is essential in promoting constructivist learning. Developing a driving question is ultimately addressed by the teacher, although learner input may be considered to help develop that question. However, once the question has been formulated, the teacher's role changes significantly, and the focus becomes more of a designer of activities and learning facilitator.

Online Instructional Strategies to Promote Constructivism

Online strategies for promoting constructivism do not differ significantly from those strategies used in a traditional classroom; the difference lies in implementation. When selecting constructivist instructional strategies, the teacher and designer must take into account the capabilities of the learning management system (LMS) or the technological tools provided. For example, a teacher who has the tools and expertise (or access to that expertise, such as an IT specialist) to develop customized complex simulations and/or learning games have options at their disposal that others may not. In addition, a primary consideration in selecting instructional strategies is whether the course is synchronous, or in real-time, or asynchronous. If the teacher has the ability to facilitate the instruction in real-time, then strategies may differ. Some of the specific instructional strategies that lend themselves to online learning are guided instruction, simulations and games, case studies, and capstone assignments.

Guided Instruction

In a traditional classroom, guided instruction is nearly always done with small, purposeful groups based on prior formative assessment. Note that such groups are comprised of learners who share a common instructional need rather than ability grouping. The teacher then asks questions to check for understanding, moderates dialogue as the learners begin to apply the skill or strategy, and uses cues to scaffold understanding when students do not respond as expected (Fisher and Frey 2010). For example, a teacher may ask, "Look at the diagram again. What else might it be telling you?"

A challenge with implementing guided instruction online is that the teacher may not be able to provide immediate cues and prompts. Even in a synchronous environment, she cannot be with all groups at all times. When using guided instruction online, establishing a system for quick-response formative assessment is essential. The use of email, threaded discussions, social media, or live chats can help to accommodate this strategy.

It is important to note that guided instruction should not be an everyday strategy for every student. Rather, to maximize its effectiveness, teachers may choose to utilize guided instruction with one group at a time while others are working on something else. This practice allows the synchronous teacher to intervene just as she would in a traditional classroom. It allows asynchronous teachers to focus on one group at a time, providing more timely feedback. Having students continuously post their thoughts on a discussion board or social media site, for example, allows the teacher to monitor and provide rapid response cues.

Simulations and Games

It is no secret that many, if not most of our youth enjoy simulations and games. Traditional classroom teachers frequently develop and implement learning games within their classrooms. Glee (2007) notes of this trend, "[B]etter theories of learning are embedded in the video games many children in elementary and high school play than in the schools they attend" (p. 5). While this statement may offend some in the educational community, the essence is that a well-designed game can provide a considerable learning opportunity that helps students to formulate knowledge. Glee (2007) also stated that games and simulations lend themselves to the committed learning principle, whereby learners may be exceptionally motivated to engage with a game, not only because it might be enjoyable, but also because they feel a commitment to the virtual world in which they find themselves. As a result, a well-designed game or simulation can motivate students to learn on their own. Many may find themselves voluntarily continuing to play—and learn—outside of school as long as they have access.

Games and simulations that can be downloaded or are offered online are a natural fit with online learning as long as learners have access to the game outside of the classroom. Games that can be downloaded to mobile devices, such as smartphones, are even more accessible. The key for the teacher is in selecting or building a relevant game that aligns with course competencies and utilizes solid learning principles. A teacher who has the tools and ability to design his or her own game or simulation makes these two elements easy to achieve, and she possibly creates learning opportunities that cannot be replicated in a classroom. For example, the University of Delaware hosts an online virtual microscope that a biology teacher may require students to view and study certain unhealthy bacteria, something that would not be viable in a traditional classroom. Teachers without the ability to build their own games must take the time to locate and vet games that provide learners with appropriate content and are based on sound learning principles.

Finding games where multiple students can take part and interact simultaneously is ideal, as a multiplayer format lends itself to constructivism more so than would many individual player games, as students must solve problems together as they occur. However, a considerable number of educational games are built for individuals. As a result, collaboration and reflection of game play is essential. While individual learners may construct meaning during game play, debriefing with peers afterwards offers another learning opportunity entirely (Lateef 2010). Learners can discuss their actions, identify outcomes, postulate regarding *better* ways to approach the game, and test it. The cycle may last as long as the teacher prefers. For example, Knowledge Matters (2015) provides a *sim* business game/simulation that requires students to build a retail store. To build it, they must select a location, decide which products to sell, determine where to place them on the shelves, select what hours to be open, and more. At the conclusion of the game, they receive a report telling them their profits or losses. If a small group of learners congregated after playing the game individually, they can compare not only strategies, but also results. This activity would allow them to predict how future actions might alter the outcomes, and they can continue to play and test those options, thereby learning or constructing the intended business principles.

Case Studies

Case studies are scenarios that present contextually rich content and can be used with virtually any school subject. They present realistic and complex situations that involve a problem or dilemma that the students (role playing as characters) must address. Case studies are often based on actual circumstances that have already taken place, so the real outcome can be seen once the case study has been analyzed (Lauckner et al. 2012). Case studies help learners to close the gap between the real and the theoretical (Barkley et al. 2005), as students examine the case study and collaboratively attempt to find solutions to the problem as well as provide their rationale for arriving at their solution.

Case studies are ideal for online learning as long as the course has properly established a communication avenue between classmates. In seeking solutions, learners must explore an often unlimited number of open-ended variables and predict outcomes based on the manipulation of those variables. Case studies may be long or short, depending on the teacher's goals, and the teacher may require learners to examine the problem in its totality, or may identify a circumscribed piece of the case on which to focus. The key to using case studies online is student communication, collaboration, and reflection (Davis 1993). One common approach to case studies conducive to online learning is to have each member of a team conduct independent outside research on the problem, then assemble to discuss findings as they apply to the case. Ideally, the assembly takes place in a live setting, such as a video chat room, so that questions and comments can be addressed immediately, thereby leading to lively, productive, and dynamic discussion. For example, an elementary school teacher might visit goodcharacter.com and select an ethical dilemma for his or her students to analyze. Students may *choose sides* and debate the case. They may or may not be required to conduct outside research on the topic before discussion ensues.

According to Lovett (n.d.) of the Carnegie Mellon Eberly Center, there is a six-step framework for utilizing case studies as a constructivist tool:

1. Provide students with adequate time to read/view and contemplate the case.

2. Introduce the case and provide guidelines on how the case should be approached. Identify the steps students should take in analyzing the case.

3. Create groups and monitor them to ensure that everyone is involved. A discussion thread, for example, is a good way for teachers to be able to monitor engagement from each group member.

4. Have groups present their solutions. Written presentation appears obvious, but if the course is asynchronous, students may opt to upload a video presentation for all to view.

5. Ask questions—both students and teacher—for clarification and deeper analysis. For asynchronous courses, this Q&A may be done using social media, chat, or discussion threads.

6. Synthesize issues raised.

Variations of these steps may be considered based on the situation and LMS. Because of the amount of discovery learning taking place with discussions, teachers should refrain from the temptation of providing partial solutions, but rather focusing more on Socratic questioning.

Capstone Experiences

Capstone experiences are multifaceted assignments that require learners to assimilate academic knowledge and skills that have been acquired over a period of time. They are designed to encourage students not only to think critically, but also to transfer knowledge in a practical, real-world situation (Hidden Curriculum 2014). A capstone project is typically completed at the end of an academic program (i.e., senior year in high school or college) and requires the application of all of the related courses in the program. However, a similar strategy can also be used near or at the end of a single course by providing an assignment that requires students to address most or all of the course's competencies.

Like other strategies used to promote constructivism, capstone experiences are conducive to online learning, but they are not intended to be used as an instructional strategy for singular lessons or units. Rather, the teacher should identify the course outcomes and design a paper or project that requires learners to address them all, and capstones do lend themselves to student collaboration and research. Continuous group reflection at each phase of the product is a critical element to ensure that learners get the most out of the assignment, and the role of the teacher is to provide continuous formative evaluation. The assignment should be introduced very early in the year, and as each series of competencies are completed during the course of the year, the teacher should identify where that particular content fits within the context of the capstone and should provide a related assignment (or, if practical, assign students that particular portion of the capstone itself). Once the instruction has been segmented as such, the teacher should provide formative feedback to ensure that students are on track. Well-designed capstones necessarily require constructivist learning, as learners must use their skills and knowledge to construct new meaning and apply it in a new situation.

Consider a technology class that is intended to teach students how to build a website. Early in the year or semester, teams of students are given an assignment to build a site for a business or organization that has been prearranged by the teacher. The ultimate outcome is to build a site for that business. The teacher might invite the stakeholders to interview with the students to help develop goals and objectives of the site, with students asking questions that help develop those goals. Throughout the year, students can build pieces of the site as the instruction permits, and they are encouraged to, outside of classroom instruction, seek web development *tricks* that can be not only used in their site, but also shared with other students in the class as part of a library of technological possibilities for their classmates. At the conclusion of the course, stakeholders are invited again to hear student presentations and review the final products, and the stakeholders determine the website that best suits their needs.

Conclusion

Ultimately, constructivism helps learners to construct their own meaning, and course designers and teachers of an online course must, in some ways, depart from traditional classroom strategies to optimize the online classroom for this type of learning. The first step in doing so is to optimize the psychosocial learning environment to create a more viable online classroom. Once that is complete, the teacher can augment learning by adapting traditional strategies to an online environment. Teachers should keep in mind the following questions as they adapt traditional teaching strategies to an online environment:

- What efforts have been made to support students in an online environment?

- What venues and mediums have been established to help students communicate and collaborate? What resources have been provided to help them work independently?

- What efforts have been made to create relevant and authentic instruction? What instructional strategies are being utilized, and how are they being modified to an online classroom?

- In what ways has the teacher become a facilitator more so than a lecturer?

By using the concepts addressed in this chapter to answer the questions above, course designers and teachers can begin to create a more constructivist learning environment, resulting in enhanced online learning.

References

Barkley, Elizabeth K., Patricia Cross, and Claire Howell Major. *Collaborative Learning Techniques: A Handbook for College Faculty*. San Francisco: Jossey-Bass, 2005.

Bennett, S., and L. Lockyer. "Becoming an Online Teacher: Adapting to a Changed Environment for Teaching and Learning in Higher Education." *Educational Media International* 41, no. 3 (2004): 231-44. doi:10.1080/09523980410001 680842.

The Consortium for Entrepreneurship Education. "Problem Based Learning and Entrepreneurship Education," 2010. http://www.entre-ed.org/_network/problem -based.pdf.

Davidson-Shivers, Gayle V., and Karen L. Rasmussen. *Web-Based Learning: Design, Implementation, and Evaluation.* Upper Saddle River, NJ: Pearson Education, 2006.

Davis, Barbara Gross. *Tools for Teaching.* San Francisco: Jossey-Bass, 1993.

Fisher, Douglas, and Nancy Frey. *Guided Instruction.* Alexandria, VA: Association for Supervision and Curriculum Development, 2010.

Gentry, Marcia, and Steven Owen. "Secondary Student Perceptions of Classroom Quality: Instrumentation and Differences Between Advanced/Honors and Nonhonors Classes." *Journal of Secondary Gifted Education* 16, no. 1 (2004): 20-29.

Glee, James Paul. *What Video Games Have to Teach Us About Learning and Literacy.* New York: Palgrave MacMillan, 2007.

Guizzardi, Renata S. S. *Agent-Oriented Constructivist Knowledge Management.* Enschede, The Netherlands: Centre for Telematics and Information Technology, 2006.

Hawkins, Abigail, Charles R. Graham, and Michael K. Barbour. "Everybody is Their Own Island: Teacher Disconnection in a Virtual School." *International Review of Research in Open and Distance Learning* 13, no. 2 (2012): 123-44.

Hidden Curriculum. 2014. In *The Glossary of Education Reform*, ed. S. Abbott. http:// edglossary.org/hidden-curriculum.

Knowledge Matters. "High School Business Simulations," 2015. http://www .knowledgematters.com

Larmer, John, and John Mergendoller. "Seven Essentials for Project-Based Learning." *Educational Leadership* 68, no. 1 (2010): 34-37.

Lateef, Fatimah. "Simulation-Based Learning: Just Like the Real Thing." *Journal of Emergencies, Trauma, and Shock* 3, no. 4 (2010): 348-52. doi:10.4103 /0974-2700.70743.

Lauckner, Heidi, Margo Patterson, and Terry Krupa. "Using Constructivist Case Study Methodology to Understand Community Development Processes: Proposed Methodological Questions to Guide the Research Process." *The Qualitative Report* 17 (2012): 1-22.

Lovett, Marsha. "Case Studies." Pittsburgh: Carnegie Mellon University Press, n.d. https://www.cmu.edu/teaching/designteach/teach/instructionalstrategies/case studies.html

Mahoney, Michael. "What is Constructivism and Why is it Growing?" *Contemporary Psychology* 49 (2004): 360-63.

Nasir, Na'ilah Suad, Amina Jones, and Milbrey Wallin McLaughlin. "School Connectedness for Students in Low-Income Urban High Schools." *Teachers College Record* 113, no. 8 (2011): 1755-93.

Rovai, Alfred P. "Sense of Community, Perceived Cognitive Learning, and Persistence in Asynchronous Learning Networks." *The Internet and Higher Education* 5, no. 4 (2002), 319-32. doi:10.1016/s1096-7516(02)00130-6.

—. "In Search of Higher Persistence Rates in Distance Education Online Programs." *The Internet and Higher Education* 6, no. 1 (2003): 1-16. doi:10.1016/s1096-7516(02)00158-6.

Simpson, Carol, and Yunfei Du. "Effects of Learning Styles and Class Participation on Students' Enjoyment Level in Distributed Learning Environments." *Journal of Education for Library & Information Science* 45, no. 2 (2004): 123-36. Education Source, EBSCOhost.

University of Delaware. Microscope, n.d. https://www.udel.edu/biology/ketcham/microscope/scope.html.

Walker, Scott L., and Barry Fraser. "Development and Validation of an Instrument for Assessing Distance Education Learning Environments in Higher Education: The Distance Education Learning Environments Survey (DELES)." *Learning Environments Research* 8, no. 3 (2005): 289-308. doi:10.1007/s10984-005-1568-3.

TPACK as Mediated Practice

Rolin Moe and Linda Polin

Abstract

Technological pedagogical content knowledge (TPACK) is a framework for professional educators developed to help those understand the interplay of three unique domains of knowledge necessary for teaching: content, pedagogy, and technology. TPACK is grounded in the work of Lee Shulman's (1986) earlier work combining pedagogy and content knowledge. Shulman along with Punya Mishra and Matthew J. Koehler (2006), the authors of TPACK, allude to the importance of contemporary learning theories such as constructivism and social learning theory as integral to the TPACK construct. This chapter presents TPACK from the historical and theoretical perspectives in order to provide a full understanding of the construct as a model for learning by doing. It also reveals practical examples and suggestions for online teachers seeking to apply this framework in their own daily teaching practice.

Introduction

During a political effort spanning more than 30 years to integrate technology into classroom instruction, one critical barrier to implementation has rarely been recognized and never successfully addressed: the lack of a theory for integration. De facto teacher preservice and in-service professional development has largely focused on *how to*, i.e., procedural understanding of tech tools, or *why to*, i.e., largely legislatively mandated and politically strident urging, but certainly not *when*. Knowing when to employ an instructional tool requires understanding something about the relationship between the features of the tool and the context in which it might be used. This is the proposition of technological pedagogical content knowledge (TPACK).

Beginning with Shulman's (1986, p. 8) concept of pedagogical content knowledge (PCK), Mishra and Koehler (2006, p. 1017) expanded the domain of teacher knowledge by incorporating technology as a third area of expertise, mediating and being mediated by the other two and generating a sweet spot of *technological pedagogical content knowledge.* Their TPACK model does not privilege technology over curriculum or pedagogy, but it emphasizes the mutually mediating effects of all three. That is, technology can and should suggest new ways of thinking about content and new pedagogical moves.

This chapter provides both a theoretical and practical framework for understanding and accessing the confluence of technology, pedagogy, and content expertise for successful teaching practices. We provide a brief review of the history of domain ontologies as a solution, followed by a more in-depth look at the relationship where the three elements merge.

Joining Pedagogy, Content, and Curriculum

In 1986, in a watershed address to the *American Educational Research Association*, Lee Shulman offered an alternative conception of the knowledge domain for teaching as a practice and profession. Shulman's proposition addressed two problems: the separation of pedagogy from curriculum and the emphasis on pedagogy as procedural moves. Shulman (1986) explains it this way:

> Mere content knowledge is likely to be as useless pedagogically as content-free [pedagogical] skill. But to blend properly the two aspects of a teacher's capacities requires that we pay as much attention to the content aspects of teaching as we have recently devoted to the elements of teaching process. (p. 9)

The domain-independent conception of teaching that viewed subject matter as interchangeable content carried by a variety of generic teaching strategies focused on transfer and storage of knowledge (Schoenfeld 1988). However, Shulman is not merely rebalancing the focus of teaching skill on content as well as pedagogy. Rather, he asserts that knowing a subject matter is not the same as being able to teach it to others skillfully or that good teaching is not the sum of good pedagogy and solid content knowledge but the interaction between the two, which results in a new knowledge domain: PCK. This theory expands content knowledge beyond concepts and information in a subject matter domain to include the epistemic structure of that domain: *What are the critical topics within the domain? How are ideas organized? How are they represented? What constitutes evidence?*

In some ways, Shulman's (1986) work is very prescient, anticipating social learning theories. His analysis of this teaching landscape begins to sound very much like that of an activity theorist, identifying mediating effects of and tensions within the sociocultural political system in which the teacher operates to accomplish teaching. Additionally, Shulman argues that "if a teacher has to 'know the territory' of teaching then it is the landscape of such materials, institutions, organization, and mechanisms with which he or she must be familiar" (p. 9). Wenger-Trayner and Wenger-Trayner's (2014) extension of communities of practice theory now invokes "landscapes" of practice, referring to the increased sophistication of a practitioner who understands not just her own practice, but a good bit about those practices that impact hers (p. 4).

From PCK to TPACK

TPACK is a theoretical model of technology integration in instruction for K–12 and adult learners. To understand the value of this model, it is necessary to recognize the advantage that a theory provides over a set of procedures. When teachers or preservice teachers are trained to do rather than to think about an instructional task, their options are limited. When things go wrong in the procedure or script or plan, they are without recourse for improvising. Yet we know teaching is a partly, if not wholly, improvised activity (Duckworth 1986, p. 481). In classrooms, teachers are called upon to make hundreds of moment-to-moment decisions. They can deduce from years of experience a set of things that seem to work, and if they are reflective about it, further deduce a working hypothesis about why. Theory scaffolds that kind of discovery and offers strong up-front support for its development. While Shulman's PCK allows for this, the influx of digital technology into the school landscape has, for many teachers, disrupted rather than mediated the relationship between pedagogy and content. Furthermore, unlike curriculum and pedagogy, Computer Age digital technology is a rapidly and constantly changing domain of knowledge. What was sufficient to define "computer literacy" in 1988 would not stand up to today's classroom technologies (Lankshear and Knobel 2005, p. 7).

For a teacher, technological knowledge means understanding the array of available tools and media sufficiently well enough to determine their possible contribution in the classroom. This is how technological knowledge mediates instruction in a content area, as seen in Figure 5.1.

Technology Knowledge (TK)

Technology knowledge (TK), also referred to as technological knowledge, is defined in terms of one's comfort with a constantly moving domain of knowledge. The emphasis is not on knowing particular applications or hardware platforms, which have a limited shelf life. Rather, the focus is on self-efficacy with regard to learning new technologies. That is, the teacher's technical fluency is defined by his/her level of engagement with technology in general, an idea which supports the value of remaining current in the digital landscape. A technically knowledgeable teacher might read *Wired* magazine, attend regional educational technology conferences, and comfortably troubleshoot or find assistance to solve technical problems.

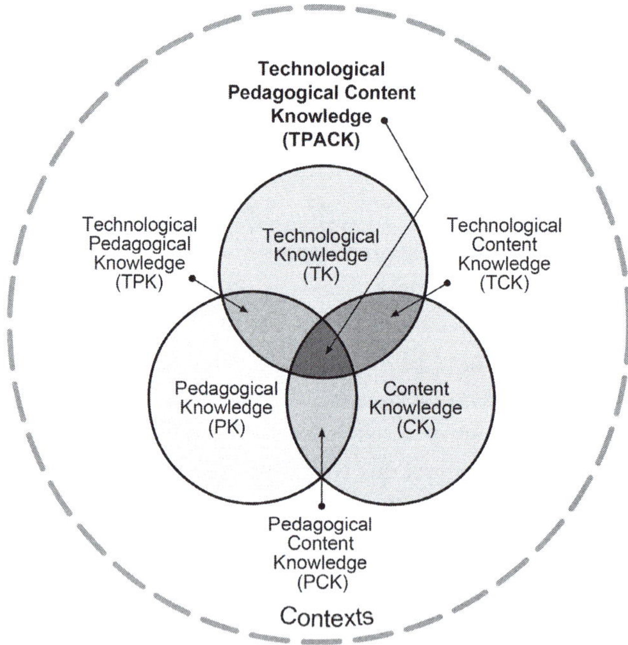

Figure 5.1   Visual representation of technological pedagogical content knowledge (TPACK)

Technology + Content Knowledge (TCK)

Technological content knowledge (TCK) views technology as an alternative delivery system and an alternative representational format for content. For example, teachers might learn about *good math software* or how Google Earth visualizations might support a human geography unit. They might also embrace a broader spectrum of formats for student work and curricular content. However, relying on content knowledge only gets the teacher so far. PCK introduces the epistemic aspects of the subject matter. For instance, what are the best ways to engage with these mathematical ideas or what are the central concepts in human geography? A teacher with TCK might know, for example, a software package for visualization and manipulation of a calculus graph or a three-dimensional view of geographical barriers to human migration.

Technology + Pedagogical Knowledge (TPK)

Technological pedagogical knowledge (TPK) assumes a view of technology as a pedagogical technique, either new or better by virtue of the features of the technology. Teachers might learn about the use of wikis for collaborative work or podcasts/vodcasts for *flipping* the classroom (Ash 2012, s7). Often, the motive behind TPK is the hope that new technologies will push teachers into different and presumably better pedagogical strategies, e.g., away from didactic sage-on-the-stage style of presentation toward workshop-like, highly interactive engagement during the class; that is, away from transmission of content and toward active construction of meaning. However, understanding the best technologies for creating and sustaining those kinds of pedagogical moves, while necessary, are not sufficient. TPK without content can lead to goal-free instructional activities, such as constructing replicas of ancient Egyptian ruins in *Minecraft*.

While both TCK and TPK capture important elements of the role of technology in teaching, by themselves they do not offer handholds for teachers trying to make immediate, contextualized decisions about what to do in their classroom with their students with regard to their particular curricular objectives. Indeed, they break up the central idea of PCK by isolating each other.

Technological pedagogical content knowledge (TPACK)

The Venn diagram in Figure 5.1 illustrates an overlap of the three domains, but is better thought of as the interaction or mediating effect of each upon the other. The content and structure of technology hardware, software, or networked services influence pedagogy and content. However, the intention of TPACK is for that influence to be intentional, designed, and relevant.

As digital technologies for education have become less about content delivery and more about construction, manipulation, representation, and distribution, they actually have a greater mediating influence on PCK. They support and encourage teachers to rethink not only how they teach, but what (Niess et al. 2009, p. 9). It does not matter if internet access is via mobile phone, tablet, or laptop. It matters that you can, for instance, produce, share, and communicate. In this way, digital technologies challenge low-tech curricular ideas and pedagogical moves by extending the range of possibility.

Thus the true value of the TPACK construct for preservice and in-service teachers lies in its integrative rather than additive approach to instructional use of technology. New media enables new pedagogy, and possibly new ways of thinking about the content of subject matter domains. And so, a teacher who has developed sophistication with TPACK is rethinking content and methods because of technical affordances of digital tools. A particular technical tool enables certain instructional moves that are only possible or best accomplished with that technology.

Acquiring TPACK

TPACK is not a feature of instruction or instructional materials. It is a knowledge base and a habit of mind that a teacher uses to guide the design of instruction. Writing about TPACK, Mishra and Koehler (2006, p. 1017) describe teachers developing TPACK or achieving TPACK, not applying or integrating it. TPACK is a framework for planning instruction, but also for improvising during instruction. It is a model or framework for making sensible use of technology in the context of one's own teaching. As such, TPACK is learned in preservice or in-service training.

Since TPACK's introduction and influence on the education community, a number of preservice and in-service programs have adopted Mishra and Koehler's approach to developing TPACK in teachers through applied design work (Doering, Beach, and O'Brien 2007, p. 43). In each case, successful implementation of TPACK is achieved through scaffolding its use in practice, through learning by designing. TPACK easily fits into a workshop style of engagement with curricular content and constructivism, where teachers through the acts of creating and doing become the source of their own learning.

The TPACK construct has a strong intuitive appeal, and in its fully realized Venn graphical representation it appears to be a simple matter of the mental acquisition of a model. However, in developing TPACK standards for mathematics, Margaret L. Niess, Emily H. van Zee, and Henry Gillow-Wiles (2011) drew upon field experiences with teachers working through the application of a TPACK framework and found teachers moved through a series of stages differentiated by the degree of comfort, commitment, and complexity. They proposed five stages of development describing a journey from acquiring an understanding of the possibilities to acting upon a fully realized TPACK construct. At the final stage, teachers' engagement with technology is truly mediational. That is, technology can result in changes to curriculum and pedagogy (p. 47).

While their developmental model offers a basis for determining teachers' depth of engagement with a TPACK perspective, it does not fully describe the process by which teachers advance. In their earliest work on the subject, Matthew J. Koehler and Punya Mishra (2005) relied on *learning by designing* as the leading activity for the development, suggesting that development of TPACK is best achieved by engaging in knowledge production activities that are supported by, and perhaps best or only constructed with, technology. Similarly, in a study using TPACK as a lens to integrate open educational resources (OERs) into a K–12 teacher preservice program, it was the immersive opportunity to transform instructional designs that most affected attitudes and learning (Kimmons 2015, p. 58).

It is important to recognize TPACK as an outlook, a perspective, and a way of thinking about instruction, rather than as a technique or procedure that is somehow applied to teaching a content area. A teacher who deeply understands the mutual mediation of pedagogy, content, and technology in the TPACK model sees curriculum and instruction differently. She does not need to think about integrating technology any more than she needs to think about integrating textbooks.

Working with TPACK

Another important aspect of TPACK is the generic nature of the model. Neither Mishra and Koehler (2006) nor Shulman (1986) prescribe a specific pedagogical approach. Thus, even with TPACK as a framework, a teacher who sees English literature as primarily about learning genres and forms of literature may see a didactic instructional model as the best instructional approach and may choose to use presentation software to support her lectures. It is not a particularly enlightened view of PCK, but the teacher's design choices demonstrate a TPACK compatible recognition of the interaction of media, content, and method.

As a further illustration, this chapter uses common core state standards (CCSS) and next generation science standards (NGSS) as a policy framework for seeing how TPACK can integrate into a classroom. Specific policy ventures come and go; however, CCSS and NGSS describe outcomes of K–12 content in ways that focus on concepts rather than information, application of concepts rather than memorization of information, and work in context rather than isolation. This discussion represents a shift in how policy references education, and this shift is indicative of the power of a TPACK approach to classroom instruction. To accomplish outcomes as noted in CCSS and NGSS, teachers need to make pedagogical changes that take them away from teacher-centric techniques such as lecture that supports a view of learning as the transfer of knowledge. Instead, they need to embrace methods that reinforce a view of learning as the use of knowledge in context. Both NGSS and CCSS standards/frameworks describe student learning outcomes best served by a constructivist pedagogical approach that makes use of authentic contexts for learning and engages students in complex, critical engagements with content (Marzano 2013).

The next section describes the interactive or mediating effect of a constructivist pedagogy, new technologies, and elements of CCSS and NGSS. It does not explain how to *do TPACK* but rather offers examples of TPACK designs from across the curriculum.

English Language Arts

CCSS.ELA-LITERACY.W.8.3—Write narratives to develop real or imagined experiences or events using effective techniques, relevant descriptive details, and well-structured event sequences.

Teachers from within the English/language arts community recognize the dramatic shift in literacy behavior and skills as a result of widespread access to the web as a consequence of the nature of Web 2.0, also known as the read/write web (Beach, Hull, and O'Brien 2011, p. 41; Lankshear and Knobel 2011, p. 16). Free and low-cost applications, ubiquity of camera phones with web access, and the rise of web communities all support rapid, frequent production, collaboration, and sharing by youth to peers. For youth, easily accessed digital information sources are privileged over print publication. Reading online, whether a 140-character Tweet or a lengthy blog posting, usually involves links to sources outside the original object, and it can often include embedded video or audio or still image clips. Multimodal and linked reading/writing is neither new nor rare. Youth are also accustomed to critiquing and remixing material they encounter online.

Understanding and valuing youth engagement with online resources pushes on the notion of what it means to be a literate consumer of content. The language arts curriculum focuses on both reading/consumption and writing/production, and curricular adjustments must address both consumption and production of digital material. The English/language arts curriculum must also take into account youth production of material for sharing with authentic audiences, including but not limited to peers. The everyday experience of youth in a networked and digital world demands rethinking what it means to be literate. This is a case of technology mediating curriculum, potentially changing what is taught and how.

A technologically proficient teacher, aware of these activities and even an active user of them, might see the potential in bringing these tools into the classroom by asking students to use them and by using them herself as part of her instructional methods. However, TPACK demands more. The teacher needs to understand how the choice of digital materials she uses affects the meaning she conveys. Likewise, students need to understand how to deliberately and effectively wield those tools to make their own best meaning clear, to understand how the medium interacts with the message. Previously, this was not a focus for language arts in a predominantly offline, print publication world.

The impact of digital literacy perspective on pedagogy may seem harder to realize than for content. However, drawing upon her PCK, the English language arts teacher should be aware of the decades-old prescription for teaching writing through engaging students in authentic writing tasks with legitimate audiences, those beyond the teacher and the classroom (Smagorinsky 2006, p. 14). Web 2.0 makes these tasks and audiences very accessible. The Wikipedia Education Program as an example purports to engage students as authors of content, held to the standards of Wikipedian nonfiction writing, mediated by the Wikipedian community, and legitimately published to a larger world, evidenced by tagline, "The end of throwaway assignments and the beginning of real-world impact for student editors."

CCSS.ELA-LITERACY.W.8.3—Write narratives to develop real or imagined experiences or events using effective technique, relevant descriptive details, and well-structured event sequences.

Since long before the internet, fans of literature have taken joy in writing their own narratives based upon and constrained by the world of the original fiction. This fanfiction acquired new power when the web opened up the possibility of publishing writing and receiving feedback from other fans in a range of online communities. The power of engagement with writing through fanfiction (Jenkins 2006, p. 44) is partly the power of having a real audience for one's writing. What makes fanfiction so incredibly useful is that it not only demands construction of the sort described in the CCSS, but also requires student writers to carefully read and comprehend the literary text to avoid contradicting or violating the original fictional world and its cultural boundaries in student-crafted tales. A teacher with a fully developed understanding of TPACK sees ways in which technology mediates pedagogical content to amplify instructional effectiveness.

Nonfiction Writing and Reading in History/Social Science

CCSS.ELA-LITERACY.RH.6-8.9—Analyze the relationship between a primary and secondary source on the same topic.

A striking feature of the internet is the vast amount of information available on virtually any topic not just in text, but also in image, graphic, and video. Despite the plethora of materials, the authority and value of any given source can be difficult to assess. Furthermore, material found online is often not constructed, tagged, or organized for instructional purposes. At the same time, relatively low-cost and easy access to production and dissemination of content in textual, video, and audio formats has given rise to a *remix* culture in which youth are able to mashup existing material in new ways, create additional novel contributions to the mix, and post it back out to a wide audience (Ito et al. 2009, p. 11; Jenkins 2006, p. 49). A TPACK teacher sees in this an authentic opportunity for students to wrestle with problems of credibility and diversity of sources and to pursue meaning-making projects that explain such things as historical events.

The teacher working from within a TPACK framework looks at technology for features that mesh with and support pedagogical content goals. A TPACK teacher with a constructivist pedagogical perspective is interested in providing opportunities for students to be historians and to participate in the taxonomy of history from events and artifacts, in ways similar to those employed by historians. Understanding a particular time in history becomes more useful, as a case of something, for example a case of civil unrest/war or a case of treaty making and breaking, relevant to current political action.

Web 2.0 production and sharing have also lowered the threshold for youth engagement in civic issues and participatory culture (Barron et al. 2014, p. 11). Efforts by teachers to engage local and global politics leaders in the classroom have been enhanced through numerous digital tools, from government websites providing access to elected officials to social media platforms such as Facebook and Twitter that allow students to develop and activate a public voice within these communities (Rheingold 2008, p. 101). What makes the digital interactions of a TPACK-mediated lesson differ from the paper copy interactions of a generation ago is not only the immediacy of the exchange, but also the transparency of the interaction, where multiple shareholders can participate as a collaboration that remains dynamic beyond a petition of government (Bertot et al. 2010, p. 55).

TPACK is not about the *what* or *how* to employ a technology, but rather the *why* and *when*. A topic such as content curation, which has been long considered a domain specific to library reference and research, is now germane to a TPACK classroom. Really simple syndication (RSS) feeds for distributing changing web content such as news allow a reader to follow many separate sources easily. A blogroll on one blog lists relevant other blogs and links allowing a reader to easily find additional information. File sharing domains and other aggregation instruments provide learners numerous platforms from which to create meaning through the collection and display of appropriate media. The creation of artifacts through these low-threshold mechanisms is, as posited in learning theories such as connectivism, an externalization of the individual learner's knowledge journey that can provide resource to extended learners both within and outside the localized environment (Siemens 2004, p. 3). The relationship between networks of learners and networks of information at the heart of connectivism provides an opportunity to link the information and contents read by networks of computers and networks of learners, in tandem with CCSS expectations of integrate qualitative and quantitative data sets within a problem analysis (CCSS.ELA-LITERACY.RH.9-10.7: Integrate quantitative or technical analysis [e.g., charts, research data] with qualitative analysis in print or digital text).

Mathematics With Meaning

CCSS.MATH.CONTENT.8.F.B.5—Describe qualitatively the functional relationship between two quantities by analyzing a graph (e.g., where the function is increasing or decreasing, linear or nonlinear). Sketch a graph that exhibits the qualitative features of a function that has been described verbally.

Mathematics is a troubling subject for many students, in part because "our education culture gives mathematics learners scarce resources for making sense of what they are learning" (Papert 1980, p. 55). Seymour Papert (1980) explicitly calls out the distance between mathematical concepts and procedures in *school math* and ideas and methods that might be invoked to accomplish something personally meaningful. School math's thin context, originally intended as a shortcut to convey the essential concepts, turns out to be a liability, depriving it of language and application that would make it easier to learn. It is considerably more difficult to have a conversation about mathematical ideas than literary ones, partly because mathematical language—not ideas, but language—is not part of everyday talk. As mathematics progresses through the grade levels, it leaves real, particular, and concrete representations and practices and heads into more abstract, symbolic, and thinly contextualized elements and tasks (Schleppegrell 2007, p. 148). It becomes harder to talk about and harder to both touch and teach.

For constructivist teachers, providing students with external representations of abstract ideas in action provides a way for engagement with those ideas. For Papert (1980), computer programming offered that opportunity; today, applications such as Geometer's Sketchpad allow students to create and manipulate graphical representations of geometric relations. There are many sites offering ideas and samples for lesson using Geometer's Sketchpad to engage with the CCSS recommendations.

Some subtopics in mathematics are more readily connected to everyday life and can be engaged with as an alternative way of describing reality. From a TPACK perspective, a teacher well aware of the rising interest in games and learning might find pedagogical value of connecting mathematical ideas to gameplay experiences. The teacher might ask students to demonstrate understanding of two dimensional graphs by writing a video game narrative based on a graph illustrating the ebb and flow of gold between two teams as a function of time or of *enemies* and *objectives* downed in a 40-minute League of Legends game (see Figure 5.2).

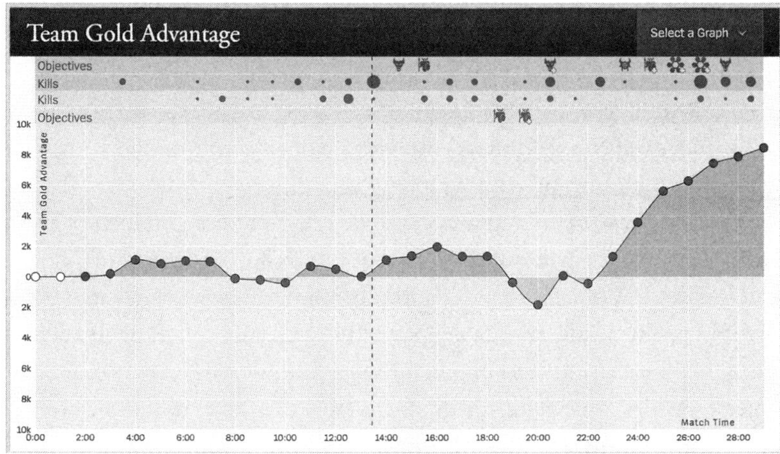

Figure 5.2   Data graph regarding the gold advantage for two teams in League of Legends. matchhistory.na .leagueoflegends.com

Or, she could introduce a calculus problem that would engage the student in the task of optimizing the balance between one game element that amplifies player health and a different element that bolsters defense (see Figure 5.3).

In League of Legends, a player's Effective Health when defending against physical damage is given by $E = \frac{H(100+A)}{100}$, where H is health and A is armor.

(1) Health costs 2.5 gold per unit, and Armor costs 18 gold per unit. You have 3600 gold, and you need to optimize the effectiveness E of your health and armor to survive as long as possible against the enemy team's attacks. How much of each should you buy?

Figure 5.3   A math question built from online gameplay. matheducators.stackexchange.com/questions/1550 /optimization-problems-that-todays-students-might -actually-encounter/1561#1561

Science and Engineering Design

MS-ETS1-4—Develop a model to generate data for iterative testing and modification of a proposed object, tool, or process such that an optimal design can be achieved (NGSS).

Teachers with a fully developed sense of TPACK are aware of new ideas in their subject matter domain because they attend subject matter conferences and/or read journals published in their field. In addition to the potential of games for learning, two rising technological trends have great potential to impact the design of math and science instruction, especially under the NGSS with its emphasis on engineering design. Those are Maker/DIY culture and computational thinking.

The cost, ease of use, and accessibility of technical production tools have given rise to widespread informal communities of makers, doers, and builders. With simple programming languages such as Scratch, low-cost 3D printers, and affordable, powerful electronic components such as Arduino, youth are able to build and share fairly sophisticated engineered objects. At the same time, and perhaps because of the rise of electronics and programming activities with low thresholds of entry, computational thinking has appeared as a new topic in education, originally under the banner of Science, Technology, Engineering and Mathematics (STEM).

Papert (1980) first coined the phrase *computational thinking* 35 years ago, and at that time he connected it to the kind of thinking and analysis typically associated with computer programming and mathematics. The concept disappeared in the intervening decade, but it was resurrected by Jeanette M. Wing (2006, p. 33) who asserted that computational thinking was the overlooked critical skill set for the 21st century. Although loosely defined in her paper, Wing's (2006) call for computational thinking transcended computer science and mathematics and was seen by many as an important access point for increasing participation in STEM majors and careers. A loose coalition of organizations including the National Science Foundation, the National Research Council, the College Board, Computer Science Teachers Association, and the International Society for Technology in Education, among others, is developing a strong definition of the domain of computational thinking that cuts across the curriculum, beyond programming and mathematics. From the perspective of a constructivist, the teacher with a TPACK sensibility sees opportunities for students to learn science concepts by building objects that make use of those concepts for some purpose: NGSS asks us to think about engineering and model building as an opportunity for applying science concepts. A Maker/DIY project asks students to construct lie detectors measuring galvanic skin response based on their understanding of relevant biochemical and Arduino technology concepts.

Conclusion

TPACK is not a response to the appearance of *digital natives*, a generation born into the internet, nor to the presumed burgeoning student body with inherent skill in the use and application of technology in everyday life. The idea that modern students have unique abilities with technology due to their growth and environment in a rapidly evolving technological world is questionable at best, as it lacks a grounding in research. Rather, use of technology by the *net generation* is considered unspectacular and in need of scaffolding and augmentation (Selwyn 2009, p. 371). Teachers should not see the appropriation of technology in response to student ubiquity and thus be in a constant game of catch-up with advances in hardware and software. Instead, TPACK can be the framing mechanism for leading students through the content, cognitive, and social expectations of formal education where technology can bolster, supplement, and transform knowledge creation and collaboration and where students grow across multiple domains (specific content knowledge, pedagogical understanding, and technological acumen) rather than exploiting one in an effort to shore up another.

TPACK, as a development construct built on the why and the when of facilitation over the what or the how, is a negotiation of external forces on formal education focused heavily on matters of content, methodology, and management. A teacher employing the TPACK framework in their classroom lessons and objectives can meet the requirements of CCSS and district management policies by an expert integration of those elements in conjunction with applicable technology for a pedagogical purpose.

The examples of TPACK listed in this chapter are evidence of the viability of an approach to instruction that understands the importance of a confluence of unique but overlapping knowledge domains that comprise the profession of teaching. As part of a greater approach to considering when and why to utilize TPACK in your courses, Table 5.1 offers a set of questions to help guide your instructional designs around considering curricular contents, pedagogical methodologies, and technological acumen. These questions are intended to offer examples of the sort of questions internalized by teachers with deep TPACK understanding that guide their instructional designs. They are not a definitive listing, but rather designed to help the reader think about the ways in which one element of TPACK mediates the other two.

Table 5.1   Guiding Questions

Thinking About Pedagogy and Content

1. What are the outcomes expected and what sort of learning experiences will best accomplish that?

2. What pedagogical strategies support those experiences?

3. What can students do to demonstrate understanding?

Thinking About Technology and Content

1. What features of technology fit with features of my content area?

2. What features of technology match the curricular approach/content?

3. How can technology move us beyond what's possible with texts and materials in the classroom?

Thinking About Technology and Pedagogy

1. What features of technology match my pedagogical style?

2. How can technology give me new strategies for instruction that still align with the pedagogical approach I have taken?

3. How can my pedagogical style generate new ways of using *old* technology?

References

Ash, Katie. "Educators Evaluate 'Flipped Classrooms.'" *Education Week* 32, no. 2 (2012): s6-s8.

Barron, Brigid, Kimberley Gomez, Nichole Pinkard, and Caitlin K. Martin. *The Digital Youth Network: Cultivating Digital Media Citizenship in Urban Communities.* Cambridge, MA: MIT Press, 2014.

Beach, Richard, Glynda Hull, and David O'Brien. "Transforming English Language Arts in a Web 2.0 World," in *Handbook of Research on Teaching the English Language Arts,* ed. Diane Lapp and Douglas Fisher. Abingdon, UK: Routledge, 2011.

Bertot, John Carlo, Paul T. Jaeger, Sean Munson, and Tom Glaisyer. "Social Media Technology and Government Transparency." *Computer* 11 (2010): 53-59.

Doering, Aaron, Richard Beach, and David O'Brien. "Infusing Multimodal Tools and Digital Literacies into an English Education Program." *English Education* 40, no. 1 (2007): 41-60.

Duckworth, Eleanor. "Teaching as Research." *Harvard Educational Review* 56, no. 4 (1986): 481-96.

Ito, Mimi, Judi Antin, Megan Finn, Arthur Law, Annie Manion, Sarai Mitnick, and Heather Horst. *Hanging Out, Messing Around, and Geeking Out: Kids Living and Learning With New Media.* Cambridge, MA: MIT Press, 2009.

Jenkins, Henry. *Convergence Culture: Where Old and New Media Collide.* New York: NYU Press, 2006.

Kimmons, Royce. "Examining TPACK's Theoretical Future." *Journal of Technology and Teacher Education* 23, no. 1 (2015): 53-77.

Koehler, Matthew J., and Punya Mishra. "Teachers Learning Technology by Design." *Journal of Computing in Teacher Education* 21, no. 3 (2005): 94-102.

Lankshear, Colin, and Michele Knobel. *New Literacies: Everyday Practices and Social Learning.* London: McGraw-Hill Education, 2011.

—. Digital Literacies: Policy, Pedagogy and Research Considerations for Education. Plenary address, ITU Conference, Oslo, Norway, October 20, 2005.

Marzano, Robert J. *The Art and Science of Teaching the Common Core State Standards.* Palm Beach Gardens, FL: Learning Sciences International, 2013.

Mishra, Punya, and Matthew J. Koehler. "Not 'What' but 'How': Becoming Design-wise About Educational Technology." In *What Teachers Should Know About Technology: Perspectives and Practices,* ed. Y. Zhao, 99-122. Greenwich, CT: Information Age Publishing, 2003.

—. "Technological Pedagogical Content Knowledge: A Framework for Teacher Knowledge." *The Teachers College Record* 108, no. 6 (2006): 1017.

Niess, Margaret L., Robert N. Ronau, Kathryn G. Shafer, Shannon O. Driskell, Suzanne R. Harper, Christopher Johnston, Christine Browning, S. Asli Özgün-Koca, and Gladis Kersaint. "Mathematics Teacher TPACK Standards and Development Model." *Contemporary Issues in Technology and Teacher Education* 9, no. 1 (2009): 4-24.

Niess, Margaret L., Emily H. van Zee, and Henry Gillow-Wiles. "Knowledge Growth in Teaching Mathematics/Science with Spreadsheets: Moving PCK to TPACK through Online Professional Development." *Journal of Digital Learning in Teacher Education* 27, no. 2 (2010): 42-52.

Papert, Seymour. *Mindstorms: Children, Computers, and Powerful Ideas.* New York: Basic Books, 1980.

Rheingold, Howard. "Using Participatory Media and Public Voice to Encourage Civic Engagement." In *Civic Life Online: Learning How Digital Media Can Engage Youth,* ed. W. Lance Bennett, 97-118. Cambridge, MA: MIT Press, 2008. doi:10.1162/dmal.9780262524827.097.

Schleppegrell, Mary. "The Linguistic Challenges of Mathematics Teaching and Learning: A Research Review." *Reading & Writing Quarterly* 23, no. 2 (2007): 139-59.

Schoenfeld, Alan H. "Problem Solving in Context(s)." *The Teaching and Assessing of Mathematical Problem Solving* 3, no. 82 (1988): 92.

Selwyn, Neil. "The Digital Native-Myth and Reality." *Aslib Proceedings* 61, no. 4 (2009): 364-79.

Shulman, Lee S. "Knowledge and Teaching. Foundations of the New Reform." *Harvard Educational Review* 57, no. 1 (1987): 1-37.

—. "Those Who Understand: Knowledge Growth in Teaching." *Educational Researcher* (1986): 8-22.

Siemens, George. "Connectivism: A Learning Theory for the Digital Age." *International Journal of Instructional Technology & Distance Learning* 1, no. 12 (2004): 3-10.

Smagorinsky, P., ed. *Research on Composition: Multiple Perspectives on Two Decades of Change.* New York: Teachers College Press, 2006.

Wenger-Trayner, Etienne, and Beverly Wenger-Trayner. "Learning in Landscapes of Practice: A Framework." In *Learning in Landscapes of Practice*, ed. Etienne Wenger-Trayner, Mark Fenton O'Creevy, Steven Hutchinson, Chris Kubiak, and Beverly Wenger-Trayner, 13-30. New York: Routledge, 2014.

Wing, Jeannette M. "Computational Thinking." *Communications of the ACM* 49, no. 3 (2006): 33-35.

Captivating the Online Learner: Frameworks and Standards for Effective Technology Integration

Chery Takkunen-Lucarelli

Abstract

Online learning, like any educational environment, requires careful and intentional instructional planning. Online learning provides many opportunities to engage students in 21st century skills and in ways that were not possible before, and online teachers should ensure that virtual learning spaces take full advantage of those opportunities. This chapter provides K–12 online teachers with an opportunity to understand how technology integration can be leveraged to optimize the learning environment in ways that engage learners. This chapter also examines frameworks such as the substitution, augmentation, modification, and redefinition (SAMR) model, 21st century skills, the International Society for Technology in Education (ISTE) standards, and the International Association for K–12 Online Learning (iNACOL) standards to help guide planning for effective technology integration in online learning.

Introduction

The online learning environment requires that students access material and interact with their teachers through web-based systems; however, because students are working *online*, teachers may falsely assume that students are engaging with technology in meaningful ways. This false assumption can lead to poorly designed online courses that do not take full advantage of the transformative opportunities that technological advances offer. It is true that navigating through the learning management system (LMS) environment can create opportunities for students to increase their technological skills. However, taking an online course does not mean that the student is utilizing technology in ways that are meaningful, empowering, and engaging. Online courses provide exciting opportunities for teachers to create engaging student activities and assessments if teachers and instructional designers are intentional in planning for these experiences, however.

Consider the following scenarios:

> Becca, a high school sophomore, is taking an online American Literature class. Her current reading assignment is to read Chapter Two of *The Scarlet Letter* by Nathaniel Hawthorne. After completing her reading assignment, she logs into her online class and reviews what she needs to complete. She responds to a discussion post on what she thought about Chapter Two. In addition, she takes an online vocabulary quiz. As she is required to respond to two of her peer's posts each week, she reads a few of the other student posts and offers comments. She reviews the requirements for an assignment and sees that she will need to write a paper on specific character traits for a character of her choosing. Since the paper isn't due for several weeks, she decides to wait to begin the assignment.

> Cooper is also a sophomore taking an online American Literature class and is also reading *The Scarlet Letter*. He begins his weekly session by viewing a video from his teacher on Voice-Thread. She provides big ideas from the reading and asks the students to consider some critical concepts. She also reminds students of what they are required to do for the rest of the week. Cooper is required to provide a video response with his own ideas, questions, or comments. He can comment to the teacher or to another student's ideas. As part of his tasks for the week, he is also required to begin creating a plan for a video documentary on the setting of the story with another student. He must create a Google Doc to share his planning with other students and invite the teacher to comment. The teacher encourages Cooper to seek out primary sources on the time period for *The Scarlet Letter*. In addition, she asks him to document how he is going to

delegate the tasks to complete the project. He begins to create a timeline and planning sheet for the documentary. He also needs to write his weekly journal where he blogs as if he is a character from the story. He skims the blog entries of a few other students and then begins to write his own entry.

Which of these two scenarios demonstrates an online learning environment that most engages the students in collaboration, research, and creativity while utilizing digital tools? Which student do you think is having a richer experience interacting with the teacher and other students? Most would agree that Cooper, the student in the second scenario, is utilizing technology in a much more effective manner. Most would also agree that the second scenario provides more opportunities for learners to collaborate, create new material, and think in complex ways. The use of the technology in the second scenario demonstrates how teachers can create online learning experiences that are engaging and empowering.

Teachers in any setting should be focused on practices that can increase student learning, and effective technology integration provides an opportunity to do so (Loertscher and Koechlin 2013). While distance and online learning have been in practice for many years in a variety of formats, recent technological advances provide exciting opportunities for online teachers to create learning activities that were not possible before. Consider how exciting it would be for students who are studying another country as part of a social studies assignment to participate in a live interview with other students from that country via Skype. Virtual learning can provide natural opportunities to engage students with technology in ways that are more difficult in onsite settings. If designed with student engagement in mind, teachers can take advantage of online collaborative tools such as Google Docs, wikis, or video hosting sites such as YouTube or virtual simulations and web-based video conferencing. The possibilities are endless. At the core of instructional practices should be *why* and *how*. The online environment presents exciting opportunities and challenges to effectively incorporate technology. One challenge facing many online teachers is that they may have had very little experience learning online; therefore, they lack models for planning online learning experiences (Yuzer and Gulsun 2014). Another challenge noted by Volkan Yuzer and Eby Gulsun (2014) is the newness of the K–12 online learning landscape. There may be fewer colleagues who teach online to share ideas with or to collaborate with to create learning experiences. However, frameworks, standards, and other conceptual ideas, grounded in research, can provide a roadmap for effective instruction that can address these challenges. The frameworks and standards provide a rationale and guidance for what that technological integration should look like.

Effective technology use can impact student achievement. Many researchers have found strong links between effective technology use in classrooms and student achievement (Green and Siegle 2002; Noeth and Volkov 2004; Valdez et al. 2000). Gilbert Valdez along with several colleagues (2000) conducted a meta-analysis of more than 800 studies involving technology and student achievement in the early 1990s. Each of these studies showed a positive impact on student learning. At every level, from preschool to higher education, a positive correlation between effective technology use and student achievement has been routinely identified (Valdez et al. 2000). In fact, in most cases, this gain in student achievement could be measured by using standardized achievement tests. In 2001, in its report to President Bush, the RAND Group stated that its studies also showed "that educational technology has begun to improve student performance and holds the potential for enabling far greater improvement" (Kirby et al. 2004, p. 20).

It has been argued that *how* technology is used is the key to improved student achievement, and expecting technology usage to increase student achievement without giving thought to *how* the technology is used in the learning environment is misguided (Green and Siegle 2002). In a study of all fourth- and eighth-grade students in Idaho, the researchers found an increase in student achievement for those students whose teachers used technology in ways that empowered students to solve programs and think critically (Green and Siegle 2002). Richard Noeth and Boris Volkov (2004) found many positive correlations between effective technology use and student achievement. For example, Noeth and Volkov (2004) found that students were more motivated when using computer technology, learned more efficiently when using computers, and were more likely to retain information. It is critical to note that simply providing access to technology (e.g., working online in an LMS) will not be enough to address low student achievement (Noeth and Volkov 2004).

As teachers design learning environments for K–12 students, they should think about their learners and the types of activities and assessments that will engage and empower them. Marc Prensky (2001), an international leader in education, discussed the possible digital disconnect between K-college learners and their teachers. Prensky labeled these K-college learners "digital natives" (p. 1) and teachers "digital immigrants" (p. 2) in part to demonstrate the different approaches to using technology. Computer technology and all of its supports such as video games, cell phones, MP3 players, and more have been around since these students were born. Prensky discussed how this digital environment has impacted the learning processes of these learners. Prensky stressed that students have typically spent more than 10,000 hours playing video games and over 20,000 hours watching television, while they have spent just 5,000 hours reading: "Computer games, e-mail, the Internet, cell phones and instant messaging are integral parts of their lives" (2001, p. 1). Prensky points out that learners, due to these experiences with the digital media, think and process information differently than past students, and teachers who have not grown up with these digital experiences typically teach in ways that do not embrace these different ways of thinking. Worse yet, is the fact that teachers do not appreciate or understand these new and different skills that their students possess. For example, digitally native learners enjoy random learning experiences and can more quickly make digital connections between tools in comparison with their teachers. Knowing this, online teachers need to carefully think about their instructional planning, keeping their *digital native* students in mind.

Some models of online learning encourage the creation of a course that is designed once and then can be taught again and again with little insight from the teacher and with little opportunity to empower students (Loertscher and Koechlin 2013). Predictability is the selling point of these types of courses, but as David Loertscher and Carol Koechlin (2013) point out, these courses can also be "deadly boring" (p. 50). In these types of courses, students have little opportunity to create content, collaborate with their peers, or work in creative and innovative ways.

In any educational setting, good instruction allows students to demonstrate their learning in a variety of formats. For example, sometimes online courses overutilize text-based discussion forums as the primary way to communicate with students, which can be limiting for some students and provides only one way of engaging with students. However, allowing students to communicate and collaborate with a peer or peers can be accomplished with different tools such as Google Docs or web conferencing programs such as Google Hangouts, Skype, and other tools such as Adobe Connect.

As stated earlier, online teachers may have the false belief that technology is integrated into the course because students are working *online* and accessing content through computers or mobile devices. By its very nature, online learning incorporates the use of technology. However, like any educational setting, the use of technology can be poor or rich. It can engage or bore. It can provide opportunities for students to be creators of new information or products, or support environments where students are merely consumers of technology. To help online teachers create compelling and powerful instructional learning environments that meet student needs and interests, research-based frameworks and standards can be leveraged to provide guidance for how to best implement technology. There are many frameworks to guide the planning of effective technology use. They have many overlapping and similar ideas and concepts that support each other. In this chapter, we examine two conceptual frameworks: the substitution, augmentation, modification, and redefinition (SAMR) model and the 21st century skills framework. We also review two sets of national education standards that provide guidance for effective technology integration: the International Society for Technology in Education (ISTE) student standards and the International Association for K12 Online Learning (iNACOL) quality online course standards.

Conceptual Frameworks

In this section, we examine two frameworks: the Four Cs from the 21st century skills framework and SAMR. These frameworks can help teachers and instructional designers think about effectively integrating technology in ways that optimize the learning environment. John Dewey (1916) stated that the "Social environment forms the mental and emotional disposition of behavior in individuals by engaging them in activities that arouse and strengthen certain impulses" (p. 13). Dewey suggests that teachers never educate directly, but indirectly by means of environment. Dewey explained this issue when he wrote, "Whether we permit chance environments to do the work, or whether we design environments for the purpose makes a great difference" (p. 15). Teachers can be intentional in their planning so that the online learning environment can capitalize on this phenomenon. When online courses are planned with intentionality to integrate technology in ways that put students in the *driver's seat* and utilize technology to create community and collaboration, there is a much higher chance for student achievement.

21st Century Skills Framework: The Four Cs

The 21st century skills framework articulated by the National Education Association (NEA) from 2012 along with the more recent version by the Partnership for 21st Century Skills (P21) from 2015, both developed by teachers, education experts, and business leaders, provides an architecture that addresses the essential skills and knowledge that students need to be successful as future citizens and students. This group of individuals formed the P21 and provides guidance and advocacy for the essential skills in the framework. The 21st century skills framework is a massive document that provides guidance for teachers and student outcomes in several areas including content knowledge, global awareness, life and career skills, as well as information literacy skills and competence with digital tools. Of these skills, Daniel Pink (2006) writes, "The future belongs to a very different kind of person with a very different kind of mind—creators and empathizers, pattern recognizers and meaning makers. These people...will now reap society's richest rewards and share its greatest joys" (p. 1). Pink, a bestselling author, has written on several topics that address the changing landscape of the future work environment. His work reinforces the need for teachers to embrace teaching in ways that empower students to think critically and to understand that the world is interconnected. His work reinforces the need for teachers to think about the skills laid out in the 21st century skills framework. Several themes strand through the 21st century skills framework. These strands include global awareness, leadership, and responsibility.

At the core of the 21st century skills framework are the Four Cs. The NEA (2012) noted that the Four Cs are the most important of the 21st century skills in preparing students for future success. They include the following:

- critical thinking
- communication
- collaboration
- creativity

The NEA (2012) writes that the Four Cs are critical to supporting students as they enter an ever-changing and more complicated work environment. Therefore, it is critical that online learning environments do not revert to *skill and drill* and lower level thinking activities. Instead, online courses should take advantage of new technological advances such as shared web spaces that include applications like wikis and blogs. These applications allow students to communicate and collaborate in asynchronous fashion across space and time, and online learning environments are positioned well for these types of rich experiences that can address the Four Cs.

A brief description of the Four Cs with an example of how this could be applied in an online learning environment follows.

Critical thinking: Critical thinking, as defined by P21 (2015), requires that students engage in problem-solving and a deep analysis of concepts and reflection. Students should solve complex problems that have multiple solutions. They should ask questions and provide different points of view on issues. For example, music students might listen to a musical passage and provide an individual interpretation. Students would then listen to the interpretations of their peers and provide a synthesis of what they believe is meant by the passage (NEA 2012).

Communication: NEA (2012) writes that communication skills for the 21st century include many of the same skills that have always been important (e.g., public speaking, writing, listening, and nonverbal communication). However, added to these core skills is also the need to have the skills to communicate through and with digital tools and with people from all over the world. For example, using a Google Doc, small groups of students in an online science class might create a list of interview questions for an archeologist on a dig site. They would then share their questions with the scientist and participation in a live Skype session with the scientist.

Collaboration: Collaboration for students can be defined as the ability to work effectively in teams with a willingness to be flexible (NEA 2012). Students working in effective collaborative teams share the goals of the project and take the responsibility to address their role in the project. For example, students working in small groups might investigate an environmental issue in their community and come up with a plan to share what they learned and to advocate for a solution. To help raise awareness of the issue, the students might create an email or social media campaign (NEA 2012).

Creativity: Students should be encouraged to develop, elaborate, analyze, and provide original work (NEA 2012). As part of creativity, students may need to work collaboratively with other students and may need to be open to hearing new perspectives (P21 2015). For example, students can apply and synthesize their learning on topics using web tools such as Smores or Prezi. They could create a demonstration or simulation to synthesize the content of a unit of study utilizing Google Slides or by creating a digital story. Students could then share their work on a class blog or in small groups to receive feedback and then refine and resubmit their work.

Thinking about the Four Cs can provide a powerful and compelling way to help teachers effectively integrate technology into the online learning activities. In fact, online environments may be better positioned than onsite classroom settings to incorporate information technology that allows students to simulate the types of activities that students might encounter in future workplace settings. Consider the growth of web-based video conferencing to host meetings and collaborative activities in the workplace, for example. Students in online courses could have many opportunities to experience participating in web-conference video sessions. They might be tasked with setting an agenda and leading a session on a collaborative project, or they may be asked to create a presentation and present their work live to a small group of their peers. In each of these cases, students are learning about how working in web-based meetings work.

David Loertscher and Carol Koeshlin (2013) point out that virtual learning yields exciting opportunities for students that are not possible in traditional face-to-face (f2f) environments. The ideas of *collaborative intelligence*, for example, where learners from across different settings help to create something new, is an exciting idea that can transform the online learning environment. Teachers can plan for learning activities that go beyond the virtual classroom walls and instead find opportunities to interact with individuals around the world.

SAMR Model

The SAMR model, developed by Ruben Puentedura (2015), provides another way to examine educational technology use. SAMR is an acronym that stands for *substitution, augmentation, modification,* and *redefinition*. At the heart of the model is the idea that, when properly used, technology can help to transform educational experiences and have a positive impact on student achievement (Puentedura 2015). What does it mean to use technology in ways that *transform* the educationally experience? Each of the four levels describes how educational technology may be used. Puentedura points out that teachers can plan instruction with technology that either *enhances* or *transforms* the educational experience with transformation being an important goal.

The bottom level, substitution, identifies technology used in ways that do not transform teaching but rather serve as a *substitute* for tasks that could be performed in other ways. For example, a student might use an iPad to take notes on a presentation. As you can see, this task could be substituted with a nontechnical tool like a pad of paper and a pen.

As you move up each level, the educational experiences of the students move towards transformation. Redefinition, the top of the four levels, describes educational tasks and experiences that would not be possible without the technological advances. For example, a group of online students might create a collaborative digital presentation using Google Slides that includes music, hyperlinks, videos, images, and recorded narration. This task cannot be substituted with a nontechnical approach.

When teachers discuss the SAMR model and instructional planning, they may use the phrase *teaching above the line* (Puentedura 2015). Teaching *above the line* means that the students are working at the modification or redefinition levels. At these levels, the educational experience is moving towards transformation. There is a significant shift in the way that the technology can be used to enhance learning when moving above the substitution and augmentation levels to modification and redefinition (Jacobs-Israel and Moorhead-Lang 2013). This *line* shifts the student to the creator rather than just the consumer of technology. The tasks that occur above the line would be impossible without the use of the technology (see Figure 6.1).

A brief explanation of each level and how this might be demonstrated in an online learning experience is provided in the following section.

Substitution: A student working in this level might complete a task that uses technology but could be substituted with nontechnical materials.

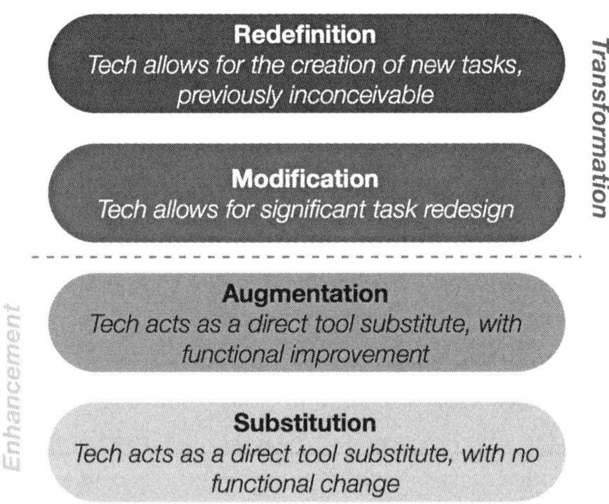

Figure 6.1   The SAMR model. hippasus.com/rrpweblog

A question a teacher could ask is, "Could the task be completed without technology?" (Puentedura 2013). If so, the technology task would be categorized as substitution. For example, a student listens to a presentation and takes notes on his laptop.

Augmentation: At this level, the technology acts as a "direct tool substitute, with functional improvement" (Puentedura 2015, p. 6). A question a teacher could ask is, "Have I added an improvement to the task process that could not be accomplished with the technology at the fundamental level?" (Puentedura 2013). In this scenario, a student might add an image and a hyperlink to a set of notes from the presentation (Jacobs-Israel and Moorhead-Lang 2013).

Modification: At this level, the tasks are "significantly redesigned." Multiple applications are normally involved in this level (Puentedura 2015, p. 6). A question a teacher could ask is, "Does this modification fundamentally depend on the new technology?" (Puentedura 2013) Melissa Jacobs-Israel and Heather Moorhead-Lang (2013) describe how students working at the modification level might create a collaborative presentation about their favorite books using Animoto. The students' slide shows could then be shared in a virtual book fair.

Redefinition: The technology provides for "the creation of new tasks, previously inconceivable" (Puentedura 2015, p. 6). A question a teacher could ask is, "How is the new task uniquely made possible by the new technology?" (Puentedura 2013). Jacobs-Israel and Moorhead-Lang (2013) give an example of students using apps such as Toontastic, which allows students to act as the creators of content as they can design their own animated films. These digital stories could then be shared with others online where they receive feedback. In this example, the task is not possible without the technological application. In another example, students could work collaboratively online to design and create their own app to solve a problem faced by society. The Mobile CSP (2015) project utilizes App Inventor, a free web-based application developed by MIT, to help students learn computer science principles as students create real apps that work on Android devices.

The tools may change, but the framework and models provide guidance. SAMR provides another way to think about technology integration in online learning environments. Teachers should intentionally plan for experiences that are above the line. In doing so, they have a better chance to engage learners and support student achievement goals.

Standards: ISTE and iNACOL

Organizations such as the ISTE and iNACOL provide a set of standards to guide effective technology integration. While the standards go beyond technology integration efforts, these standards provide a foundation to guide this aspect of instruction. What is now possible in the virtual world would not have been possible even a few years ago, and these standards can guide teachers to make the most of these new technologies. In this section, an overview of each set of standards is provided along with ideas on how they can help teachers plan for effective technology integration.

ISTE

ISTE's (2007) standards for students are organized into six categories. As you review the six categories of the ISTE standards for students, you may want to think about the ways that the standards align with the Four Cs and SAMR. You will see many similarities on how each of the models support each other.

The six categories of the ISTE (2007) standards for students are as follows:

1. Creativity and innovation: Students demonstrate creative thinking, construct knowledge, and develop innovative products and processes using technology.

2. Communication and collaboration: Students use digital media and environments to communicate and work collaboratively, including at a distance, to support individual learning and contribute to the learning of others.

3. Research and information fluency: Students apply digital tools to gather, evaluate, and use information.

4. Critical thinking, problem-solving, and decision making: Students use critical thinking skills to plan and conduct research, manage projects, solve problems, and make informed decisions using appropriate digital tools and resources.

5. Digital citizenship: Students understand human, cultural, and societal issues related to technology and practice legal and ethical behavior.

6. Technology operations and concepts: Students demonstrate a sound understanding of technology concepts, systems, and operations.

A review of the six broad categories of the ISTE student standards shows that they reinforce the Four Cs as well as the SAMR model. Students engaged in online collaboration can be taught to apply the ideas of digital citizenship, as noted in ISTE Standard Five (digital citizenship). Students working online have the opportunities to work with others across the country and the world, interacting with other individuals and groups of people. James Banks (2014), an international leader in multicultural education, reinforces the need for students to understand the cultural and social issues that are required to do this well. He highlights in his book, *An Introduction to Multicultural Education*, a set of changing demographics, trends in global migration, and rapid globalization that are transforming the world and the way that we interact with each other. He writes, "Citizen education should help students acquire the knowledge, attitudes, and skills needed to function in their nation-states as well as in a diverse world society" (Banks 2014, p. 28).

Online courses that require students to collaborate with others in other locations and provide support for this work can help students achieve this goal. The ISTE standards underlie the importance of creating learning environments that can best prepare students for their future.

iNACOL Standards

iNACOL is an organization devoted to the quality of online courses and programs. They have done extensive work to create evaluation criteria to help teachers and other stakeholders of online courses and programs understand the critical components of effective online courses. The criteria are thorough, extensive, and focus on 11 broad areas as noted in the 2012 publication, *National Standards for Quality Online Teaching*. These 11 standards, organized A-K, provide guidance for online teachers to design courses that engage students and create rich learning experiences.

Each category (A-K) has several areas that reinforce each of the frameworks as well as the ISTE standards highlighted and discussed in this chapter. Several of the criteria presented here are perfectly aligned with the ideas discussed earlier and reinforce the idea that how technology use matters. For example, criteria under several of the A-K categories support collaboration, digital citizenship, communication, and use of emerging technologies. In the following section, samples of these criteria from the broad categories A-K that are directly related are highlighted. As you review these sample criteria, consider how these ideas support the other frameworks and standards previously reviewed.

From Standard A:

> The online teacher knows and understands the role of online learning in preparing students for the global community they live in, both now and in the future (iNACOL 2011, p. 4).

From Standard B:

> The online teacher knows and understands the use of an array of grade-appropriate online tools for communication, productivity, collaboration, analysis, presentation, research, and content delivery (iNACOL 2011, p. 5).
>
> The online teacher knows and understands the use of emerging technologies in a variety of mediums for teaching and learning, based on student needs (iNACOL 2011, p. 5).

From Standard C:

> The online teacher knows and understands the techniques and applications of online instructional strategies, based on current research and practice (e.g., discussion, student-directed learning, collaborative learning, lecture, project-based learning, forum, small group work) (iNACOL 2011, p. 6).
>
> The online teacher knows and understands the process for facilitating and monitoring online instruction groups that are goal-oriented, focused, project-based, and inquiry-oriented to promote learning through group interaction (iNACOL 2011, p. 6).

From Standard E:

> The online teacher knows and understands the responsibilities of digital citizenship and techniques to facilitate student investigations of the legal and ethical issues related to technology and society (iNACOL 2011, p. 9).

From Standard H:

> The online teacher knows and understands the reach of authentic assessments (i.e., the opportunity to demonstrate understanding of acquired knowledge and skills, as opposed

to testing isolated skills or retained facts) are part of the evaluation process (iNACOL 2011, p. 12).

From Standard I:

The online teacher knows and understands the role of student empowerment in online learning (iNACOL 2011, p. 14).

From Standard K:

The online teacher knows and understands critical digital literacies and 21st century skills (iNACOL 2011, p. 16).
The online teacher knows and understands appropriate use of technologies to enhance learning (iNACOL 2011, p. 16).

iNACOL's (2011) mission states, "The International Association for K–12 Online Learning (iNACOL) is to ensure all students have access to a world-class education and quality online learning opportunities that prepare them for a lifetime of success" (p. 2). Clearly, the iNACOL standards support this mission and reinforce the Four Cs from the 21st century skills framework, the SAMR model, and the ISTE standards for students highlighted in this chapter. These sample iNACOL standards criteria provide a compelling mandate for online teachers to design online learning experiences and courses that are rooted in effective technology use.

Conclusion

Effective online learning design takes time, creativity, and hard work. Like all good teaching practices, online instructional planning must focus on student learning and requires effort backed by research. What is now possible in the virtual world would not have been possible even a few years ago. These technological advances should be harvested and optimized to incorporate the very best of online teaching and learning. The frameworks and standards highlighted in this chapter provide guidance and offer a way to examine the level of technology use to support student learning. Loertscher and Koeshlin (2013) reinforce this point:

If "learning" is what we are after, whether blended or totally online, then a move must be initiated from locked-in, content-driven packages to participatory knowledge-building experiences. Learners need to be free to work individually, cooperatively, and collaboratively, with the best information available in technology-rich learning environments. (p. 53)

Online teachers should do their best to plan for and teach in ways that empower and engage learners. They should provide opportunities for students to prepare for an ever-changing world. Harnessing the power of emerging technologies provides new and exciting methods to transform online learning and therefore helps students reach their potential.

References

Banks, James. *An Introduction to Multicultural Education.* Boston: Pearson, 2014.

Dewey, John. *Democracy and Education.* Champaign, IL: Project Gutenberg, 1916.

Green, Clifford, and Del Siegle. The impact of SES and teacher exposure to technology on student achievement gain scores. In *Annual Meeting of the American Educational Research Association,* New Orleans, LA, 2002.

International Association for K–12 Online Learning. "National Standards for Quality Online Teaching," version 2, 2011. Accessed July 12, 2015, http://www.inacol.org/wp-content/uploads/2015/02/national-standards-for-quality-online-teaching-v2.pdf.

International Society for Technology in Education. "ISTE Standards," 2007. Accessed July 30, 2015, https://www.iste.org/docs/pdfs/20-14_ISTE_Standards-S_PDF.pdf.

Jacobs-Israel, Melissa, and Heather Moorhead-Lang. "Redefining Teaching in Libraries and Schools: AASL, Best Apps, Best Websites and the SAMR Model." *Teacher Librarian*, 41, no. 2 (2013): 16.

Loertscher, David, and Carol Koechlin. "Online Learning: Possibilities for a Participatory Culture." *Teacher Librarian*, 41, no. 1 (2013): 50.

Kirby, Sheila Nataraj, Jennifer Sloan McCombs, Scott Naftel, Heather Barney, Hilary Darilek, Frederick Doolittle, and Joseph Cordes. "Reforming Teacher Education: A First Year Progress Report on Teachers for a New Era," 2004. Accessed June 30, 2015, http://www.rand.org/pubs/technical_reports/TR149.html.

Mobile CSP. "Mobile Computing in App Inventor." Last modified June, 2015. Accessed July 9, 2015, http://mobile-csp.org/.

National Education Association. "Preparing 21st Century Students for a Global Society: An Educator's Guide to the 'Four Cs,'" 2012. Accessed June 25, 2015, http://www.nea.org.

Noeth, Richard, and Boris Volkov. "Evaluating the Effectiveness of Technology in Our Schools: ACT Policy Report," 2004. Iowa City: American College Testing. ERIC ED483855.

Partnership for 21st Century Learning. Home Page. Last modified 2015. Accessed June 13, 2015, http://www.P21.org.

Pink, Daniel. *A Whole New Mind*. New York: Riverhead, 2006.

Prensky, Mark. "Digital Natives, Digital Immigrants." *On the Horizon* 9, no. 5 (2001). Accessed June 28, 2015, http://www.marcprensky.com/writing/Prensky%20-%20Digital%20Natives,%20Digital%20Immigrants%20-%20Part1.pdf.

Puentedura, Rueben. "The SAMR Ladder: Questions and Transition." Last modified October 25, 2013. Accessed July 8, 2015, http://www.hippasus.com/rrpweblog/archives/000112.html.

—. "The SAMR Model: Background and Examples." Accessed July 8, 2015, http://www.hippasus.com/rrpweblog/archives/2012/08/23/SAMR_Background Exemplars.pdf

Valdez, Gilbert, Mary McNabb, Mary Foertsch, Mary Anderson, Mark Hawkes, and Lenaya Raack. *Computer-Based Technology and Learning: Evolving Uses and Expectations*. Oak Brook, IL: North Central Regional Educational Laboratory, 2000.

Yuzer, Volkan, and Eby Gulsun. *Handbook of Research on Emerging Priorities and Trends in Distance Education: Communication, Pedagogy and Technology*. Hershey, PA: IGI Global, 2014.

Online Student Teaching: From Planning to Implementation

Lori Feher and Kevin J. Graziano

Abstract

Online learning is growing exponentially, and with the continued advancements in technology, this growth is not likely to slow down. An online learning environment has the potential to meet the needs of many students who cannot function in a traditional setting. Today, about one third of higher education students have taken at least one online course (Allen 2013, p. 10) and across the country many school districts are offering online K–12 education. With the evolution of online learning, it is imperative that teacher preparation programs not only offer online courses, but also prepare preservice teachers to teach online. This chapter describes an online student teaching partnership between Nevada State College (NSC) and the Nevada Learning Academy (NLA), a 6–12 online school in the Clark County School District.

Introduction

Student teaching, for many colleges and universities, is the culminating field experience for education majors desiring to become teachers. Though the required hours to complete student teaching varies from institution to institution, new teachers consistently characterize student teaching as "the most valuable aspect of the education program" (Levine 2006, p. 39). Student teaching provides prospective teachers with the opportunity to test the theories, knowledge, pedagogy, practices, and classroom management techniques that they learned in their undergraduate and graduate teacher education courses. Simulating the experience of teaching is difficult to do in a college classroom, and the student teaching experience takes prospective teachers out of their classrooms and puts them into actual K–12 schools. It is a chance for students to be personally mentored by someone with experience and exemplary teaching skills. In a report by the National Council on Teacher Quality, it is noted that a strong student teaching experience has the power to dramatically improve the vision of teaching excellence (Greenberg, Palmerance, and Walsh 2011, p. 1). Excellent mentor teachers can transmit effective instructional techniques and important teaching lessons.

The teacher preparation program at Nevada State College (NSC) requires 16 weeks of supervised student teaching. In addition to student teaching in the classroom, student teachers attend weekly seminars facilitated by a college instructor. Student teachers argue that they learn more during student teaching than in their four years in the classroom. With the growth of online learning and modern advances with technology, it is important to find new, creative, forward-thinking ideas to take the student teaching experience to the next level. Online student teaching promises to do just that.

The Need for Online Student Teaching

All around us, new technologies are changing the way the world functions. People rely on technology to communicate, entertain, work, compose, create, and learn. Cell phones allow us to access the internet, anytime and anywhere. Information is literally at our fingertips. The world of education is evolving as well, and school districts across the country are incorporating technology into the classroom. Tablets and iPads, interactive white boards, student response systems, ebooks, and countless numbers of websites are being used in classrooms at every grade level. In order for teachers to keep up with modern technology and be highly skilled educators, they must not only know their content and pedagogy, but also be trained in teaching with technology. Teacher education needs to focus on how technology can become part of the teaching process, as teachers need to be able to use technology not only as a resource, but also as a teaching tool.

As the digital revolution continues to progress, we are seeing fully online programs as well as individual online courses offered (and often monitored) within the brick-and-mortar K–12 school setting. All fifty states, including Washington, D.C., now offer some virtual experience in

K–12 education (LaFrance and Beck 2014, p. 160). According to *Keeping Pace with K–12 Digital Learning*, 30 states have fully online schools operating at the statewide level, and it is estimated that over 315,000 students attended these fully online schools in the 2013–2014 school year, a year-over-year increase of 6.2 percent (Watson et al. 2014, p. 5). It is also projected that by 2019, 50 percent of all high school courses will be delivered online (Christensen et al. 2008).

Since 2010, 14 states have enacted laws to initiate or expand online coursework: Florida, Georgia, Idaho, Indiana, Iowa, Maine, Nevada, New Mexico, Ohio, Oregon, Tennessee, Utah, Virginia, and Washington (LaFrance and Beck 2014, p. 162–163). Some states such as Michigan, Alabama, New Mexico, and Idaho have passed legislative measures requiring K–12 students to complete at least one online learning experience by the time they graduate high school (Kennedy and Archambault 2012b, p. 185). Florida has mandated that all school districts provide online learning opportunities to all K–12 students. Idaho has adopted online teaching standards and is also the second state after Georgia to establish a state-level online teaching endorsement (Kennedy and Archambault 2012a, p. 35).

Despite these advances in online education, only 1.3 percent of teacher preparation programs are preparing teachers in settings other than traditional, brick-and-mortar classrooms (Kennedy and Archambault 2012b, p. 195). As education changes, teacher educators must also change. This requires an alteration in our training programs. The need for teacher preparation programs to train teachers in the online setting is apparent. According to Kathryn Kennedy and Leanna Archambault (2012b), K–12 online education is not presented as something that will completely replace traditional face-to-face (f2f) learning (p. 197–198). Traditional and online learning can be combined to provide the best educational experience possible for K–12 students.

In 2007, Iowa State University (ISU) was awarded a grant that helped initiate the movement of online training in teacher preparation programs. This initial virtual school field experience offered practical experiences in Iowa Learning Online (ILO) to first- and second-year preservice teachers. The preservice teachers were enrolled in a one-credit course at ISU, requiring them to spend 15 hours in ILO. The cooperating teacher provided guided observation and hands-on experiences, allowing the preservice teachers to interact with K–12 online students, parents, other online teachers, and course facilitators (Kennedy and Archambault 2012a, p. 36).

Online Student Teaching: A Case Study From Nevada

NSC is a four-year public college located in Henderson, Nevada. About 50 percent of its students are from culturally diverse backgrounds. When NSC opened in 2002, 177 students were enrolled at the college. In 2003, student enrollment increased 222 percent.

Approximately 50 student teachers graduate with a teaching degree each year from NSC. Students in the school of education are required to student teach for 16 weeks during their final semester in the program. Traditionally, this student teaching placement has been in a conventional f2f K–12 setting. However, with the increase in online learning, NSC created an online student teaching program that is combined with an f2f student teaching placement.

In 2013, NSC created a partnership with the Nevada Learning Academy (NLA), known as Virtual High School at that time. NLA is the first virtual high school in the Clark County School District. NLA is a full-time online school that serves nearly 13,000 students (Watson et al. 2014, p. 38). When NSC decided to pilot online student teaching in the fall of 2013, there were many uncertainties. Along with creating criteria for student selection into the online student teaching program and modifying observation and evaluation procedures for online student teachers, there needed to be a plan for incorporating both f2f and online student teaching experiences into the semester. This dual placement requires innovative scheduling and flexible mentors in both settings, as students selected for this dual placement must student teach in a conventional high school setting as well as in an online setting.

Teaching in an f2f classroom cannot be replicated in an online-only environment. NSC did not want to completely replace f2f student teaching because traditional schools typically employ NSC student teachers after student teaching. However, with the increasing prevalence of online programming through NLA and other blended and on-site programs, the intent was to expand and enrich student teaching by providing experiences in both f2f and online settings. The experience that is gained in an online setting is not confined to online teaching alone, and many skills that students who complete their online student teaching learn are valuable in an f2f classroom.

In implementing this dual experience, the online student teacher teaches two f2f classes at a traditional high school. The two classes are scheduled back-to-back, usually in the morning, which allows the student to arrive early and prepare with the cooperating teacher. After teaching two classes, the student teacher travels to the NLA building. The number of online classes that the student teacher is assigned varies depending on class size. Some classes may have 150 students and, in those situations, the student teacher is only assigned to one class. Other NLA online classes are much smaller, and, in these cases, the student teacher may be assigned to teach one class and then act as a teaching assistant in other classes. The student teacher spends all 16 weeks in this dual placement.

Though the virtual setting is more flexible, it requires that the student teacher meet physically with the NLA cooperating teacher daily during the first few weeks of the semester. The meetings allow the student teacher to check in with their cooperating teacher, discuss any relevant technology issues, and receive valuable mentoring. The student teacher continues to meet in person with the cooperating teacher in the online setting at least twice a week throughout the semester.

Kathryn Kennedy, Cathy Cavanaugh, and Kara Dawson (2013) believe that communication with a supervising teacher is key to students' experience in a virtual school field placement (p. 58). Kennedy, Cavanaugh, and Dawson (2013) studied the experiences of three preservice gradate teachers who voluntarily participated in a virtual field placement with online teachers. They found that it was essential for communication to be constant and deep in order for the preservice teachers to feel their relationship with their supervising teacher advanced their professional development as future teachers. The preservice teachers desired to hear what life was like for the supervising teacher as an online instructor in the K–12 environment and wanted to understand how they could fit into that new learning environment (Kennedy, Cavanaugh, and Dawson 2013, p. 59).

Selecting Student Teachers for the Online Placement

Since student teachers are placed in both online and f2f classes, a selection process has been created to determine which students would be accepted into the program. The dual placement requires more work for the student teacher, and it is important to ensure that the students selected for this type of placement possess essential skills such as being highly organized, possessing strong written communications skills, and having significant previous experience with technology.

In 2015, Leanna Archambault and Jean Larson surveyed 325 K–12 online teachers and identified the most important attributes an online teacher must have to be highly effective. The following section describes the results of Archambault and Larson's (2015) survey.

The most frequently cited attribute necessary to be an effective online teacher was the ability to communicate using a variety of methods, including phone, text, email, and video chat. Being structured, focused, prepared, and organized were also important characteristics for an effective online teacher, as stated by 37.8 percent of the respondents.

Seventy-two (27.8 percent) of respondents said online teachers who are engaging and have a solid understanding of their content area were said to be highly effective online teachers. In addition, a strong desire to learn, a willingness to continue professional development, and an understanding of the best practices for teaching online were included as important attributes. Several teachers also mentioned the value of having prior experience with traditional classroom teaching as a key to successful online teaching.

According to 55 of the respondents (21.2 percent), an effective online teacher must also be flexible and able to multitask. Flexibility is essential because of the ever-changing nature of online teaching. A fifth of all respondents (54, 20.8 percent) stated that effective online teachers are self-motivated with a strong work ethic. A friendly, supportive attitude, along with being patient, approachable, and caring were also mentioned as being important characteristics for effective online teachers by another fifth of the respondents (53, 20.5 percent).

Thirty-nine respondents (15.1 percent) listed comfort with technology as an important attribute for an online teacher. Many teachers described the value of an ability to "read data to determine if students are making learning progress" as well as being able to provide technical support to online students. It was also noted that online teachers should be willing to try and adapt to new technologies (p. 66).

Thirty-six respondents (13.9 percent) noted that providing students with punctual responses was an essential trait for an online teacher. Several participants mentioned how critical quick and frequent feedback was to a successful online course. Online teachers also reported the need for an ability to motivate and build relationships with students, even though these relations must be created through digital forms of communication.

Seventy-nine respondents (31.3 percent) explained that their preparation for online teaching was self-taught, indicating that they learned the process by teaching themselves and by "actually doing it." Leanna Archambault and

Jean Larson (2015) argue experience and practice are always a component of the learning process and this is true in learning how to teach an online class. Self-teaching and practice were the methods of training reported by many of the respondents.

The aforementioned attributes were considered as students were selected for NSC's online student teaching program. Both NSC and NLA agreed that placement of a single online student teacher would be best during the first year of the partnership. The young man who we selected was an English major in NSC's secondary education program. He had a high GPA and very high scores on his Praxis II exams. He had experience with online learning. He was an English major and had excellent writing skills. He wrote meaningful and timely responses to his students. He went above and beyond to get students to think more deeply about the material through thought-provoking questioning. His feedback was also specific to students' responses, which enabled him to connect with students on a more personal level. He was very successful as an online student teacher and was, in fact, hired at the NLA after graduation.

The success from our first online student teacher helped solidify the importance of selecting highly qualified students for the online student teaching program. Before candidates are selected, NSC and NLA staff meet with all secondary education majors who are interested in online student teaching. The benefits, challenges, and placement requirements for online student teaching are discussed. Students then volunteer for placement at NLA. A number of students choose not to volunteer for this placement, which may be due to factors such as having to travel between two schools, time commitment, workload, or simply a lack of interest. Once students who are interested in online student teaching have been identified, their GPA and Praxis scores are taken into consideration with the selection process. No student with a GPA below a 3.0 is considered for the program.

It is important to select students who are organized, dedicated, and understand that the workload is more difficult, as these students are planning lessons and taking on teaching responsibilities in both f2f and online classes. Online student teachers must also have excellent writing skills because a majority of the teaching and communication with online high school students is through writing. Not only do online student teachers need to know their content, but also be able to explain it in writing, using language that students can understand. Online student teachers must be able to communicate electronically in a mature, appropriate manner. It is important to select student teachers who are also organized and self-motivated. The high school students taking classes in an online setting are completing assignments on their own schedule, which means that assignments are coming in at different times. From a teacher's perspective, this format and the need to jump from one assignment to another can be difficult and confusing.

Since NSC's program of online student teaching is relatively new, we have not had the opportunity to prepare students to teach online. This deficit is a common practice among teacher education programs. Despite a growing body of literature related to K–12 online teachers, Archambault and Larson (2015) argue there is limited research that focuses on the characteristics and teacher preparation of K–12 online teachers (p. 50). The literature to date has focused primarily on the quality of K–12 online programs as well as student perceptions rather than on specific information regarding the preparation of those who teach online K–12 classes (Archambault 2011, p. 75). Because there are so few opportunities for pre-service teachers to be exposed to proper training in the techniques and methods for online teaching, most of this form of training occurs once a teacher is hired to teach online (Archambault and Larson 2015, p. 78). For this reason, teacher education programs need to provide coursework that includes online pedagogy curriculum as well as instructional design work in online learning environments (Kennedy and Archambault 2012a, p. 47).

Examples of possible preparation for an online teacher might require the completion of a course in online teaching methods, specialized instruction on recognizing and handling cyberbullying, preparing online modules, or finding online educational resources for high school students. All of these experiences would be helpful in preparing students for online teaching. NLA does provide tutorials, technical support, and trainings to help the student teachers become familiar with the learning management system (LMS) and other software programs such as Apex, and Softchalk. Teacher educators need to give preservice and in-service teachers a chance to unpack their beliefs, deconstruct their experiences, and reflect on how their past relates to their new learning opportunities (Kennedy and Archambault 2012a, p. 45).

What Does Online Student Teaching Look Like?

NLA began its program with purchased curriculum content, though they are transitioning to building their own content that supports the Clark County School District's values (Watson et al. 2014, p. 39). NSC student teachers are not involved in the process of curriculum development, but this does not mean that student teachers do not create lessons. For example, they create various alternate ways to explain and clarify these predesigned lessons for students who are unable to understand the lesson as it is originally presented. This reteaching requires an extensive knowledge of the content and an ability to present material in ways that reach various learning styles. The student teachers also hold a weekly online session that all their students are required to attend. During this time, the student teacher connects with students, provides further clarification on course materials, answers questions, and encourage students to participate more fully in the class.

Student teachers grade all assignments and respond to all students electronically. They are responsible for making calls to students and parents to ensure that students are keeping up and staying on task. The student teacher must continually reach out to their students and encourage them to stay on a steady pace to ensure that they are successful in the class, and parents are called when needed to inform them of pacing or academic issues. The student teacher must be available to meet with students who need additional help. They can meet online for discussions and tutoring or they can meet at the NLA Student Center for f2f tutoring.

The student teacher works with the cooperating teacher as a teaching assistant for the first few weeks until she is trained on the procedures and technical aspects of teaching online. During this time, the student teacher begins by creating an introduction of herself for the class. She also helps grade papers, upload grades, and become comfortable with software programs, and she may be asked to research online resources that can help struggling students. Initially, she may meet with her cooperating teacher daily, but as she becomes more comfortable, she can work from home and meet less often. The cooperating teacher retains full access to everything that the student teacher does online during the semester.

Evaluating Online Student Teaching

One of the biggest challenges, from the college's perspective, was identifying how to observe and evaluate online student teachers. A supervisor from the college is assigned to evaluate each student teacher. In a traditional setting, the supervisor visits the school and completes a minimum of eight observations. Since there is not a physical classroom, observing online student teachers requires some adjustments. First, student teachers must take a much more active role in the observation. Student teachers are required to capture screen shots of various items and artifacts and send them to their NSC supervisors. These artifacts include assignments and projects created by student teachers as well as examples of their students' work. They also submit snap shots of discussions and feedback that they provide students in their classes. Gradebook and rubric snapshots as well as announcements are other examples of observation artifacts.

The student teaching supervisor also relies on the cooperating teacher to send a collection of screen shots, a process that ensures the supervisor is seeing a true variety and not just the student teacher's best examples. Student teachers must also send the link to the online recording of their live sessions to the supervisor. Supervisors can attend live sessions, which is preferable, but they also have the opportunity to review them at a later time. Supervisors also meet with the student teachers every other week and have them open previous assignments from the LMS so that the supervisors are able to see all feedback and grading completed by the student teachers. NSC relies heavily on the feedback from the cooperating teacher to know things such as the following:

- Are assignments graded in a timely manner?
- Does the student teacher reach out to struggling students beyond just providing feedback on papers?
- Does she contact parents when necessary?
- Does she find appropriate resources to help students who may need additional support?

These questions reflect the standards that have been created to assess effective online teaching. These standards originated from professional organizations such as the Southern Regional Education Board's (SREB) Essential Principles for High-Quality Online Teaching, the National Education Association's (NEA) Guide to Teaching Online Courses, and the International Association for K12 Online Learning's (iNACOL) National Standards for Quality Online Teaching. These standards do not solely concentrate on preparing teachers for online learning; they also cater to meaningful technology integration in general and can be applied to the vast spectrum of K–12 online learning programs (Kennedy and Archambault 2012a, p. 37). Online student teachers at NSC are given an abridged copy of the iNACOL standards. Students use the iNACOL standards to self-evaluate their own teaching each week and discuss progress with their supervisors.

Most recently, NSC faculty and staff created an online observation PDF form to help NSC supervisors complete their observations in the field more easily. Supervisors can open the form while at a school and complete an observation on a tablet or iPad. They click on the drop-down menu to rate the student teacher in different areas. The online observation form also has text areas where supervisors can make written comments. The supervisors email copies of the observation to themselves, the student teacher, and the Student Teaching Coordinator. Supervisors also have an option to store copies of the student teacher's observations on the College's internal computer drive for other NSC faculty and staff in the school of education to view.

Challenges of Online Student Teaching

Online student teachers from the Spring 2015 semester were surveyed and asked to comment on the challenges of online student teaching. Table 7.1 highlights their responses.

Even though teachers working with K–12 students online are self-motivated, place a high value on learning and education, and enjoy the challenge and process of using technology for teaching (Archambault and Larson 2015, p. 49), NSC online student teachers found it challenging to motivate students. Without the f2f interaction, motivating students often involved making phone calls to students and sending students text messages and/or emails. This is not only time-consuming, but also requires that comments are written in a way that encourage students to work harder, turn in assignments in a timely manner, and reach for their fullest

Table 7.1

Challenges of Online Student Teaching
Transitioning from face-to-face to online
Motivating students
Difficulty contacting students
Time management
Writing insightful comments within time constraints
Effectively communicate in writing
Building rapport

potential. In Heather E. Duncan and John Barnett's (2009) study of the preservice teachers' experiences in an online course designed to teach about online teaching, students recognized motivation, time management skills, commitment, and reciprocity as qualities necessary to collaborate successfully in an online environment (p. 367).

Having to also make numerous parent and student required phone calls was a challenge for the online student teachers. In an f2f classroom, a student teacher does not generally need to call or email the student or parent. Directions, encouragement, discussions, and follow-up can all be done in class or before or after school. Although the student teacher in the online setting can send out a single announcement or instructions to all students, she may need to answer repeated questions related to the announcement or instructions. Also, individual parent contact in the f2f classroom is fairly minimal. A parent may be contacted directly if there is a behavior problem, but outside of this, there are few phone calls made to parents. Parents at NLA, though, are regularly kept informed when students are not keeping pace with the lessons.

Time management was another major challenge for the online student teachers, mainly due to their dual placements. Student teachers had many responsibilities in both their f2f and online environment, and these responsibilities differ. Keeping a schedule and meeting requirements of both settings involves organization, preparation, and time management. Having to do weekly grading in two different grading programs, preparing teaching lessons for the f2f class, recording live sessions for the online class, grading papers in two different formats, and contacting online students requires more juggling than most student teachers are asked to do. Additionally, the online student teachers reported that because they have the flexibility to work away from the office, it is easier to forget something that they needed to do. The lack of a set schedule means that online student teachers must find a way to stay organized.

Online student teachers need to be organized so that they can stay on top of missing work on an ongoing basis. They need to be flexible enough to move from one type of assignment to another when grading. Preparing live weekly sessions is also challenging for this reason. Online student teachers must judge what is important to discuss in the weekly live session, based on what they see in the weekly assignments that students submit. Though most of the students are working on the same topic, they are often at different stages of the learning process.

Time commitment was also an obstacle for the online student teachers, as they continuously grade large volumes of student work. It is important to give constructive comments that encourage deeper thought, and it is also essential to provide feedback that includes probing questions to stimulate interest in the subject. It is time-consuming to do this. Using a rubric is helpful, but it does not eliminate the need to motivate and engage students in what they are learning. Many online classes may have 100–150 students, yet student teachers are still trying to individualize their responses. It is important to prepare student teachers by making them aware ahead of time that providing meaningful feedback is an ongoing demand so that they can work on this skill. Providing examples of individualized, insightful comments is also beneficial. A good cooperating teacher should model this skill, and a good supervisor offer suggestions for improvement.

It is not surprising that building rapport with students was more challenging for our online student teachers. All student teachers, however, were able to make meaningful connections with their students. In fact, many student teachers were surprised by the number of online students who shared more personal information than most of the f2f students. Perhaps, the lack of f2f contact is what enables some students to feel more comfortable sharing personal information. A number of students online described experiences in which they were bullied or rejected in a typical school settings, and they seemed to appreciate and need the connection that a teacher provides. Having opportunities for one-on-one communication with the teacher may, in some cases, foster these connections.

Although the student teachers accepted into the online student teaching program have been excellent writers, it is still a challenge to communicate effectively in writing. Comments provided to students in an online class need to be appropriate, clear, succinct, and accurate. We all make mistakes as teachers, but these mistakes become more noticeable when they are in writing. It can be a challenge to write responses to students that are both understandable and professional.

In Christian Wilkens et al.'s (2015) study of online graduate preservice teachers, one student highlighted the importance of communication as foundational for the online environment. She explains, in order for online teaching to be most effective, teachers have to be sure that they are communicating with students on a consistent basis by providing feedback to assignments and posting updates about the course and its material. Doing so keeps students from disengaging as well as helps to create a routine for everyone involved (p. 152). Archambault and Larson (2015) argue that strong communication skills are equally important for both f2f teachers and those teaching online. However, communicating at a distance is critically different, as neither the student nor the teacher has access to the rich nonverbal cues and feedback elements of human communication (p. 79).

Benefits of Online Student Teaching

Online student teachers from the Spring 2015 semester were also asked to comment on the benefits of online student teaching. Table 7.2 highlights their responses.

Since the online student teachers at NLA did not write the curriculum, they all agreed that this was a benefit of student teaching in a virtual setting. Although they were still responsible for designing weekly live session lessons and creating new approaches to deliver the content, they agreed that this was not nearly as time-consuming as daily planning of entire lessons.

In an online environment, teachers may need to find ways to motivate students more efficiently, but correcting bad behavior is not generally a problem. Many of the student teachers felt that a lot of their time in the f2f setting was spent trying to get the class under control. A single student can cause enough of a problem to ruin a lesson. Even minor infractions can interfere with the teaching-learning process. In the online setting, the types of classroom disturbances seen in f2f classrooms do not generally exist.

Table 7.2

Benefits of Online Student Teaching
Few lesson planning and behavior issues
Provides another alternative for future teaching
Better parent support
Freedom to be able to grade anytime, anywhere
Increased computer competency and confidence
Can individualize instruction more easily
Can supplement instruction more easily

Another benefit of online student teaching reported by student teachers was the fact that parent involvement was generally high. Since it is a requirement that teachers keep parents apprised of student progress at regular intervals, this kept the parents involved in the educational process and seemed to lead to better relationships between the students, teachers, and parents.

Student teachers found that having the flexibility to grade student work and communicate with students at the touch of the keyboard was also a benefit to online student teaching. When they found something online that they thought would help students understand a concept better, they would simply send the information out as an email. They also valued that work does not get lost. All resources, gradebook items, student work, and the curriculum are in one location.

Since online student teachers spend so much time on the computer, teaching online increased their computer confidence and competence. Online student teachers learned to explore online tools and resources that supplemented their lessons. Online student teachers cite this as one of the most important benefits of online student teaching. They did not realize that there are volumes of resources on the internet that could motivate and engage students in learning. They found that educational games, tutorials, and videos help students understand a concept.

Online student teachers agreed it was a benefit to use teaching tools acquired online in an f2f class. Technology is utilized by students of all ages outside of the classroom. Teacher preparation programs and teachers themselves would be remiss not to capitalize on the use of online resources and technology in the classroom. Student teaching in an online setting helps to foster growth and confidence in student teachers' technology skills. It exposes them to resources that they may not have found and utilized otherwise. Teachers who leave the online environment to teach in an f2f environment take technology skills and knowledge with them and ultimately become better teachers.

Having the ability to engage struggling students in individual, differentiated instruction was another benefit reported by online student teachers. Online student teachers have more opportunities to find online resources for each individual student based on their unique needs. Since these students are comfortable on the computer and are sitting in front of the computer for instruction, they are more likely to use these resources. Preservice graduate teachers who completed virtual field experiences online also reported similar benefits, notably gains in their ability to provide explanatory feedback, provide clear instructions, meet the individual educational needs of students, and to differentiate instruction (Wilkens et al. 2015, p. 156).

Tips for Success for Teacher Preparation Programs Considering Online Student Teaching

Though any new endeavor will have its successes and challenges, the following recommendations should help improve the online student teaching experience.

1. Teacher preparation programs should have a selection process in place that allows faculty and staff to select qualified students. Student teachers need to go into this experience with the realization that there will be successes and benefits and also that it will require more work.

2. It is necessary to select supervisors who are comfortable with technology and are computer savvy. This is not because they need computer skills in order to supervise but rather because having a background and knowledge of educational technology can help the supervisor act as a mentor as well as a supervisor.

3. It is advisable to examine the online program at the virtual school that you partner with for online student teaching. Selecting a virtual school where the curriculum content lessons were predesigned was important for online student teachers at NSC.

4. As with any student teaching placement, the selection of quality mentor teachers is crucial to its success. It is important to meet with the mentor teachers prior to the semester to ensure that they not just are great teachers, but also possess qualities of excellent mentors. They need to be willing to share their expertise and skills and have a positive attitude and enthusiasm about their jobs. Great mentors are open to new ideas and allow their student teachers to be creative while being able to use constructive comments to help them be successful. Mentors should be approachable, compassionate, and fair. They should also be teachers who are recommended by the principal based on their professional standards.

5. NSC chooses to continue using dual placements, which ensures that our students get experience in both settings. In doing this, it is important to work out a schedule that allows the student

teachers to make the most of the time management aspect of this placement. Placing students in f2f classes that begin the day or end the day allows the student teacher to collaborate before or after school without having to travel back to the school. This also gives the student teacher the opportunity to meet and collaborate with the online teacher in an f2f setting, especially for initial training.

Tips for Success for Student Teachers Placed in Online Student Teaching Experiences

1. Come into student teaching prepared. Student teachers should research or create their own online materials, activities, videos, podcasts, and tutorials ahead of time that can be used in online teaching.

2. Use a planner. It is recommended that student teachers keep a list of things that they need to do and check them off as they complete them. This is especially important in an online setting where student assignments are coming in at different times.

3. Remember that written feedback is extremely important to a student who sees (or hears) you once a week. Your words need to be constructive but also motivating. There is a lot of room for miscommunication when you are writing comments to students; choose your words carefully.

4. Call students as often as possible. When students are struggling, a comment on a paper is not always enough. In the f2f setting, you are able to pull students aside and speak to them. In a virtual setting, a phone call or online meeting is your way of pulling them aside. Get comfortable doing it.

5. Read what your students are saying. Since writing will often be your main method of communication, it is important to read everything. Students will often share insights about their personality and their struggles. It is an opportunity to connect with your students.

6. Get the parents involved. This can be as simple as a general announcement to all parents that keeps them informed of upcoming projects or deadlines.

7. When learning the system, write things down. Online student teaching is very fast-paced and much of what you need to

know, in terms of the technology and software, may be new to you. Do not assume that you will remember what your mentor teacher is telling you. There is much to learn.

8. Know your content! Take the time to understand what you are teaching. You must find different ways to teach the content to students who do not *get it* in the initial delivery mode. Find alternative approaches to teaching your content.

9. Use what you are learning in the f2f setting as well. Not only will this benefit your f2f students, but it will also make you more comfortable with the technology. There are many websites and online resources that you can use to supplement a lesson and make it more engaging. Your f2f students will appreciate this.

10. Make a connection with your cooperating teacher and college supervisor. You can learn so much from mentors with experience.

11. Bring enthusiasm and passion to all that you do. Your students will see it, appreciate it, and be motivated by it.

Conclusion

The feedback from student teachers who have taught online at NSC has been very positive. Though it is more work, every student teacher in this setting has expressed that they would "most definitely" choose this dual placement again. Since NLA hires so few teachers each year, most of our student teachers have gone on to teach in f2f settings. These teachers comment that the skills and resources that they gained during their virtual training have greatly improved their success in the classroom. Because teacher education programs are responsible for preparing the future generations of teachers, it is important that programs begin preparing teachers for an ever-growing and expanding field of K–12 online learning in all of its forms, including blended, hybrid, and fully online (Kennedy and Archambault 2012b, p. 195). The use of technology in our classrooms has no doubt led to a need for change in the way we educate our teachers. Online student teaching is a step in that direction.

References

Allen, Elaine, and Jeff Seaman. *Changing Course: Ten Years of Tracking Online Education in the United States.* Oakland, CA: Babson Survey Research Group and Quahog Research Group, 2013.

Archambault, Leanna. "The Practitioner's Perspective on Teacher Education: Preparing for the K–12 Online Classroom." *Journal of Technology and Teacher Education* 19, no. 1 (2011): 73-91.

Archambault, Leanna, and Jean Larson. "Pioneering the Digital Age of Instruction: Learning From and About K–12 Online Teachers." *Journal of Online Learning Research* 1, no. 1 (2015): 49-83.

Christensen, Clayton, M., Michael B. Horn, and Curtis W. Johnson. *Disrupting Class: How Disruptive Innovation Will Change the Way the World Learns.* New York: McGraw Hill, 2008.

Duncan, Heather, E., and John Barnett. "Learning to Teach Online: What Works for Pre-Service Teachers." *Journal of Educational Computing Research* 40, no. 3 (2009): 357-76.

Greenberg, Julie, Laura Palmerance, and Kate Walsh. *Student Teaching in the United States.* Washington, DC: National Council on Teacher Quality, 2011.

Kennedy, Kathryn, and Leanna Archambault. "Design and Development of Field Experiences in K–12 Online Learning Environments." *The Journal of Applied Instructional Design* 2, no. 1 (2012b): 35-49.

Kennedy, Kathryn, and Leanna Archambault. "Education Programs Offering Preservice Teachers Field Experiences in K–12 Online Learning: A National Survey of Teachers." *Journal of Teacher Education* 63, no. 3 (2012a): 185-200.

Kennedy, Kathryn, Cathy Cavanaugh, and Kara Dawson. "Preservice Teachers' Experience in a Virtual School." *American Journal of Distance Education* 27, no. 1 (2013): 56-67.

LaFrance, Jason, A., and Dennis Beck. "Mapping the Terrain: Educational Leadership Field Experiences in K–12 Virtual Schools." *Educational Administration Quarterly* 50, no. 1 (2014): 160-89.

Levine, Arthur. *Educating School Teachers.* Washington, DC: The Education Schools Project, 2006.

Watson, John, Larry Pape, Amy Murin, Butch Gemin, and Lauren Vashaw. *Keeping Pace with K–12 Digital Learning.* Mountain View, CA: Creative Commons, 2014.

Wilkens, Christian, Kelli Eckdahl, Mike Morone, Vicki Cook, Thomas Giblin, and Joshua Coon. "Communication, Community, and Disconnection: Pre-Service Teachers in Virtual School Field Experience." *Journal of Educational Technology Systems* 43, no. 2 (2014-2015): 143-57.

PART 2

Supporting Diverse Learners

Flipped Learning: Making the Connections and Finding the Balance

Kevin J. Graziano

Abstract

Flipped learning, an instructional model that reverses typical in-class lectures and at-home exercises or homework, is on the rise in classrooms across the nation. As a subset of blended learning, the flipped model of instruction often involves the use of a learning management system (LMS) to house the lecture content that students access before hands-on experiences in the classroom. Flipped classrooms have frequently served as a teacher's gateway to fully online teaching. Through a critical analysis of the literature and reflections from first-hand experience flipping a classroom, this chapter explores the origination, growth, and characteristics of flipped learning and discusses its unique benefits and challenges. This chapter also shares data from teachers who have flipped their classrooms and offers viable solutions and recommendations to guide the successful implementation of flipped learning.

Introduction

There is a buzz in academic circles, at all grade levels, focused around the flipped classroom. Flipped learning has been discussed and praised in newspaper and magazine articles, online blogs, internet websites, and professional education conferences. In a flipped learning model, the teacher creates video lectures, screencasts, or video podcasts (vodcasts) that teach students academic content outside of class, freeing up valuable class time for more engaging and collaborative activities typically facilitated by the teacher (Milman 2012). In the flipped classroom model, teachers move from the "sage on the stage" to the "guide on the side" and roam the class looking for ways to scaffold learning (Siegle 2014, p. 51). The teacher's role as a course designer shifts from structuring in-class time to structuring advance or preparatory class experiences through the creation or curation of learning resources that can be consumed asynchronously as needed (Davies, Dean, and Ball 2013, p. 565). With technology-driven teaching methods being a major component of flipped learning, the approach has gained popularity among K–12 teachers as an effective online teaching method.

Flipped learning has been defined as facilitating low-level (terms, definitions, and basic concepts) learning outside of class and high-level (application-based) learning within class (Sarawagi 2013). Others have described flipped learning as a mindset (Siegle 2014, p. 51) or a result of teachers using different tools to meet individual students' needs (Stumpenhorst 2012) rather than a method. Whether a mindset or method, flipped learning has gained popularity due to modern technology.

For some educators, myself included, a *flipped* journey may begin with doubt, resistance, and a lot of unanswered questions. Judy E. Gaughan (2014), who attended her first flipped workshop in 2011, left the workshop wondering, "Would videos cater to and encourage what sometimes seems like an increasingly illiterate student body? Would creating videos of lectures just be hand-feeding the students at a time when they should be learning to engage with materials on their own? Would video lectures somehow diminish or deny the value of what [educators] are already doing?" Gaughan, like many novices to flipped learning, wondered what would happen when new information needs to be added to a video or when it is necessary to refine a particular argument, and asked herself, "Would I be reluctant to flip my class because it would require remaking a complete video?" (p. 222)

Through a critical analysis of the literature and reflections from my personal experience in a flipped classroom, this chapter will likely leave you with more answers than questions. In doing so, it explores characteristics of flipped learning, including a discussion of its growth and origination and its benefits and challenges. This chapter also offers viable solutions and recommendations to the challenges of flipped learning and shares data from teachers who have flipped their classrooms.

Flipped Learning and its Origination

The concept of the flipped classrooms originated at Harvard University in the early 1990s when Eric Mazur (1991) incorporated computer-based instruction to guide his physics students through a unit outside of class. In 2006, Jonathan Bergmann and Aaron Sams (2012b), high school chemistry teachers from Colorado, began using online, taped lectures to reach students who were frequently absent. They found that the video lessons could serve as instructional resources outside of class and freed up class time for more meaningful work on content.

It is important to distinguish between a flipped classroom and flipped learning. According to the Flipped Learning Network, these terms are not interchangeable. Flipping a class can, but does not necessarily, lead to flipped learning. Many teachers may have already flipped their classes by having students read text outside of class, watch supplemental videos, or solve additional problems, but to engage in flipped learning, teachers must incorporate the four pillars of flipped learning into their practice (Flipped Learning Network 2014, p. 1).

The four pillars of a flipped learning include the following: (1) flexible environment, (2) learning culture, (3) intentional content, and (4) professional educator. In a flexible environment, the first pillar, teachers establish spaces and time frames that

- permit students to interact and reflect on their learning
- observe and monitor students continuously and make adjustments as appropriate, and
- provide students with different ways to learn content and demonstrate mastery

In the second pillar, the learning culture, students

- have opportunities to engage in meaningful activities without the teacher being central
- participate in activities that are accessible through the teacher's provision of scaffolding and differentiation, and
- learn and progress through a system of ongoing and formative feedback

With intentional content, the third pillar, teachers

- prioritize concepts in direct instruction for learners to access on their own, and

- create and/or curate relevant content (typically videos) for students

The role of the professional educator, the fourth pillar, requires teachers to

- make themselves available to all students for individual, small group, and class feedback in real-time
- conduct ongoing formative assessments during class through observations and record data to inform future instruction, and
- take responsibility for transforming practice (Flipped Learning Network 2014, 2)

In February 2014, *Sophia* (a provider of online professional development and college readiness programs) and the Flipped Learning Network conducted online independent surveys on flipped learning with more than 2,300 teachers, which revealed that the number of teachers who have flipped a lesson in their classroom increased from 48 percent in 2012 to 78 percent in 2014. According to the survey results, the majority of flipped teaching still occurs in high school. In the Flipped Learning Network survey, 80 percent taught flipped classes in secondary schools with 15 percent in grades K–5. Of those teachers who flip, 96 percent said they would recommend the flipped classroom to a colleague. Additionally, Herreid and Schiller (2013) surveyed 15,000 members of the National Center for Case Study Teaching in Science Listserv to see if STEM teachers were using the flipped method of instruction, and 200 teachers reported that they teach in a flipped classroom.

During the fall of 2014, approximately 522,000 K–12 students, teachers, administrators, parents, and community members participated in the annual online Speak Up Survey (2014) on educational technology. For the third consecutive year, more than 4,000 building and district administrators from approximately 2,600 school districts have seen significant increases in flipping their classrooms. Over the past three years, school leaders at all grade levels have seen increases from 23 percent to 32 percent of teachers using videos found online, with a slightly larger overall increase in the number of teachers who are creating their own videos moving from 19 percent to 29 percent (Speak Up Survey 2014, p. 1).

When school technology leaders from the Speak Up Survey were asked about popular approaches to digital learning that have had positive results in schools, they specifically selected *flipped learning* 48 percent of the time. They also selected digital content, which includes videos, simulations and animations 84 percent of the time. Two thirds of those same respondents selected digital media tools for student content creation as a popular and promising approach.

Many school administrators are now expecting new teachers to know how to flip their classrooms prior to completing their certification process. In 2013, 41 percent of school leaders indicated that preservice teachers should know how to set up a flipped learning classroom. In 2014, that increased to 46 percent. Of the same group, 68 percent indicated that preservice teachers should come to their new jobs with the ability to create and use video, podcasts, and other media in the classroom (Speak Up Survey 2014).

These statistics clearly show that flipped learning and the need for innovative online teaching methods are in the mainstream and on the rise. So, what does it look like, and what are the benefits and challenges of flipped learning?

Benefits of Flipped Learning

There are a variety of ways that teachers implement a flipped classroom. The teacher's main role in a flipped classroom is a facilitator of knowledge. Direct instruction is blended with constructivist learning pedagogies so that individualized differentiated learning is facilitated. Learning is not limited to the classroom, and students can personalize their learning by moving at their own pace and directing their efforts based on their individual needs. Through these scaffolded and self-paced options, students are not left behind by class discussions that go too fast, and they are less likely to become bored by class time that is spent covering content they already know (Davies, Dean, and Ball 2013, p. 565). When students become accustomed to the flipped approach of learning, they develop an increased sense of responsibility for their learning and they work with their teachers to achieve common goals (Greenberg, Medlock, and Stephens 2011, p. 10).

Katrina Keene (2013) discusses several benefits to flipped learning. She states that flipping can help busy students work ahead and struggling students who may need more time with the teacher. Flipping helps students of all abilities excel, as all notes, concepts, and class materials are online for students who need extra help and it allows students to "pause" and "rewind" their teacher (p. 66).

With flipped learning, student-teacher interaction increases. Teachers, as facilitators, provide more one-on-one time with students. Students see their teacher in an online virtual format as well as in person, allowing teachers to build meaningful relationships with their students both online and in person. When teachers are able to build solid relationships with their students, students are more likely to trust their teachers and are motivated to do well (Schultz et al. 2014, p. 1335). Flipping also increases student-to-student interaction. In the online world, students have access to peers through discussion boards (Keene 2013, p. 66), and research shows that learners learn more effectively if they are actively involved in the process rather than being passive thinkers (Webb et al. 2004).

In addition to higher levels of motivation to do well in the classroom, students' level of interest, engagement, and enthusiasm increase with flipped learning (Fulton 2012, p. 23; Moore, Gillett, and Steele 2014, p. 424). Flipped learning can also change a teacher's approach to classroom management. Since learning occurs in small groups, students feel less threatened by classroom participation (Keene 2013, p. 66).

Another benefit to flipped learning is that it changes conversations with parents. Simply put, flipping educates parents. The focus is no longer on behavior in the classroom. Instruction is the focus of conversation, which lessens or eliminates the *behavior* conversation with parents. Parents begin getting involved in their child's education as videos provided online can be viewed and studied together. Flipping also makes teaching transparent. Parents and others can see online what is being taught and can access the curriculum (Keene 2013, p. 66).

Video analytics can also be a benefit to flipped learning since the flipped classroom utilizes online multimedia. Video analytics will not only let teachers know when and how many times a student accesses a video, for example, but will also allow teachers to see when they are pausing, what part of the video they repeat, and how long it takes to get through the video (Enfield 2013). LMSs are able to provide some of these data.

Challenges of Flipped Learning

Flipped learning is not without challenges and criticism. Del Siegle (2014) discusses five problems with flipped learning (p. 52). First, he writes, for flipped classrooms to work, students must have access to computers and the internet from home. Socioeconomic status plays a large role in accessibility, and often determines prior exposure to technology both in the home and in the educational setting (Ching, Basham, and Jang 2005). Second, students need to be motivated to complete the home assignments, whether they are watching a video, exploring a website, or observing a presentation. Third, lecture, whether it is delivered live or on video, may not necessarily be the best way to learn because it may be too fast for those who already know the material and too slow for those without sufficient background. Fourth, fully flipped learning is unscalable from both the teachers' and students' perspective (Freedman 2011). Fifth, most teachers do not have the time or skills to create all the needed lessons for students to watch. Amy Roehl, Shweta Reddy, and Gayla Shannon (2013) report teachers spent about two hours per topic to create videotaped lectures and digital slide presentations with voiceovers (p. 45). In addition, the monetary expenditure needed to produce instructional materials may be problematic for flipped classrooms, and, in the end, students might not even watch the videos. Hence, there may be a lack of accountability for students to complete the out-of-class instruction (November and Mull 2012).

Other concerns with flipped learning include the role of teachers being diminished, students' experience with out-of-class instructions not being interactive (November and Mull 2012), poor quality video production, conditions in which the students view the videos out of class, inability for teachers to monitor comprehension, and use with English language learners and students with learning disabilities (Milman 2012).

While repetitive instruction is important in face-to-face (f2f) classes, it appears to be less important and sometimes frustrating for learners in video instruction (Enfield 2013, p. 25). Jacob Enfield (2013) also warns teachers that, while class time may be freed up by flipping the classroom, new challenges for teachers may surface on how to effectively use class time, which may be especially challenging for teachers who are accustomed to the traditional teaching practice of direct instruction (p. 26). Teachers who use traditional lectures in class may find it challenging to post their lectures online.

Another interesting challenge for teachers considering or using flipped learning is that students tend to expect instructional videos to be edited so that there are no errors or unneeded pauses (Enfield 2013, p. 26). Enfield argues that it can be very challenging for teachers to make changes to online content once it has been posted to the learning management system (LMS), as making adjustments to course content requires teachers to use the original technology used to create the course content and then resave the content and upload it to the LMS, all of which can be very time consuming for teachers.

Despite the growing number of flipped courses, quantitative information on their effectiveness remains sparse. Studies currently available often lack measures of student learning, and many studies make "apples to oranges" comparisons of active learning in flipped classrooms to traditional lecture courses with no active learning (Lape, Levy, and Yong 2015, p. 1). Jamie L. Jensen, Tyler A. Kummer, and Patricia D. Godoy (2015) argue flipped classrooms do not result in higher learning gains or better attitudes compared with the nonflipped classroom when both utilize an active learning, constructivist approach (p. 1). Current studies on flipped learning are also limited due to the fact that so many potential causative mechanisms are being changed between treatments (e.g., shifting to active learning, including additional technology, using additional teaching materials, and implementing peer instruction) that it is difficult, if not impossible, to disaggregate data (Jensen, Kummer, and Godoy 2015, p. 2).

Bryan Goodwin and Kirsten Miller (2013) conclude that, to date, there is no scientific research base to indicate exactly how well flipped learning works. Preliminary nonscientific data suggest that flipped learning may produce benefits, and the lack of hard scientific data does not mean that teachers should not flip their classrooms. Goodwin and Miller write, "If we only implemented strategies supported by decades of research, we would never try anything new. Until researchers are able to provide reliable data, the best we can do is to ask whether the purported benefits of flipped learning reflect research-based principles of effective teaching and learning" (p. 78).

Viable Solutions to Overcome Flipped Challenges

There are viable solutions for teachers to consider with many of the aforementioned challenges. Teachers in schools across the nation wear multiple hats in the classroom and juggle numerous responsibilities and obligations out of the classroom. Teachers often struggle to find time to grade, write, reflect, and be creative, let alone create videos for tomorrow's lesson. One solution to a lack of time for creating multimedia is to have schools and school districts offer summer technology institutes or "boot camps" where teachers develop online content alongside an instructional technologist and instructional designer. Teachers can also locate and curate free teaching and learning materials from open educational resources (OERs) at this time. These opportunities should be ongoing, offered over several weeks in the summer or during extended periods of time when teachers are available, and should provide stipends to participants.

One solution to the concern that students may not have access to technology outside of school is to offer an afterschool program for students to use computers. Schools with large lower-income populations have been experimenting with ways to deliver content before or after school in the library, on students' mobile devices, on hardware available for checkout at the school library, or on burned DVDs for students who have DVD players (Finkel 2012). Finkel adds that students who cannot get to the videos at home can watch them during study hall or before class in the library or even in class if they prefer (p. 32). Another solution is to establish partnerships with local libraries, feeder schools, community colleges, or nearby universities where students can go to access the internet and watch videos out of class. Schools implementing 1-1 laptop or tablet initiatives are also ideally poised to support flipped learning approaches.

As noted in this chapter, students would probably not watch multiple videos outside of school for multiple subjects every night. A solution is to only flip portions of classroom instruction and make shorter videos for students to watch. In fact, Bergmann and Sams (2014) recommend that videos should not be longer than 60 to 90 seconds per grade level. They suggest, for example, if you are making videos for 10th graders, each video should be less than 15 minutes (p. 27).

Another solution is to have students use the jigsaw cooperative learning strategy to view selected videos or sections of videos (Aronson and Patnoe 1997). Students can be assigned to different videos on the same topic and then report back to class the next day on their video content, or students can be assigned to the same video and watch sections of the video rather than the whole video. Brain research tells us that the novelty of any stimulus tends to wear off after about 10 minutes and, as a result, learners tend to check out after 10 minutes of exposure to new content. After that, they need a change of stimulus or an opportunity to step back and process what they are learning (Medina 2008).

As noted in this chapter, it can be overwhelming for a teacher to create all the needed lessons for students to watch (Siegle 2014), and resources, hardware, and software may be expensive on a restrictive budget. One solution is to rely on free online resources from OER Commons or the Khan Academy, which provide free educational videos on a variety of topics from algebra to organic chemistry. YouTube and TED Talks also feature useful, free educational videos.

There is free software available to teachers who wish to create their own online content as well. Camtasia Studio is best known for screencasting. It allows users to record on-screen activity, edit content, and add interactive elements. Jing and Screencast-o-matic are also popular and free screencasting software. Most LMSs have built-in features that allow teachers as well as students to record audio and video. Teachers can rely on technical support from technology specialists on staff to get started with these features. A general rule of thumb is to allow 30 minutes to create a 10-minute video (Bergmann and Sams 2012a, p. 25). The benefit for students is that—unlike an f2f lecture—the video content can be paused and replayed on an as-needed basis.

Lecture capturing software, such as Echo360, allows teachers to record classroom action and interaction, then turn them into lessons that students can replay on any device in real-time or any time after class. Lecture capturing is helpful for teachers who teach on-campus and online and wish to capture and share on-campus lectures with online students. Teachers can also consider creating online, multimedia posters using Glogster. Glogster allows users to create interactive posters with text, graphics, images, audio, video, and web links. Glogster is also available as an app for iPad users. VoiceThread is another option for teachers to consider as they develop interactive slideshows. VoiceThread allows the teacher to create slideshows that hold images, documents, and videos. Students can then leave comments using text, voice, or video formats. Both Glogster and VoiceThread allow teachers to incorporate innovative, nontraditional videos that engage students with online content. Teachers can also use student-created content to supplement their instruction and engage learners online.

Bergmann and Sams (2014) believe it is worth the time and effort for teachers to create their own videos. They write, teaching is inherently about human interaction and teacher and student relationships. Students recognize that when teachers create their own videos, they are taking the time to "teach" them (Bergmann and Sams 2014, p. 27). Students from Amanda J. Moore, Matthew R. Gillett, and Michael D. Steele's (2014) study of flipping high school math classes suggest that the presence of a teacher, either through narrated voiceovers or a camera presence, may be an important factor in the success of using videos (p. 424).

The iTunes U app gives users access to free education content on thousands of topics. Other useful apps include the ShowMe iPad app. ShowMe allows teachers to create lessons using a whiteboard. The app is free and there is no limit what you can teach. Users can retrieve lessons created by other users from chemistry, history, math, sports, or arts.

Educreations is another popular app that allows users to record voice and iPad screens to create video lessons that students can access anytime. Educreations allows users to share videos via email, Facebook, Twitter, Edmodo, or YouTube, and even download and store them in Dropbox or Google Drive. Videolicious and Nearpod are other recommended video apps that teachers should explore. The photovoice app is also gaining popularity in schools. Users take a photo (or select any image already on an iPhone), record a brief audio commentary about the photo, and then save the photo with the accompanying audio. Teachers and students can create photovoice projects that are content specific for students to view outside the classroom (Graziano 2011, 2014; Graziano and Herren 2009).

Teachers can also consider Creative Commons, a nonprofit organization that enables the sharing and use of creativity and knowledge through free legal tools. Creative Commons is a gateway to a wealth of openly free licensed products ranging from songs and videos to scientific and academic materials.

Application of Flipped Learning

Although there is a lack of empirical data on flipped learning, countless teachers continue to flip their instruction with positive outcomes such as improved academic performance and higher test scores (Roshan and Roshan 2012; Yarbro et al. 2014), increased student engagement (Hamdan et al. 2013), increased homework completion rates (Yarbro et al. 2014), fewer disciplinary problems (Hamdan et al. 2013; Yarbro et al. 2014), and a decrease in the amount of preparation time required for each class meeting and in the amount of time spent on remediation (Enfield 2013). Similar results of improved academic performance, increased engagement, and positive student attitudes towards flipped instruction have been reported by various disciplines, practitioners, and researchers (Datig and Ruswick 2013; Gaughan 2014; Kay and Kletskin 2012; Ruddick 2012; Talley and Scherer 2013).

In 2013, I took a more student-centered approach to flipping my undergraduate second language acquisition course. By way of background, I teach a language acquisition course every fall semester to undergraduate preservice teachers onsite at a partnership school. I use a Teach, Apply, Reflect model of instruction. The first hour of class is a seminar (Teach) where I actively engage students in lectures on course content. Students are assigned to a classroom teacher for the second hour of class. They observe the classroom teacher each week for 16 weeks. Students observe best practices used by the teachers (Apply) and relate them to content learned during the first hour of seminar. The last hour of class allows students to debrief (Reflect) on classroom observations during the second hour of class.

Lessons were flipped for 12 weeks during the semester. Students watched videos and podcasts I selected or created on course content. All students were required to watch the videos and podcasts outside of class. Students were randomly assigned to groups of two to three students and voluntarily signed up to teach a lesson during the first hour of class (Teach) on a selected chapter of interest from our textbook along with the accompanying videos and podcasts. A different group of students taught one lesson per week. The lesson had to include all eight components of the Sheltered Instruction Observation Protocol (SIOP) lesson plan (Echevarria, Vogt, and Short 2013). I met with all students prior to their delivery of the lesson to ensure their lesson included active learning strategies and engaging, meaningful activities and in-class assignments. Every lesson also had an informal assessment created by students. I delivered direct instruction after each group taught their lessons to reinforce concepts and new knowledge. Not only did this model of flipped learning allow students to receive more one-on-one time from me before, during, and after class to support their learning, but it also afforded the opportunity to interact with the classroom teacher they observed each week and strengthen their connections of course content from theory to practice.

Conclusion

Technology experts predict by the year 2025 there will be an ambient information environment where accessing the internet will be effortless and most people will tap into it so easily it will flow through their lives *like electricity* (Anderson and Rainie 2014). I hope by 2025 the divide between those who have and do not have access to the internet, broadband, and cell phones will be obsolete, and everyone will have broadband access at home similar to household utilities that most individuals utilize on a daily basis. In the meantime, we need to identify innovative and practical options to bring the internet and modern technology to students who do not have access. It is important that school administrators reach out to colleagues, parents, and community organizations to identify and develop strategies for securing access to hardware, software, and the internet for all students in and out of school. This degree of access will aid students in

the development of 21st century skills that will transfer from class
classroom and to life after graduation.

School administrators should also provide support to teachers who may
need to learn the latest technology that will allow them to flip their classrooms. With anything new in education, teachers need time and support
to roll up their sleeves and experiment. Teachers should be able to work
with others in a supportive environment where they can ask each other
questions, share ideas, create, and reflect. School administrators should
consider offering professional development opportunities throughout the
school year so teachers together with their colleagues and collaborators can
acquire the necessary skills to make videos and other multimedia suitable
for instruction.

Teachers should start small and identify colleagues who favor flipped
instruction, share resources, observe colleagues online by enrolling as
guest users in courses with flipped instruction, follow flipped discussion
and online forums, participate in blogs on flipped instruction, and join
special interest groups (SIGs) or the Flipped Learning Network. Teachers
should also document their individual and collective experiences using the
flipped model of instruction. These experiences can be shared at regional
and national conferences and published in educational journals, which will
contribute to the research on flipped learning.

The experiences from flipping a classroom and familiarity with LMSs,
technology, and online best practices may serve as a gateway for teachers
to teach online. Teachers may be inspired from the experience and seek
opportunities to transition from f2f teaching to online or hybrid teaching.

It is important to note that the flipped model of instruction might not
work for all teachers and students or with all grades and subject matters.
Not all teachers will succeed with it, and some students may prefer traditional classroom approaches (Hamdan et al. 2013). The limited amount of
data available in the literature on flipped learning, however, is promising
and supports a classroom environment that is student-centered. Teachers
at all levels of education seem to have caught onto flipped instruction, and
it does not seem to be going away anytime soon.

References

Anderson Janna, and Lee Rainie. "Summary: 15 Theses About the Digital Future,"
    2014. http://www.pewinternet.org/2014/03/11/digital-life-in-2025/.

Aronson, Elliot, and Shelley Patnoe. *The Jigsaw Classroom: Building Cooperation in the
    Classroom*. New York: Longman, 1997.

Bergmann, Jonathan, and Aaron Sams. "Before You Flip, Consider This: Leaders of the Flipped Classroom Movement Say Each Teacher Will Have a Different Experience, but Securing School Leadership Support, Time, and IT Resources Will Be Important to Every Effort." *Phi Delta Kappan* 94, no. 2 (2012a): 25.

—. *Flip Your Classroom: Reach Every Student in Every Class Every Day*. Washington DC: International Society for Technology in Education, 2012b.

—. "Flipping for Mastery." *Educational Leadership* 71, no. 4 (2014): 24-29.

Ching, Cynthia C., James D. Basham, and Eunice Jang. "The Legacy of the Digital Divide: Gender, Socioeconomic Status, and Exposure as Predictors of Full-Spectrum Technology Use Among Young Adults." *Urban Education* 40, no. 4 (2005): 394-411.

Datig, Ilka, and Claire Ruswick. "Four Quick Flips: Activities for the Information Literacy Classroom." *College & Research Library News* 74, no. 5 (2013): 249-57.

Davies, Randall S., Douglas L. Dean, and Nick Ball. "Flipping the Classroom and Instructional Technology Integration in a College-Level Information Systems Spreadsheet Course." *Educational Technology Research and Development* 61 (2013): 563-80.

Echevarria, Jana, MaryEllen Vogt, and Deborah Short. *Making Content Comprehensible for English Learners: The SIOP Model*. Boston: Pearson, 2013.

Enfield, Jacob. "Looking at the Impact of the Flipped Classroom Model of Instruction on Undergraduate Multimedia Students at CSUN." *TechTrends* 57, no. 6 (2013): 14-27.

Finkel, Ed. "Flipping the Script in K12." *District Administration* 48, no. 10 (2012): 28-30.

Flipped Learning Network. "The Four Pillars of F-L-I-P," 2014. http://flippedlearning.org/domain/41.

Freedman, Terry. "8 Observations on Flipping the Classroom," 2011. http://www.ictineducation.org/home-page/2011/10/20/8-observations-on-flipping-the-classroom.html.

Fulton, Kathleen P. "10 Reasons to Flip." *Phi Delta Kappan* 94, no. 2 (2012): 20-24.

Gaughan, Judy E. "The Flipped Classroom in World History." *The History Teacher* 47, no. 2 (2014): 221-44.

Goodwin, Bryan, and Kirsten Miller. "Evidence on Flipped Classrooms is Still Coming In." *Educational Leadership* 70, no. 6 (2013): 78-80.

Graziano, Kevin. "The Everyday Realities of Palestinian College Students Living and Studying in Israel: A Photovoice Study." *International Journal of Progressive Education* 10, no. 1 (2014): 32-45.

—. "Working With English Language Learners: Preservice Teachers and Photovoice. *International Journal of Multicultural Education* 13, no. 1 (2011): 1-19.

Graziano, Kevin, and Craig Herren. "Students as Researchers: A Photographic Approach to Teaching High School Economics." In *Justice, Care, and Diversity: Addressing the Needs of All Students in Catholic Secondary Schools*, ed. Edmundo Litton and Shane Martin. Arlington, VA: National Catholic Educational Association, 2009.

Greenberg, Brian, Leonard Medlock, and Darri Stephens. 2011. "Blend My Learning: Lessons Learned From a Blended Learning Pilot." http://www.blendmylearning.com/2011/12/06/white-paper/.

Hamdan, Noora, Patrick McKnight, Katherine McKnight, and Kari Arfstrom. "A Review of Flipped Learning," 2013. http://flippedlearning.org/domain/41.

Herreid, Clyde, and Nancy A. Schiller. "Case Studies and the Flipped Classroom." *Journal of College Science Teaching* 42, no. 5 (2013): 62-66.

Jensen, Jamie L., Tyler A. Kummer, and Patricia D. d. M. Godoy. "Improvements From a Flipped Classroom May Simply be the Fruits of Active Learning." *CBE-Life Sciences Education* 14 (2015): 1-12.

Kay, Robin, and Ilona Kletskin. "Evaluating the Use of Problem-Based Video Podcasts to Teach Mathematics in Higher Education." *Computers and Education* 59 (2012): 619-27.

Keene, Katrina. "Blended and Flipping Distance Education." *Distance Learning* 10, no. 4 (2013): 63-69.

Lape, Nancy, Rachel Levy, and Darryl Yong. "Probing the Inverted Classroom: A Study of Teaching and Learning Outcomes in Engineering and Mathematics." *EDUCAUSE Learning Initiative* (2015): 1-5.

Mazur, Eric. "Can We Teach Computers to Teach?" *Computers in Physics* 5, no. 1 (1991): 31-38.

Medina, John. *Brain Rules: 12 Principles for Surviving and Thriving at Work, Home, and School.* Seattle: Pear Press, 2008.

Milman, Natalie. "The Flipped Classroom Strategy: What is it and How Can it Be Used?" *Distance Learning* 9, no. 3 (2012): 85-87.

Moore, Amanda J., Matthew R. Gillett, and Michael D. Steele. "Fostering Student Engagement With the Flip." *Mathematics Teacher* 107, no. 6 (2014): 420-25.

November, Alan, and Brian Mull. "Flipped Learning: A Response to Five Common Criticisms," 2012. *NovemberLearning.com.* http://novemberlearning.com/educational-resources-for-educators/teaching-and-learning-articles/flipped-learning-a-response-to-five-common-criticisms-article/.

Roehl, Amy, Shweta Linga Reddy, and Gayla Jett Shannon. "The Flipped Classroom: An Opportunity to Engage Millennial Students Through Active Learning Strategies." *Journal of Family & Consumer Sciences* 105, no. 2 (2013): 44-49.

Roshan, Stacey, and Wendy Roshan. "My View: It's Never Too Late to Begin Flipping Your Classroom," 2012. http://schoolsofthought.blogs.cnn.com/2012/08/24/my-view-its-never-too-late-to-begin-flipping-your-classroom/.

Ruddick, Kristie W. 2012. "Improving chemical education from high school to college using a more hands-on approach." PhD diss., University of Memphis.

Sarawagi, Namita. "Flipping an Introductory Programming Course: Yes You Can!" *Journal of Computing Sciences in Colleges* 28, no. 6 (2013): 186-88.

Schultz, David, Stacy Duffield, Seth C. Rasmussen, and Justin Wageman. "Effects of the Flipped Classroom Model on Student Performance for Advanced Placement High School Chemistry Students." *Journal of Chemical Education* 91 (2014): 1334-39.

Siegle, Del. "Technology: Differentiating Instruction by Flipping the Classroom." *Gifted Child Today* 37, no. 1 (2014): 51-55.

Speak Up Survey. "Speak Up 2014 National Research Project Findings Flipped Learning Continues to Trend for Third Year," 2014. http://flippedlearning.org/domain/41.

Stumpenhorst, Josh. "Not Flipping for Flipped," 2012. http://www.stumpteacher.com/2012/12/not-flipping-for-flipped.html

Talley, Cheryl P., and Stephen Scherer. "The Enhanced Flipped Classroom: Increasing Academic Performance With Student-Recorded Lectures and Practice Testing in a 'Flipped' STEM Course." *The Journal of Negro Education* 82, no. 3 (2013): 339-47.

Yarbro, Jessica, Kari Arfstrom, Katherine McKnight, and Patrick McKnight. "The 2014 Extension of the 2013 Review of Flipped Learning," 2014. http://flippedlearning.org/domain/41.

Webb, Eileen, Alan Jones, Philip Barker, and Paul van Schaik. "Using E-Learning Dialogues in Higher Education." *Innovations in Education and Teaching International* 41 (2004): 93-103.

Virtual School-Home Communication

Dianne L. Tetreault

Abstract

Online learning is on the rise. Statistics show that the number of students taking at least one online course has rapidly increased since 2002. Today's students are quite computer savvy and are often referred to as digital natives. They use many types of technology on a daily basis. From the perspective of an experienced K–12 online teacher, this chapter discusses the importance of making the home–school connection via a multitude of technology-based tools. This chapter also offers online teachers and family members simple activities that promote improved teacher-parent/guardian involvement and foster the quality and level of communication that is essential to student success.

Introduction

Online learning is rapidly increasing in K–12 education. This trend is growing in both the sheer number of online programs and in the number of teachers, students, and families who participate in online programs. Many students are attracted to online learning because they believe it gives them more control over their learning and that they have more support from their online teacher.

This shift in educational models changes the dynamics of K–12 teaching and learning. In online settings, parents or guardians who assist their children are often referred to as "learning coaches" as they take on the role of advocate and advisor: "Learning coaches are student managers and guides for their own children, [motivating] them to press on and [guiding] them through the curriculum" (Hasler, Waters, and Leong 2014, p. 52).

Educators have long been aware of the importance of the connections to be made between home and school, and in the case of online learning, these connections take on a new level of significance. With the goal being to improve student retention and success, this chapter discusses how teachers in online programs can establish and sustain a home-to-school connection with parents and caregivers.

The means of communication in an online school are substantially different from those found in a traditional one. In a traditional setting, in-school or after-school communication with students and families are often based on a daily and time-bound schedule. Correspondence is often managed through email messages, phone calls, or through a parent portal or student information system. While these same unidirectional or asynchronous tools are used in the online setting, virtual schools are optimized to support communication that is ongoing and dynamic (Sivy 2014).

One of the most important factors in the success of a virtual school program is a policy and infrastructure that drives good, clear communication between students and teachers as well as teachers and parents. Florida Virtual School (FLVS) supports open and ongoing communication through its use of its ConnectYard portal that integrates email, text, and social media networks within its learning management system (LMS) (Namahoe 2012). Students and teachers are able to send and receive messages through their preferred device platforms, and all these messages are stored in the LMS itself. A great benefit is the ability to connect students, teachers, parents, and staff using social media without requiring them to change their behaviors. This system features social media tools, including trending topics that enable users to follow popular discussion topics, as well as capabilities to support online tutoring and study groups. Teachers can also track messages to ensure students receive them and send communications to individuals or entire classes.

The virtual experience can differ depending on the type of program in which a student is enrolled. Regardless, all virtual experiences require a strong collaboration between the home and the online school. In many cases, the enrollment counselor or school guidance counselor is the first avenue of communication, as she often guides the parent through enrollment, placement, and registration. Once this is complete and the student is enrolled and placed with a teacher, the teacher takes over. Teachers in online settings communicate via email, telephone, online live lessons, web meetings, and other tools. The teachers closely monitor all student progress and report to parents. Teachers often conduct live online sessions through their virtual office to ensure mastery of content. Teachers also have the ability to develop interventions if a student is struggling. These interventions might include one-on-one tutoring, video or screencasts, or additional web resources to further explain the content. The teacher is the manager of the online content and its delivery and—especially on the elementary or middle school level—she communicates with the parent often. Additionally, many fully online programs implement a structure in which parents or guardians serve as *learning coaches*. A learning coach is not responsible for creating course content or assessing student work. However, for younger students, these coaches can be essential partners in the participation and success of online learners.

Digital Immigrant Versus Digital Native

Today's students are not like students of the past. Many of our students' lives are already filled with technology. Students today spend countless hours texting, emailing, participating in chat rooms, manipulating photos, playing video games, and expressing themselves in many different forms of multimedia. Students born when digital technology was increasingly ubiquitous and widespread are often referred to as digital natives (Prensky 2001). These individuals have often grown up using technology tools for a plethora of uses every day. On the flip side of digital natives are the parents or caregivers who may be in the category of digital immigrants (Prensky 2001). Digital immigrants are the ones who came to use technology later in the game. Some digital immigrants are still trying to figure out this game while the digital natives know no other way. As teachers, if we are not speaking the same language as students, then how can we expect them to learn? This, in turn, gives rise to a disconnect with the rate at which students, parents, home, and school communicate.

Strategies for Effective Communication Between Home and the Online Learner

A productive and successful learning environment includes one where parents are invited and encouraged to participate in their child's education. Researchers have found that parents of students in K–12 online programs often help them with organization, technology, and time management (Hasler, Waters, and Leong 2014). Therefore, establishing good communication with parents is a promising strategy to improve achievement among online learners.

It is true, however, that parent involvement in the day-to-day efforts of their child can vary widely, and this is true of those in online as well as brick-and-mortar settings. Just because a child is learning online does not mean that the parent is hovering over the child's daily lessons. Regardless of the age or grade, communication is essential. Facilitating communication within the fast-paced world that both students and parents live in can be challenging. It is still the teacher's responsibility, though, to communicate with parents and ensure that they are aware of the child's successes and struggles with the curriculum. The quality and frequency of this communication leads to better understanding among all parties involved.

The online teacher may at times find the fostering of communication to be frustrating or demanding. However, positive outcomes typically prevail. Research conducted and compiled by the National Association of School Psychologists in 2008 indicates that effective, responsive, well-planned home/school communication has the following results:

- improved test scores
- improved grades
- more positive student attitudes
- lower dropout rates
- less high-risk behavior
- enhanced relationships between school and community
- increased parental support for school's initiatives and programs
- improved parental opinion of and regard for the school
  (Lavoie 2008)

Research is clear about the kinds of parental involvement that lead to student learning. Anne T. Henderson and Karen L. Mapp (2002) analyzed eighty studies of parental involvement in K–12 schools, and some of their key findings provide clear guidelines for effective communication:

- Family involvement that is linked to student learning has
  a greater effect on achievement than more general forms of
  involvement.
- Family involvement that supports student learning at home is
  linked to improved student achievement.
- Families of all cultural backgrounds and education and income
  levels can have a positive influence on their children's learning.
- Family involvement efforts that recognize cultural and class
  differences, address family needs, and build on families'
  strengths are effective in engaging diverse families.

A survey distributed to members of the International Association for K12 Online Learning (iNACOL) shares some of the strategies that online teachers and schools are using to keep parents and families involved (Bryans-Bongey 2015). Based on feedback from iNACOL members and school representatives who completed the survey, a majority of these online teachers and administrators stated that parents volunteer time and effort to promote and enrich the school community. According to these respondents from roughly 30 different online schools, approaches for parent involvement in the online K–12 classroom include the following:

- Parents or community members serve as guest speakers or presenters in an online class (65 percent).
- Parents are involved in some form of Parent-Teacher Association (41 percent).
- Parents are involved in virtual or face-to-face (f2f) field trips (41 percent).
- Parents and/or family members participate in supplemental f2f events (35 percent) .
- Parents participate in fundraising events (18 percent).
- Parents take part in group web meetings (18 percent). (Bryans-Bongey 2015, p. 15)

While many parents seem engaged in their child's education, the online arena demands vigilant and ongoing communication on the part of the teacher. As a teacher, it is important that you communicate and connect with parents, guardians, and families. The way this is done may vary based on teacher or family preference and/or available communication tools. Like our online students, many parents and guardians are connected with digital devices that allow them access anytime and anywhere. Establish a plan and start your communication early. Whether you use wiki, website, blog, or social media like Twitter, Instagram, or Facebook, consider tools that meet the lifestyle needs of parents, guardians, and families as well as your own.

The age of the child in a virtual program is an important factor in approaches used to establish and maintain good communication with parents or guardians. For the younger elementary child, the parent often acts as a learning coach, establishing and maintaining daily routines. The learning coach typically stays in touch with the student's teacher via phone, email, or online meetings. The teacher and the parent should establish contact early in the school year to discuss how they will work together to ensure the success of the child. In other instances, particularly in middle school and high school, the student is a more independent learner. Regardless of how much communication is needed throughout the school year, it is essential to communicate contact information, office hours, and any other procedures or venues that support a free flow of questions, comments, and student support on an as-needed basis.

Many virtual programs require a welcome call to both student and teacher/guardian. These welcome calls are an introduction and a critical component in getting things started on the right foot. A good rule of thumb is to block a 20-minute time span for each welcome call. During the call, the teacher introduces herself and provides essential contact information. Discussions should center on pacing guides and general policies for learning. The teacher should also review expectations and how parents will be contacted and kept informed of their child's progress. Oftentimes, there may be discussions relating to technology requirements or materials. Lastly, the teacher should discuss the course content, how the student will be assessed, and other content-related information.

The online program in which the student is enrolled often requires the use of a specific LMS. There are several content delivery systems such as Blackboard, Canvas, Desire2Learn, among others. These systems all require teachers and students to log in with a username and password, ensuring that online discussions, grades, and other sensitive information is visible only to those who need it. These platforms organize and present course content, and they offer a rich array of communication tools that support the ability to send and receive email, post grades, and support ongoing access for parents. Through private gradebook comments and opportunities for synchronous and asynchronous communication via discussion boards, online journals, in-course messages, and web meetings, these systems often let the teacher tailor their communication to individual students. This type of feedback is student-centered and provides parents with timely information as to how their child is progressing.

It is important that students in an online setting feel that their teacher is present and cares about their success. Therefore, it is essential that the teacher personalize her communication. Frequent contact is also necessary. An online teacher's spare time should be used to keep in touch and build professional relationships with her students.

Teachers should remember to communicate early at the first signs of a struggle and provide detailed feedback on assignments. Teachers should show the students that working toward a goal may require revisions and discussions with the teacher. Teachers should be providing detailed feedback to students. Doing so provides guidance, fosters the teacher-student connection, and ensures that students are more apt to work towards the goals set forth. Sometimes, the same students who may avoid a phone call will respond quickly to an email or text message. It is important to know your students and to keep track of their communication preferences.

Online teachers should keep a comprehensive log of all types of various communications. Oftentimes, an LMS will have a separate file system to allow the teacher to keep a log of communications for future reference. Although teacher communication is essential, it is really up to the teacher which method or methods to offer and employ based on convenience, student-needs, and the specific objectives of the communication. A virtual online teacher can use a variety of tools for communication. The next section takes a brief look at social media as an opportunity for communication and the ongoing exchange of ideas.

Social Media

Web-based solutions create a virtual open window into effective communication. In an article by Jason Tomaszewski (2012), studies suggest that approximately 70 percent of all organizations engage in structured collaboration using online social learning tools such as blogs, wikis, and podcasts. The use of online tools like social media sites and services has also increased in the K–12 school setting. Social media can be an excellent way to increase communication reach as well as to further engage our learners to enrich their online content. These resources can build a community of learners and allow for collaboration and the sharing of ideas.

Social media and apps such as Facebook and Twitter have allowed us to communicate in real-time. Using social media and apps within the educational setting can serve to enhance the experience of those participants.

There are several advantages to using social media to connect home and school. Social media is designed to be user-friendly and allow for cross-cultural communication. Other benefits include minimal technical requirements, multimedia sharing capabilities, and the opportunities for extending the reach of one's message. Social media tools encourage back-and-forth type of communication, and many of these tools are applicable in a pure virtual setting, a blended setting, or a brick-and-mortar setting.

Teacher Resources to Foster the School-Home Communication

Here is a brief list of social media and other online resources that teachers can use to enhance their ability to support open and ongoing communication with online students and their parents:

Facebook: Less sensitive material and general information can be kept on a facebook page. This link—www.schooltechnology.org/blog/2010/08/18 /creating-facebook-page-school-edtech-elearning—is a good resource for help in creating a school-type facebook page.

Edmodo: A social networking space designed for online learning environments, Edmodo (https://www.edmodo.com/) allows a teacher can post discussions, create student polls, upload additional documents for enrichment or remediation, and develop calendars and many other types of virtual learning experience. The parent receives a class code to access the space and can keep up on their student's online learning.

Poll Everywhere: This is an easy-to-use polling tool that can be accessed from any smartphone to solicit responses and opinions from parents. As an online teacher, Poll Everywhere (https://www.polleverywhere.com/enter prise) can be used during online collaboration meetings with students. Additionally, it can be used to collect parent feedback on a certain assignment or more general concerns. When compared to making numerous phone calls or waiting for parents to respond to emails, this is a faster way to elicit responses and gain insight.

Wetxt.com: Also used to create groups to invite parents to join, Wetxt (www.wetxt.com) is a new service offering free group text messaging. Wetxt works with 10 major cellular service providers to support the ability to send text messages to large groups at once. In addition to creating and sending initial messages, Wetxt offers an option for sending *reply all* messages. Messages can be sent from a mobile device or from an email account. A mobile calendar helps teachers keep track of items that need to be sent out as text messages.

Google for Education: Google offers a wide variety of creative apps for learning and communication including Google Voice and Google Hangouts. Google Voice and Google Hangouts promise Google-powered simplicity. You can send and receive messages from your phone, Gmail, or desktop. You are able to answer voice calls and listen to voicemails from the browser, and Google Voice even transcribes your voicemail messages. Google spreadsheets can be shared with parents/guardians and by providing them with editing rights to the spreadsheet; it can be used as a centralized signup sheet for appointments (https://www.google.com/edu/).

Classdojo: Any online teacher can adapt this classroom management app to fit their needs within the virtual setting. You may not use it to manage behavior, but instead use it to encourage students and give feedback on specific skills they are trying to master. The students will not be sitting in front of you, but in many cases you will know when they are online and working. Send your students messages, and use Classdojo (https://www .classdojo.com) to share updates with parents.

Remind101: This simple app can solve various communication obstacles between the virtual teacher and the parent. App security can be an issue, so this app does not display any phone numbers and all communication stays within the Remind101 (https://www.remind.com/learn-more) interface.

SchoolWay: Teachers can configure SchoolWay (myschoolway.com/parents) to send activity updates, assignment reminders, and other notifications.

Blogs and Wikis: Blogs and wikis are great tools to engage parents and students in an open dialogue. The teacher can set up a post and request comments from parents that facilitate an ongoing discussion. You may want to use a combination of the two; look at EduBlog (edublogs.org) and WikiSpaces (wikispaces.com) as possible tools.

Skoolbag: A mobile school app, Skoolbag (www.skoolbag.com.au/) allows teachers to create customized content for single-point parent communication.

Vimeo: Students can share their work in video format with teachers and parents through Vimeo (https://vimeo.com/).

Bonfyre: A networking app, Bonfyre (https://bonfyreapp.com/) allows users to create clubs, sports, and study groups, and improves parent-to-teacher communication.

SurveyMonkey: Create and publish online surveys in minutes using SurveyMonkey (https://www.surveymonkey.com/), and view your survey results graphically and in real-time.

Here are a few scheduling tools that make it easy for teachers, parents, and students to schedule appointments:

Doodle: Doodle (doodle.com/features) offers a wide selection of online solutions that radically simplify the process of scheduling appointments, ranging from the group event *poll* that does not require registration to the professional version.

Flash Appointments: With easy one-page scheduling, Flash Appointments (www.flashappointments.com/index.htm) allows the student to select from a preset menu designed by the teacher to set up various types of online appointments. Appointments populate to a calendar in real-time.

Cyber Safety and Digital Citizenship for the Online Learner

The ability to exhibit digital citizenship, to be information-literate, and to use the internet safely are important attributes and skills for 21st century learners. Teachers can assist parents and students by providing them with basic information and resources on cyber safety. There are several tips for keeping students safe. These should be reviewed with students and parents/guardians in an effort to make a child's online learning experience positive and free from distractions. The LMS is a secure system that requires all teachers and students to log in. However, even in the closed and password-protected setting of the online classroom, it is possible for students to behave unkindly and inappropriately. Therefore, it is important to teach students to alert an adult if they feel uncomfortable or threatened online.

Following are suggested safety rules and procedures to discuss with students:

1. A student should tell parents right away if they come across something that makes them feel uncomfortable.

2. Teach students not respond to any messages that are mean or in any way make them feel uncomfortable. Let them know it is not their fault if they get a message like that.

3. Teach students to refrain from giving out their passwords to anyone (even best friends) other than their parents.

4. Teach students to check with their parents before downloading or installing software or doing anything that could possibly hurt their computer or mobile device or jeopardize their family's privacy.

5. Teach students how to be a good online citizen and not do anything that hurts other people or is against the law. (Safekids .com 2015)

It is important for teachers at all grade levels to help students develop skills of digital citizenship such as those described in the International Society for Technology in Education's (ISTE) standards for students (2007). These essential attitudes and behaviors involve creativity, communication and collaboration, research and information fluency, critical thinking, digital citizenship, and expertise with technology operations and concepts. When teachers proactively teach, model, and encourage respectful and cooperative behavior, students are better able to learn these essential digital citizenship and literacy skills, and the entire online community stands to benefit.

Conclusion

It is clear that online teaching and learning offers both challenges and opportunities that may not exist in the f2f setting. Fortunately, through the use of careful planning, deliberate outreach, and interactive or collaborative tools, it is possible to open and maintain positive communication between virtual school and home. Regardless of the instructional format, all parents should have opportunities to become meaningful participants in their child's education. A child's academic success is greatly enriched when teachers and parents are partners in the process.

Online teachers can and should initiate meaningful conversations that allow both parents and students to participate. Teachers should be sure to choose the communication tools that work for the parent. Not all parents are the same, and using multiple communication methods makes the parent feel connected in a more comfortable way.

Keep in mind the following questions: Are your methods getting parents to respond? Which of the methods yields the best results? Surveys? Emails? Phone calls? Texting? Video conferencing? Web meetings? Are you using a combination of approaches to support whole class as well as one-to-one communication? For example, while class websites, newsletters, or blogs are a great way to communicate with all family members, other tools and strategies are needed for personalized communication.

Teachers should respond to parents in a timely manner and acknowledge their communication. Even if it is not possible to answer parent inquiries right away or in the detail required, let them know that their request or concern has been received. A responsive approach as well as more general and proactive efforts to cultivate communication with all parents will go a long way in fostering relationships.

Relationships are at the heart and soul of teaching and learning and are built on communication. Ongoing communication in an online teaching and learning environment must be deliberately designed on the part of the teacher. Just like their counterparts in more traditional programs, parents of students in virtual settings from kindergarten to high school need open communication and timely information. They want to know when their child's progress is slipping, and they want insight on how to help their children improve. They want to be kept informed of live online sessions and collaboration activities that require online attendance. Parents and teachers have the same goal in mind: success of the student. Communication is key to reaching this goal. An effective home-school connection fosters growth in children and confidence in the virtual school setting.

References

Bryans-Bongey, Sarah. "Meeting the Holistic Needs of K–12 Online Learners: Designing Schools for the Future," Fall 2015. *Internet Learning Journal,* 4(2), 7-24. http://www.ipsonet.org/publications/open-access/internet-learning/volume-4-number-2-fall-2015.

Hasler Waters, Lisa, and Peter Leong. "Who is Teaching? New Roles for Teachers and Parents in Cyber Charter Schools," *Journal of Technology and Teacher Education* 22, no. 1 (2014): 33-56.

Henderson, Anne T., and Karen L. Mapp. "A New Wave of Evidence: The Impact of School, Family, and Community Connections on Student Achievement," 2002. https://www.sedl.org/connections/resources/evidence.pdf.

International Society for Technology in Education. "Standards for Students," 2007. https://www.iste.org/docs/pdfs/20-14_ISTE_Standards-S_PDF.pdf.

Lavoie, Rick. "The Teacher's Role in Home/School Communication: Everybody Wins," 2008. http://www.ldonline.org/article/28021/.

Namahoe, Kanoe. "Florida Virtual School Adopts New Communication Portal," 2012. http://thejournal.com/articles/2012/07/11/florida-virtual-school-adopts-new-communications-portal.aspx.

Prensky, Marc. "Digital Native, Digital Immigrants." *On the Horizon* 9, no. 5 (2001). http://www.marcprensky.com/writing/Prensky%20-%20Digital%20Natives,%20Digital%20Immigrants%20-%20Part1.pdf.

Safekids.com. "Kids' Rules for Online Safety," 2015. http://www.safekids.com/kids-rules-for-online-safety.

Sivy, Mark. "Virtual School Leadership," 2014. https://virtualschoolleadership.wordpress.com/2014/09/19/virtual-school-internal-communication/.

Tomaszewski, Jason. "Study Suggests Benefits of Social Media in the Classroom," 2012. *Education World.* http://www.educationworld.com/a_curr/study-suggests-social-media-has-place-in-classrooms.shtml.

Universal Design for Learning (UDL) and Online Learning

Luis Pérez, Kendra Grant, and Elizabeth Dalton

Abstract

Universal design for learning (UDL) is a curriculum design framework, one which considers learner variation as based in neuroscience. Developed by the Center for Applied Special Technology (CAST) in 1991, UDL bases its core principles on the brain's affective, recognition, and strategic networks. The three core principles of UDL are multiple means of engagement, representation, and action and expression. This chapter provides background on UDL and relates UDL principles, guidelines, and checkpoints to online instruction and learning. Real examples of UDL infusion in an online learning course provide models for further exploration and application of UDL as a model framework for K–12 online instruction.

Introduction

We know that one-size-fits-all instruction is ineffective in meeting the needs of the diverse learners we see in our classrooms. Unfortunately, we often see this approach applied to online environments, where providing everyone with the same content, the same pathway for learning, and the same assessment makes managing the instruction easier. Whether instruction is delivered in a face-to-face (f2f) or online environment, the reality is that addressing variation in what students bring to the learning experience and what they need to be successful is primary to any effective course design. In addition, online learning brings unique challenges that may include learner isolation and a lack of engagement and support.

We three authors created an online professional learning opportunity to explore how one framework, universal design for learning (UDL), could counteract some of the potentially negative aspects of online learning. This chapter focuses on the insights we gained as we developed this course for educators, many of which can be applied to your K–12 online instructional practice.

Universal Design for Learning (UDL)

Developed by the Center for Applied Special Technology (CAST), UDL offers a curriculum design framework based on the foundations of neuroscience, universal design (UD) in the physical environment (Center for Universal Design 2008), and constructivist principles (Vygotsky 1962). To meet current learner needs, UDL provides guidance to systematically address learner variation through purposeful and proactive design of goals, assessments, methods, and materials in different types of instruction, including that which takes place in online environments. The three core principles of UDL—multiple means of engagement, representation, and action and expression—and the guidelines developed to support implementation also provide direction for educators to purposefully build variability into lessons and teaching (CAST 2011). In this chapter, we provide an overview of the UDL framework and explore how it can be used to support K–12 online instruction.

UDL is a framework that guides supported and improved teaching and learning (Rose and Meyer 2002). This is accomplished by effectively addressing the widely varying needs of students in the general education classroom from the onset, through innovative curriculum design rather than through individual retroactive adjustments and accommodations. In *Teaching Every Child in the Digital Age,* David Rose and Anne Meyer (2002) embraced technology and its ability to reduce barriers, provide access to information and, when applied appropriately, provide broader access to learning. CAST and UDL itself reflect a break from a medical model in which treatments or solutions are specifically and reactively designed to address those "in the margins" to one that focuses on an initial design that supports learner variability at the outset, and with the goal of developing expert learners (Meyer and Rose 2005, p. 1).

UDL has three core guiding principles:

1. multiple means of engagement with the goal of creating purposeful, motivated learners

2. multiple means of representation with the goal of developing resourceful, knowledgeable learners

3. multiple means of action and expression with the goal of supporting strategic, goal-directed learners (Meyer, Rose, and Gordon 2013)

Each principle in the UDL framework has three more detailed guidelines to support educators in the development and implementation of goals, methods, materials, and assessments that work effectively for the widest range of learners in any type of learning environment (CAST 2011). The UDL guidelines follow a horizontal as well as a vertical organization. Horizontally, the guidelines address variability along three primary brain networks identified in neuroscience:

1. *The affective network (multiple means of engagement)*: This network, located in the center of the brain, monitors the learner's internal and external environments in order to set priorities for behavior. It determines what a learner finds motivating or threatening in a given learning environment as well as his or her ability to persist when challenges arise. By providing supports for this network, we can minimize frustration and make it more likely that a learner will achieve the goals of a given learning activity.

2. *The recognition network (multiple means of representation)*: This network, located in the back of the brain, recognizes patterns in the information received through the senses. This ability to recognize patterns differs between novices and experts, who bring differing amounts of background knowledge to each learning experience. Accounting not only for these different levels of background knowledge and experience, but also developing learners' abilities to acquire and organize new information in order to translate it into new knowledge is key to effective UDL implementation in this learning network.

3. *The strategic network (multiple means of action and expression)*: This network, in the front of the brain, is involved in planning, organizing, and executing purposeful actions such as writing an essay or solving a math problem. A key UDL goal with regard to this network is to reduce barriers that are present when the goals of a lesson or unit are combined with the means for achieving

them. An example would be requiring that all learners write an essay demonstrating their understanding of an important event in a history course. Such a requirement could put certain learners who have motor difficulties that make typing slower or more painful at a disadvantage. By providing other options such as the recording of answers using the microphone or camera on a mobile device, we can ensure all students can demonstrate their understanding on a level playing field.

While each network is often discussed separately for ease of explanation, in practice the three brain networks are highly interdependent. Barriers in the recognition and strategic networks can result in frustrated learners who are less motivated to continue with a given learning activity. Conversely, highly motivated learners often find ways to get around barriers in the recognition and strategic networks, although our goal as teachers and designers should be to minimize the need for such workarounds.

Vertically, the UDL guidelines are organized to emphasize extrinsic factors at the bottom (what the teacher or instructional designer does to empower learners to be successful) to intrinsic ones at the top (what learners do to empower themselves to be successful). Recognizing and integrating this organizational pattern is often the step missing from many UDL implementations, where the focus remains solely on the extrinsic factors that are foundational to UDL. These factors by themselves will not result in expert learners who take ownership of their own learning. In keeping with the UDL principle of multiple means of representation, Figure 10.1 offers an infographic entitled "The Key Goal of UDL: Developing Expert Learners" (Grant 2015). It provides a visual representation of the UDL principles and guidelines, highlighting the vertical organization of the UDL guidelines. The UDL goal of developing expert learners is at the top, reflecting the ultimate aim of any UDL-based learning environment.

The potential for UDL to be achieved in an online learning environment is high, primarily due to opportunities for variation of content and concept representation available through different digital online tools. Digital resources tend to be, by their nature, more flexible than traditional analog ones. With a print textbook, for example, separate versions need to be purchased for learners with low vision who need the text enlarged as well as for those who are completely blind and require a braille version. With a digital version of the same textbook, however, learners who need the text enlarged can do so by changing a setting within the application

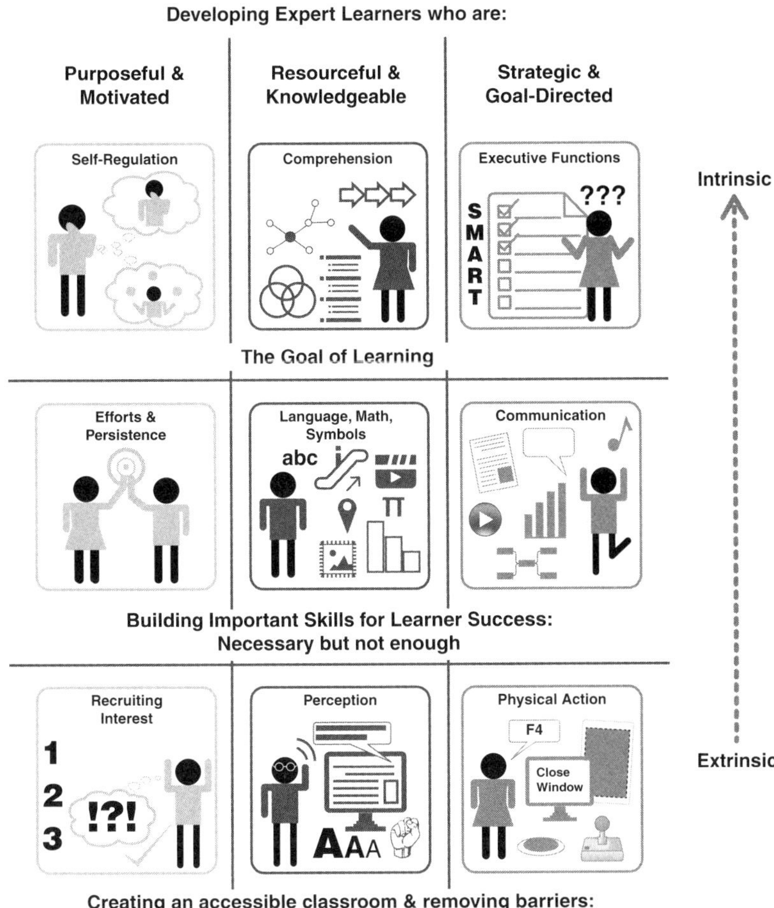

Figure 10.1   Online learning and UDL

used to display the book. Similarly, those who are blind can use a screen reader to have the content read aloud using text to speech, a feature that is often built into many operating systems today.

As is often the case with a universal design approach, features such as text-to-speech that help those "in the margins" are often useful and helpful to other learners (Meyer and Rose 2005, p. 1). Actually, text-to-speech could be used by any reader who struggles with decoding, even if he or she has not been diagnosed with a disability such as dyslexia, or by an English language learner who could benefit from hearing the correct pronunciation spoken aloud as he or she reads the text. As with the UD movement in architecture and product design, UDL starts by considering barriers that prevent equitable participation by those in the margins but always with the goal of creating flexible environments that work for all.

In addition to potential reliance on flexible learning materials, online learning has a number of other advantages for diverse learners. For those who have difficulty with navigation due to poor vision or motor challenges, the convenience of accessing lessons from home can be a great asset. Furthermore, for those who struggle with social interactions, the online environment provides a more anonymous form of interaction. For those who are shy, an online environment could provide more opportunities for participation than in a traditional f2f classroom, reducing direct interpersonal threats for the student, thereby increasing their willingness to engage and participate.

To realize the potential of online learning for all learners, special attention needs to be paid to accessibility best practices. Without such a focus, barriers will remain in place and may prevent certain learners from enjoying the benefits of such environments. A common problem is that while digital resources tend to be more flexible, they are not always accessible for those who rely on assistive technology (AT). As quoted by Mindy Johnson (2015), senior instructional designer at CAST, "born digital does not mean born accessible." Teachers and instructional designers need to pay attention to accessibility best practices in order to ensure such digital resources do not replicate the barriers that would be present in an f2f classroom. An example is the reliance on scanned PDF documents in many online courses. When these documents are scanned as images, they do not present useful information to those who need the content described aloud because they are blind. On the other hand, when these documents are scanned as text (through a process known as optical character recognition or OCR), they are accessible to not only those who use screen readers due to a disability such as blindness, but also to those who would rather hear the content read aloud during a long commute. While accessibility is an important consideration for any UDL implementation, it is even more important in online learning environments where digital content is the primary way learners engage with the content, each other, and the teacher.

In the remaining sections of this chapter, we explore how to incorporate a number of accessibility best practices and UDL principles, guidelines, and checkpoints into the design of online courses (CAST 2011). Our suggestions are based on a course we delivered to two cohorts of teachers in the springs of 2014 and 2015 (Dalton, Grant, and Pérez 2014). This course is available for review at www.sooc4learning.com. Key goals of the course were to teach in-service teachers how to utilize the latest apps for mobile devices in order to implement UDL in their classrooms, while at the same time modeling key aspects of UDL in the design of the course. While the course was aimed at a professional audience, many of the same design considerations are easily transferrable to support online courses developed for K–12 learners. Note that the design approaches and references that follow make use of the UDL checklists and checkpoints that are available on the CAST.org website.

Multiple Means of Engagement

Provide Options for Recruiting Interest

Engagement is a big topic in education circles these days—so big, that in the latest version of the UDL guidelines it is mentioned first, whereas before it was the third principle. We know that without interest most learners give little effort and retain even less. In recognizing that what learners find engaging and worthy of their effort varies from one person to another, it is important to build choice into your courses, which will vary depending on your learners' experience with online learning, their age, and their command of technology. As you design learning tasks, consider creating a variety of ways for the students to show you what they know. Rather than assign one culminating task such as an essay, expand their choices and consider providing an open choice option approved by you for more advanced learners, choices that will help make learning meaningful and relevant to all your learners in accordance with UDL checkpoint 7.2 (optimize relevance, value, and authenticity). Also, let students choose the tool or app they use. This models the UDL checkpoints 4.1 (vary the methods for response and navigation), 5.1 (use multimedia for communication), and 5.2 (use multiple tools for construction and composition). For younger students, provide them with one or two tools, expanding upon their choices as they gain skills. Providing students with a choice of media and tools is a simple way to honor the varying skills, abilities, and interests of all learners.

Provide Options for Sustaining Effort and Persistence

While gaining learners' attention and interest is key, learning to sustain effort and persist in the face of challenge is an important part of learning. When such challenges arise, supports need to be in place, especially in online environment when the perception of being *alone* can quickly become overwhelming. To strengthen learners' abilities to persist, we recommend you provide both synchronous and asynchronous support to address varying schedules and preferences for interaction. While your learning management system (LMS) may have an automated response email when learners struggle, fail to sign in, or show waning effort, our course confirmed for us that teacher presence is paramount. You need to be available, with a system of timely responses in place that meets both your learners' and your own needs. By being available, you address the UDL checkpoint 8.3 (fostering collaboration and communication) and you model what sustained effort and commitment looks and sounds like.

Effort can also be sustained through features that assist learners in tracking their progress toward the completion of learning goals. In our course, we incorporated digital badging as a way to document completion of the tasks and as a tangible recognition system for weekly progress and final completion of the course. These badges were linked to the appropriate International Society for Technology in Education (ISTE) 2015 standards in order to document the skills and dispositions addressed in each week of the course. Many LMSs have built-in badging. In addition, Classbadges (2015) has an excellent system to organize, award, and share student badges. To better address UDL principles related to engagement, carefully consider how you will use badges. Competency-based badges, with a set of criteria to be met, can help learners maintain effort and persistence, while skill-based badges, focused on intrinsic abilities, can support self-regulation.

Provide Options for Self-Regulation

Self-regulated learners take initiative and drive their own learning. They are reflective and make adjustments as needed with a reduced need for prompting from the teacher. To encourage this type of reflection, provide learners with self-reflection rubrics, encourage them to post their thoughts in a learning community, and build reflection into your instructional tasks. Electronic portfolios are excellent ways for learners to select some of their best products then reflect on what they learned and how they can improve. Providing continuous formative feedback for each learner addresses UDL checkpoint 8.4 (increase mastery-oriented feedback) and UDL checkpoint 9.1 (promote expectations and beliefs that optimize motivation). While it requires commitment to respond to learners consistently, this commitment, as we experienced in our online course, is often reflected back in the quality of the tasks and reflections posted.

Multiple Means of Representation
Provide Options for Perception

While UDL today is an approach that aims to make the curriculum work for all learners, we cannot forget that it started as an effort to reduce barriers to learning for those "in the margins" (Meyer and Rose 2005, p. 1). Thus, it remains important to address the accessibility of learning materials for those with sensory or other limitations when designing an online course based on UDL. Many LMSs now model best practices for web accessibility in their design; however, it is best to review the support they include. Also, even if the LMS you select is accessible, it is the content shared within the system that will ultimately determine the accessibility of your course. At a minimum, you should provide descriptive text equivalents for images and other visuals to make them accessible to screen reader users along with closed captioning for any videos. This practice of including closed captioning not only makes the content accessible for those with a hearing loss, but also becomes a valuable aid to other learners (including those who are not fluent in the target language). It can serve as a support for reading development, as well. If you are creating your own videos, then we recommend you create a script first as it not only results in a more polished presentation, but also facilitates the captioning process. After you upload a video to YouTube, it is a relatively simple process to upload the corresponding transcript and let YouTube accurately time the captions. Resist the temptation to rely on the automatic captions provided by YouTube itself, as these are not yet sufficiently accurate to provide an accessible solution. Ideally, you should also link to the transcript used to create the captions, since some learners may require more time to process the information and the rate of presentation of the captions may be too fast for them.

Finally, you should carefully consider the selection of colors for handouts, videos, and other visual representations to ensure there is sufficient contrast between the text and the background. Clean layouts with sufficient contrast not only work well for those with low vision, but also make the information easier to scan and process for everyone. Size of text is also important for clarity in reading. A minimum of 14-point san serif text is recommended for large print for those with low vision or those with reading or tracking difficulties; however, 18-point text is preferred. Fortunately, this does not mean you need to create all your online course content using 18-point text because when text is digital, it can be enlarged quite easily.

Provide Options for Language, Expressions and Symbols

The ability to easily hyperlink to definitions of unfamiliar terms and concepts is a unique advantage of digital resources that can be used to support learners' varying levels of language competence and background knowledge (UDL checkpoints 2.1—clarify vocabulary and symbols and 3.1—activate or supply background knowledge). The first time you use a specialized term (such as UD or variability in our course), you should link to the appropriate definitions on the web. Doing so ensures everyone in the course is starting from a common definition of terms that are essential to understanding the content. Digital content also supports the use of the text-to-speech features now built into most devices as an aid for decoding text (UDL checkpoint 2.3). It is important to ensure your content, especially PDF documents, are accessible. Many PDFs are actually images, making them inaccessible to screen readers. Finally, use a variety of media to illustrate important concepts in a way that appeals to learners' preferences for different modalities (UDL checkpoint 2.5—illustrate through multiple media). You can use cartoons and other visuals to provide alternative representations of text-based content. Videos can also be an effective way to present content in an engaging manner. However, we caution against the simple recording of a traditional f2f lecture that is then presented online. For our course, videos were created with the Powtoon service for a more engaging presentation through the careful use of images, color, and animation. In addition, we edited the content of our videos to create a concise 10-minute video with links to additional information rather than the typical 45- to 60-minute lectures. In our estimation, these are rarely viewed in their entirety. Lastly, do not forget to include closed captioning in your own instructional videos, too.

Provide Options for Comprehension

At the highest level of multiple means of representation, the goal is not only to provide access to the content, but also to assist learners in making sense of the information in order to translate it into useful knowledge. This task may be complicated by the fact that learners bring differing levels of background knowledge to the learning task, or have different native languages or cultures to where you may need to provide some of that background knowledge for some learners in the form of links to additional online resources that fill in the gaps for those learners. For example, if you provide overview videos to introduce key concepts, supplement them with a number of additional online resources to provide background knowledge (UDL checkpoint 3.1—activate or supply background knowledge) and multiple ways for learners to access the information. Clearly label these additional resources to provide easy access to them. Expert learners are highly resourceful and capable of organizing information in a way that makes sense to them, but novice learners may lack this skill.

To aid with comprehension, guiding questions can be provided to highlight the key ideas and concepts for novice learners (UDL checkpoint 3.2—highlight patterns, critical features, big ideas, and relationships). For example, you may want to include a series of guiding questions to focus the learner's attention on the key ideas presented in the video or text. Furthermore, novice learners may need some guidance in how to proceed through the content in an efficient manner. In our course, the link to each video on YouTube was supplemented with a table of contents linked to the specific point in the video where each item was discussed. This additional feature was included to further organize the content for learners in keeping with UDL checkpoint 3.3 (guide information processing, visualization, and manipulation).

Multiple Means of Action and Expression

Provide Options for Physical Action

Just as some learners may have sensory limitations that make it difficult for them to access the content in an online course, so do some learners have motor limitations that make interaction with the learning environment more difficult. For example, some learners may not be able to use a mouse; thus, they rely on the keyboard for all or most of their interaction. One issue we discovered early in the design of our course website was a lack of accessibility for keyboard users with the pull-down menus that were used to simplify the course navigation and organize it around the three key principles of UDL. This issue was addressed with the installation of a WordPress plugin that provided keyboard accessibility for the pull-down menus in order to meet the requirements of guideline 2.1 of the W3C's (2012) "Web Content Accessibility Guidelines" as well as UDL checkpoint 4.2 (optimize access to tools and assistive technologies). For those using a different platform to deliver an online course, it is important to test for keyboard accessibility and to not limit accessibility considerations to screen reader users. A simple test is to disconnect the mouse (or flip it over), and then try to navigate the interface using just the keyboard by pressing the tab key to advance and shift tab to go back. On a keyboard accessible site, every interactive element (hyperlink, form element, and navigation element) should have an outline or other visual cue to indicate when it has focus, and it should then be possible to make a selection by pressing the Space or Return key on the keyboard.

Provide Options for Expression and Communication

By expanding the options learners have to demonstrate their understanding, we can tap into their creativity and significantly increase their engagement with learning. Most platforms used for online learning support the submission of course products in a variety of formats including video and audio. While we used a Google+ community (as it has a number of advantages as a tool for collaboration and engagement), you may not have this option and may be required to use other tools associated with your district's LMS. If you are a Google Education district, you will have access to many of the Google tools and apps we used, including YouTube and Google drive. If your district uses a traditional LMS, then you should have access to a shared drive or repository that allows for the easy inclusion of multimedia. This repository can encourage a range of responses rather than only text for posting, reinforcing the UDL checkpoints 5.1 (use multimedia for communication) and 5.2 (use multiple tools for construction and composition).

For some learners, starting an activity from scratch can be an overwhelming prospect. For them, providing a number of exemplars that demonstrate skillful work can be helpful. We did this in our course by adding a new page to our course website each week with links to the products submitted by the course participants. By seeing the variety of ways that activities could be completed and mobile devices and apps could be used to implement UDL, the learner's self-efficacy was further facilitated and supported (Meyer, Rose, and Gordon 2013).

Provide Options for Executive Function

The ability to plan and execute purposeful action is one of the highest level skills a person can possess. Some learners who do not possess this skill can become easily distracted and as a result may not complete assigned tasks in a timely manner. For those learners, you should provide a number of aids to show how the course itself is organized and when important deadlines occur. For example, provide at the beginning of your course a course syllabus in two accessible formats: a page within the LMS and an attached PDF document tagged for screen reader access. This syllabus should provide a clear statement of the course, guiding questions, and learner expectations, as well as brief descriptions of the assignments and assessment methods. To help learners plan their schedules, a calendar with the key dates for assignment submissions and additional meet-ups online should be listed.

Many LMSs now also have automated reminders. While this is efficient, where possible personal contact such as a weekly reminder emails will help ensure learners are up-to-date on what is expected of them. The digital badges discussed in the section on multiple means of engagement are another tool for learners to track their progress as they complete tasks. Other aids you can provide to support learners' executive functioning include checklists and rubrics. These are especially important for longer projects that require a number of steps for successful completion. Finally, consider becoming teacher participants, or *lead learners* within your own course, providing direct models for students with your own work and demonstrating your own decision-making and executive functioning. Such full participation as someone who is learning right along with your class can help to break down barriers and help guide students on the path to become truly expert learners.

Conclusion

Online learning that is designed with accessibility in mind can be a great fit for implementing UDL in order to meet the needs of diverse learners. UDL provides multiple pathways for learning so that individual learners can find what grabs their interest, sustains their effort, and develops their learning expertise. As you design your course, consider how you will build engagement, support access to content, and provide options for learners to demonstrate what they learned. Designing this flexibility into your course will help ensure the unique learning needs of each student are addressed. UDL involves intentional planning for learner variability from the start, rather than the retrofitting of the curriculum to accommodate individual needs after the fact. It is a front-loaded approach to curriculum design that may require more time during the planning phase, but it will produce the kind of flexible learning environments needed by an increasingly diverse student population. UDL marries the science and art of teaching and learning into a powerful solution for today's online and f2f classrooms by combining insights from neuroscience, best practices in pedagogy, and the flexibility afforded by digital content and tools.

References

Center for Applied Special Technology. "What is Universal Design for Learning?" 2014. http://www.cast.org/udl/index.html.

—. "Universal Design for Learning Guidelines Version 2.0," 2011. Wakefield, MA: Author. http://www.udlcenter.org/aboutudl/udlguidelines.

Center for Universal Design. "About Universal Design," 2008. Durham, NC: North Carolina State University, College of Design. https://www.ncsu.edu/ncsu/design/cud/about_ud/about_ud.htm

Classbadges. Home Page, 2013. http://classbadges.com/.

Dalton, Elizabeth, Kendra Grant, and Luis Pérez. 2014. "SOOC: A New Model for Online Professional Learning Communities Focus: Universal Design for Learning." In *Proceedings of World Conference on E-Learning in Corporate, Government, Healthcare, and Higher Education,* 1918-26. Chesapeake, VA: AACE, 2014.

Grant, Kendra. "The Key Goal of UDL: Developing Expert Learners," 2015. http://kendragrant.wix.com/udlnow#!expert-learners/cs6t.

International Society for Technology in Education. "ISTE Standards," 2015. http://www.iste.org/STANDARDS.

Johnson, Mindy. "UDL." Personal communication. 2015.

Meyer, A., and D. H. Rose. "The Future is in the Margins: The Role of Technology and Disability in Educational Reform." In *The Universally Designed Classroom: Accessible Curriculum and Digital Technologies,* ed. D. H. Rose, A. Meyer, and C. Hitchcock, 13-35. Cambridge, MA: Harvard Education Press, 2005.

Meyer, Anne, David Rose, and David Gordon. *Universal Design for Learning: Theory and Practice.* Wakefield, MA: Center for Applied Special Technology, 2013.

Rose, David, and Anne Meyer. *Teaching Every Child in the Digital Age.* Alexandria, VA: Association for Supervision and Curriculum Development, 2002.

Vygotsky, Lev. 1962. *Thought and Language,* ed. E. Hanfmann and G. Vakar. Cambridge, MA: Massachusetts Institute of Technology Press.

W3C Web Accessibility Initiative. "W3C's Web Content Accessibility Guidelines (WCAG) Overview," 2012. http://www.w3.org/WAI/intro/wcag.

Helping Special Education Teachers Transition to K–12 Online Learning

Richard Allen Carter, Jr., James D. Basham, and Mary Frances Rice

Abstract

For the special education teacher, the online course environment represents challenges and opportunities that are different from those experienced in the traditional face-to-face (f2f) setting. This chapter presents practical and research-based applications to guide special educators in the exciting and sometimes complex online environment. The chapter is framed around five key issues that address teachers' and learners' successful transition into fully online or blended learning environments: (1) the development and implementation of Individualized Education Programs (IEPs), (2) curriculum making and the timing of instructional delivery, (3) facilitating learner independence and self-determination, (4) communication with learners and their families, and (5) collaboration with families and colleagues to build relationships that support student learning.

Introduction

As special education teachers provide increasing amounts of instruction online, they are faced with a number of new situations that require sophisticated judgment to navigate (Archambault 2011). Online learning represents a departure from traditional teaching because most interactions with both educators and subject matter happens via the internet and does not occur synchronously. In traditional education, school buildings are natural places for communities to form. Educators and students converge at the same time in the same places for the same reasons and their time together is well regulated in order to facilitate interactions that are both planned and spontaneous. For example, students with disabilities are more likely to interact with librarians who are eager and willing to help with research projects because classroom teachers have informed the librarians or because other students have been discussing the project in a librarian's earshot. A librarian may also pass by students in the hallway and talk to them or become aware of areas of interest by virtue of living in the same community (shopping at the same stores, spending time with friends, having their own children in the school and so forth). Because of this physical and time-bound embeddedness, incidental guidance for academic work and relationships of trust are likely to emerge organically, and may not even be noticed as having developed.

By contrast, in online learning, students who want or need access to expertise will have to deliberately seek it from people who are essentially strangers. Much of work completed during the day for student enrolled in online coursework is free of teacher support as a trade-off for allowing the students to control their learning path and pace. The resources around subject matter for learners who are working largely independently are immense online, and can be overwhelming. For learners with disabilities, discerning and processing these resources on their own can present challenges (Greer, Rice, and Dykman 2014). Since the parent is the person in closest proximity to the learner and since their parent is the person with whom they already have the strongest relationship it makes sense that the parent would become the primary source of expertise. If teachers care about making sure that parents are supported in this role and they, as teachers, desire to put forward their knowledge and grant access to the wealth of expertise on the internet, they will have to be more deliberate in their work with students.

The conditions of learning environments that require extra deliberation and new kinds of expertise can be daunting to teachers who are new to the profession or whose teaching experiences have not required them to make intensive use of internet and other technologies to meet the needs of learners with disabilities (Basham and Marino 2013). The purpose of this chapter is to use research that offers insight about online learning in order to help special education teachers conceptualize their work. The primary questions that are answered in this chapter include the following:

- How can special education teachers help learners new to online learning transition successfully?

- What can special education teachers do to uphold
  Individualized Education Programs (IEPs) in online learning
  environments?
- What are the possibilities for curriculum design in online
  learning environments?
- How can learners with disabilities use technology to
  become independent and self-determined in online learning
  environments?
- How can special education teachers maintain communication in
  online learning environments?
- How can special education teachers promote collaboration in
  online learning environments?

These questions will be attended to using relevant theories as they apply to practice. The practice-orientated nature of the chapter is developed using illustrations and explanations from teachers. The intent is for readers to see how theory informs practice on key issues of teacher work with learners with disabilities in online learning environments.

How Can Special Education Teachers Help Learners Transition Successfully to Online Learning?

A fully online school does not have terms or semesters. Learner enrollment in online schools is ongoing, and learners come into and out of courses at high rates. Even learners in blended settings display more erratic entry and departure patterns. Learners with disabilities come into online schools for many reasons. Some typical reasons include the desire of time to do extra activities beyond school or to have new experiences with technologies. Learners also have medical needs that preclude regular daily attendance in a brick-and-mortar school, behavioral issues that an IEP team hopes an online school environment will ameliorate, or even a sense of alienation after a string of hard experiences with a traditional school (Rice and Carter 2015). These decisions for placement in an online school require sensitivity and confidentiality, yet it is crucial that the online teacher be aware of not only the reason for placement, but also the events that preceded the placement as part of a records review.

Teachers we have interviewed emphasized the range of learners with and without disabilities that come into their courses. All interviews were conducted in confidentiality, and the names of interviewees were withheld by mutual agreement and the names throughout this chapter are pseudonyms. One teacher told us:

> Some students in our virtual school have parents that have a lot of resources and want to advocate for their children by pulling them out of traditional school. They can afford lots of activities; seeking out online learning is just one part of that. You also have kids who come into online learning with few material resources. I've had so many homeless kids. A girl left me a message last Friday from a motel. They got evicted. She can call me, but how am I going to call her? You never know how long students are going to last in the course. (Interview with teacher, April 2014)

The realities that this teacher presents suggest actions for teaching in an online environment. First, special education teachers do not assume they understand why learners with disabilities have come to an online environment; instead, they seek out that information. Second, teachers expect to deal tactfully with learners who are in an online school around information about the disability as well as any personal circumstances. Third, teachers develop orientations to learners around their strengths rather than their disabilities. All learners who enroll in online schools are looking for a way to learn that allows them to meet their other needs. Their families need to trust that they can learn effectively online with support. Students with disabilities need advocates to help them meet their educational and personal goals as well as understand how to implement their disability plans. Teachers should be interested in making sure that students have positive experiences in online school to the greatest extent possible.

In addition, social and political inequalities that exist are less visible until learners come into online environments. Not all families have equal access to the internet and related technologies, and not all families use this access in the same manner (van Duersen and Van Dijk 2014). Teachers, including those who work with students with disabilities, are at the forefront of making sure families have access to technologies or that they can navigate through material when access is limited.

Having access to the online school environment may not be enough to ensure that a learner is successful in his or her online coursework. There are also skills associated with these resources like installing software updates, troubleshooting skills, and organizational skills for keeping the devices charged and available for use that families must develop or pool to support online learning (Carter and Rice 2015). Not having access through connectivity or not having access to skills can cause learners with disabilities great anxiety as they engage with their coursework. Finally, teachers should avoid making assumptions about why learners may or may not be logging on every day for their coursework or responding immediately to texts or emails.

What Can Special Education Teachers Do to Uphold IEPs in the Online Learning Environment?

The IEP plans are legal contracts between learners with identified disabilities, their families, and the school that serves them. These documents outline what services are necessary, who provides the services, and where the services are to be delivered. In addition, the IEP outlines present levels of achievement and stipulates measurable learning goals. A learner with an IEP may have academic goals, behavioral goals, and/or social goals. An IEP team must create goals for the learners that attend to learner needs while providing opportunities for online teachers to monitor learner progress toward the goal. According to current disability laws, IEP documents are created yearly with a re-evaluation occurring within a three-year period, provided the family and school deem it necessary (Iowa Legislature 2009).

What is written in the IEP is legally binding. Therefore, an IEP for learners engaging in online schooling must be written with goals that serve the learner and can be met in that environment. IEPs are rarely written with consideration of the online environment and the affordances of the environment (Rice, East, and Mellard 2015). Thus, when learners with disabilities enter online environments, online school teams should immediately consider revisiting and rewriting the IEP to consider the required resources for online learning as well as how to generalize the technologies that the learner may already be using, such as a screen reader. Resources include, but are not limited to, unrestricted access to a computer, reliable internet connectivity, appropriate software/updates, assistive technology (AT), and working knowledge of how to access the online curriculum and internet to support learning. Table 11.1 highlights some of the important considerations for building a viable IEP for a learner in an online environment.

Discussing required resources with the family, particularly in regard to AT, is the best way to determine if the learner has access to the appropriate technologies for online learning. An assessment such as the student, environment, task and tools (SETT) framework is a resource for helping IEP teams determine appropriate accommodations and services

Table 11.1

Making IEP Plans Meaningful for Online Learners.

- IEP goals should be relevant to the online learning environment
- Appropriate assistive technology should be acquired and tested for functionality
- Required resources should be discussed with the parents in advance
- Learner data should be used to inform IEP plans
- Provisions should be made for ongoing communication and collaboration with other professionals charged with serving the online learner

(Zabala, Bowser, and Korsten 2004). The SETT framework is commonly associated with assistive technology; however, it does provide additional structures for identifying resources that learners will need to engage with curriculum in online learning environments. If these major resources are not readily available, the IEP team should put these in place before the learner begins the work.

Unfortunately, many online teachers, even when they are special education teachers, are not always responsible for generating the IEP goals (Greer, Rice, and Carter 2015). Instead, teachers create these goals in the traditional brick-and-mortar school in the area in which the learner lives as opposed to where the online school resides. A learner's traditional brick-and-mortar school (often called the home school, not to be confused with homeschooling) is in a different physical location with a different set of resources from where learners attend online school. In the cases where the home school creates the IEP, the online special education teacher is left as the lone person responsible for implementing IEP goals that were probably not created with the online environment in mind. Clearly, such an approach is not the recommended practice, as it pushes the online professionals into a situation wherein they are attempting to support brick-and-mortar style needs and goals in an online setting.

What Are the Possibilities for Curriculum Design in Online Learning Environments?

There is neither a shortage of content to teach nor a shortage of people who have opinions about what should be taught. This stuff can be called many things, but for the purposes of this chapter, we refer to it as subject matter. Subject matter is not curriculum, but only one element of it. According to the curriculum scholar Joseph Schwab (1969), curriculum is made when a teacher and learners engage in activity in a particular milieu, or context. The purpose of the activity that teachers and learners engage in is to learn specific subject matter, ways of thinking, knowledge, or even skills. While public policy and the media are overly concerned about only the subject matter, modern understandings of curriculum are likely more focused on the context of the learning itself. Similar to brick-and-mortar style instruction, teachers in online environments should be able to design the context for supporting learning; this is part of the curriculum making process.

Schwab's (1969) ideas have currency in the online environment since they complement other evidence-based frameworks for instructional design. For example, universal design for learning (UDL) is an evidence-based framework that is focused on supporting the variability of needs across the learning environment. Currently, UDL is being emphasized in a number of schools around the world, states across the nation, and individual leading school districts. UDL is also a primary focus in the implementation and research around online and blended learning in both K–12 and higher education settings. At its basic level, the framework emphasizes providing multiple means of engagement, representation, and action/expression in every learning experience, according to the Center for Applied Special Technology (CAST) (2011). Overall, UDL seeks to provide flexibility that is sufficient for successfully teaching all learners in both brick-and-mortar and online environments. Basham and Marino (2013) indicate that UDL is a process of iteratively designing environments focused on meeting the needs of all learners. To support the integration of UDL, the Universal Design for Learning Implementation and Research Network (UDL-IRN) has developed a number of tools, including the five-step instructional planning process (Basham 2011). See Figure 11.1 for suggested steps in the instructional planning process.

Regardless of the language used to discuss curriculum development, meeting the needs of learners with disabilities is a matter of flexible informed thinking about appropriate activities that offer options and facilitate engagement with subject matter. With the possibilities afforded by technologies, there are more chances than Schwab (1969) could have imagined. Now, given ready resources, learners can generate valuable content with teachers and other learners. In a traditional school milieu, teachers have been known to present learners with the same learning activity in the same space with the same resources. This approach is chronotopic. When education is chronotopic, it occurs in a particular sequence that has

UDL Instructional Planning Process

Step 1: Establish Clear Outcomes

Step 2: Anticipate Learner Variability

Step 3: Establish the Assessment Plan

Step 4: Design the Instructional Experience

Step 5: Reflection and New Understandings

UDL IRN http://udl-irn.org/

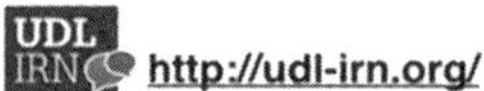

Figure 11.1 UDL instructional planning process

been proscribed formally or through tradition. It does not matter who the learners are and it does not matter who the teachers are (Rice and Coulter 2012). The online environment has the potential to liberate teachers and learners from this uniformity. The teacher's new responsibility is to help learners do activities that reflect, not chronotope, but kairos. In kairotic teaching, the instruction is responsive to the individual needs of the learner. The right activity comes in front of the right learner at the right time (Artemeva 2008). Kairos is possible without the internet and other technologies in the traditional f2f classroom, but it is much easier to create kairotic moments with students online.

The difficulties with moving curriculum design/delivery from a chronotopic effort to a kairotic one will come in several forms. An online teacher may be given technology tools and told to use them with learners without having control over how these tools fit into the larger rhythms of activity in a course. Teachers may be given programs that are really more like textbooks online that dictate the subject matter entirely (Rice and Greer 2014). In this scenario, teachers often realize that the text containing the subject matter is too difficult for learners with disabilities to read (Greer, Rice, and Deshler 2014), that there are too many vocabulary words the learners do not know, and support within the program is limited for helping them learn these words (Deshler and Rice 2015). Frustration may result when teachers understand curriculum planning and UDL principles but are unable to enact them.

When these things have happened to teachers with which we have worked, they have made efforts to take responsibility for curriculum making by pulling small groups of learners together using classroom social tools and teaching learners reading strategies using appropriately leveled text. They have also designed other activities to help learners with new words, created additional technological resources to learn concepts, and turned the learners back to the required subject matter. Following is a story where a high school teacher was working with learners to write essays about a specialized topic:

> The Letter from Birmingham Jail is a wonderful message about working together and not having racial injustice and all of that, but the prompt is asking them to analyze Martin Luther King's stylistic elements. Learners with disabilities always have trouble with the idea that they are not supposed to write about the injustice, but about the style. It's almost entirely vocabulary, they don't know the term stylistic elements and then they do not know associated terms. So I ask them to read the first sentence of the assignment and then I say, "Are there any words or phrases in here that you don't understand?" And most of them say, "Well, yes. It's fine. I know it. I understand." And then when I say, "Do you know what stylistic elements are?" then they start admitting they don't. And this is wonderful because then I can teach them. (Interview with teacher, April 2014)

Notice how this teacher is excited instead of irritated when her learners do not know something. That is key to true, rigorous curriculum making—to be brave enough to find out what the learners do not know and then to find a way using both technological resources and instructional strategies to help them learn it.

How Can Learners With Disabilities Use Technology to Become Independent and Self-Determined in Online Learning Environments?

The goal of any educational environment should be to develop independent learners. Independence is especially important to help learners with disabilities (Shogren et al. 2013). When establishing the online environments, everyone involved in the learners' education should focus on utilizing technology to offer opportunities to engage in self-determined ways.

Supporting independent and eventually self-determined behavior begins with ensuring sensory as well as cognitive accessibility to all of the necessary content, tools, knowledge, and skills as part of curriculum making. Important questions to consider include how the learners engage within the environment, how they process and comprehend information, and how they are afforded appropriate options for taking action or expressing their understanding. Embedding the UDL framework within the design of the online environment as well as within the daily practices that take place within the environment is critical to provide independence and self-determination (Smith and Basham 2014).

In order to further support self-determination, online special education teachers often have to rely on vendors and developers to appropriately align to the UDL framework. These developers are supposed to consider accessibility options and then system design to support UDL (Smith and Basham 2014). As additional support, there is a five-step UDL instructional planning process for considering how to integrate UDL into instruction (Basham 2011). The steps are in order: (1) establish clear outcomes, (2) anticipate learner variability, (3) make a measureable outcomes assessment plan, (4) establish the sequence of instructional experience, and (5) reflect about the instruction for new understandings. Taking this proactive approach is contingent on teachers having established the relationships to uncover the particularities of learners and their disabilities and acquired forms of expertise necessary to claim the right to make judgments about instruction.

Beyond UDL, considerations should also be made for specific technologies and practices needed to support individual learners that may not be supported within such a broad framework. That is, if learners with more intensive needs exist within the online environment, then specially-designed technologies or assistive technologies and more individually-based instructional interventions may be needed to support the learners and can be considered as part of the IEP process. Adults who are responsible for interacting with learners in the online environment (e.g., teachers, parents, related service providers) should continually reinforce or perhaps even negotiate and collaborate to promote the use of assistive and other support technologies until learners are able and willing to use them on their own.

How Can Special Education Teachers Maintain Communication With Learners and Families in Online Learning Environments?

For most of human history, physical presence was necessary for participation in activities and events. Eventually, recording technologies—first audio, then video—made it possible to create permanent records of events.

The emergence of video recording devices in smartphones that could also *tag* online photo and video made it possible to search recordings. Most people call these spaces where events are shared social networks, but danah boyd (2010) calls these *networked publics* to emphasize how digital technologies have shifted what it means to witness, to participate, and to attend activities and events. The implication of these understandings is that learners and teachers experience the school day in a fully online environment differently than in a brick-and-mortar setting. The online school relies on recorded, replicated technological resources that they can make available for learners. With educator planning and online tools, it is possible for students to learn through creation, collaboration, and distribution, but such constructivist opportunities are not the norm without the use of flexible approaches such as those consistent with UDL.

A high quality brick-and-mortar environment provides learners constant f2f interaction with teachers and related service providers, opportunities to learn in the whole school environment, and access to a host of both physical and digital resources focused on supporting the learner's needs. The fully online learning environment eliminates time constraints as well as many physical or social barriers associated with traditional schooling, but, in so doing, limits f2f experiences with teachers in real-time. Instead, what real-time learners have with teachers has to be efficient, of high quality, and delivered in various ways. Related disability services must also be provided in the online environment.

Young people who participate in online learning enjoy using technology and so do their teachers. However, these teachers are also aware of the issues around technology, particularly in regard to relationships and communities. One special education teacher we interviewed described this concern as she discussed an assignment in which her learners had to articulate a social problem:

> What is really interesting that is a lot of my students are writing about the overuse of technology. And this is for their online class! But I find it really fascinating that the students are concerned that people really are overusing their cellular phones and ironically, losing communication with the human race. (Interview with teacher, May 2014)

Learners in this teacher's class are interested in communicating with technology, but it does not always give them a sense of connection. A learner with disabilities in a high quality brick-and-mortar classroom typically interacts with many individuals throughout the school day, including other learners, teachers, and related service providers or school staff. These interactions extend the community of the learner in important ways. In online learning environments, especially a fully online school, it is possible for learners to feel isolated. Isolation stems from the fact that they have to reconceptualize social interactions and what counts as support in a community of learners online (Garrison and Arbaugh 2007). As a result, learners like ones in the example above are left struggling with what this special education teacher described. Therefore, teachers in these environments are responsible for helping learners manage these feelings and learn to participate in online communities to become truly networked publics (boyd 2010).

To help learners feel connected to their school and their work, online teachers often create communication schedules that are considerate, comprehensive, and consistent. Table 11.2 explores these elements of communication that apply to online teachers in general and are especially applicable to special education teachers. To be considerate, the teacher takes into account how the disabilities impact the learner's work schedule and any other commitments or constraints on the learner's time. To the greatest extent possible, the teacher determines what time of the day learners plan to be most engaged in the content, preferred times of communication for the learners and the family members, preferred methods of communication, and who the family desires to be involved in the communications. The answers to these questions will guide when and how synchronous communications will occur between the teacher, learner, and her family members.

Communications must also be comprehensive. A comprehensive schedule is one that builds in appointments to connect and engage with online learners, and such a schedule should provide for a variety of communication patterns among teachers, learners, families, service providers, and peers. Moreover, online teachers should build in these communicative patterns in advance to check on academic successes and challenges, comfort with the curriculum, and satisfaction with progress.

Finally, communication in online schools needs to be consistent. Establishing routines for communication with learners and families is important because it helps teachers advance the learning agenda as well as allows them to save time for listening to family or learner concerns. An online teacher who just attends to the academic needs of learners will likely come across as impersonal and institutional to families; a teacher who just discusses

Table 11.2   The Three Cs

The three Cs	What It Looks Like	The Benefit
Considerate	Online teachers plan learning opportunities using the information families have provided. Examples of this include preferences as to: • Contact times • Communication methods • Participants in conversations about the learners academic and social progress	Teachers are able to use information to relieve undue burdens on the learners and families and support the learners' socialization in the online school.
Comprehensive	Online teachers communicate with learners and families about multiple aspects of online learning. • Academic and social successes and challenges • Comfort with content • Satisfaction with performance	Teachers communicate a holistic knowledge of the learners' performance in the online learning environment based on continual reassessment of learners' strengths and needs.
Consistent	Online teachers communicate with learners and families: • On a regular schedule • Promptly as issues arise • Using predictable, negotiated patterns and norms	Teachers use communication as a tool for establishing and maintaining momentum for course completion.

problems and concerns will likely be perceived as negative and unprofessional. Online teachers have to manage their time with families to ensure that they can be predictable, reliable, and familiar to them.

How Can Special Education Teachers Promote Collaboration in Online Learning Environments?

There are many ways to think about the role of a teacher (Shim 2008). The philosopher Plato regarded teachers as guides into objective knowledge through the reasoned understanding of causes. In the Eastern tradition, Confucius regarded teachers as leaders of self-cultivation. In the 1960s, Martin Buber (1970) argued that teachers' primary role was relationship building with their learners. A few years later, the Brazilian educator Paulo Freire (1973) was adamant that teachers were supposed to foster critical consciousness of oppressed situations.

It is likely that online special education teachers will have to take on all these roles in some form or another. All of these roles are both desirable and possible in online teaching. However, what we have found is that teachers and administrators agree that building relationships with learners is not only the most important role an online teacher has, but also may be the hardest thing to do (Rice and Carter 2015). The way to accomplish this difficult task of relationship building is through frequent, pleasant, fact-filled and/or fact-finding contact with learners, their families, and other teachers. Teachers can also establish their presence through the use of individualized comments, collaboration, active engagement, and the use of multimedia methods to connect with students and communicate via their individual voice (Garrison and Arbaugh 2007).

Here is what one teacher said about her role as a relationship builder working with learners with disabilities in a fully online school:

> We make welcome calls to new students. Sometimes those calls are quick: an introduction, a prompt to watch a new student orientation, and a schedule for another call when the family has more time. Then we call a lot to make sure that everything is on track with student work and to answer questions. And you have to listen to what they tell you. You can't say, "Where's Julie?" and hear, "Oh, Julie has been hospitalized," and have your response be, "Oh, hey, yeah, thanks a lot, keep me posted, and she needs to submit work." You have to be prepared to find out more information and offer sympathy and support. I call 20 to 25 students daily and then I have my grading and my small group lessons, and virtual meetings with other staff. When I taught in a brick and mortar school as a special education teacher, I didn't really have much communication with the parents; I could barely get them to attend an IEP meeting, but here I talk to them a lot and many are even happy to hear from me. I feel I have good relationships with the parents as well as students. If they are doing well I can celebrate that with them and then move them on to the next thing. (Interview with teacher, April 2014)

As this teacher illustrated for us, the relationship-building efforts of online special education teachers begin as soon as possible, even before learners officially enroll in a course. Before teachers begin to plan for how they will educate learners with disabilities in the online learning environment, it is imperative that they spend time getting to know the learners and their families (Rice and Carter 2015). As we have said previously in this chapter, scheduling conversations with the learners and families via telephone calls or video conferencing tools will facilitate those conversations. Initial conversations represent an opportunity to learn about who the learners truly are and learn about the family members who support them. All teachers in an online school have to be proactive about seeking one another out to ask for help with specific learners and about keeping good records so that they speak helpfully and with confidence when talking with families of learners with disabilities (Greer, Rice, and Carter 2015). Following, a special education administrator details more about his record keeping and relationship building activities:

> If a parent calls and says, "Hey, I wanted to send you a copy of my child's IEP," I will give them my contact information, fax, email, whatever they want. I would then hang up from that phone call. I would log that I spoke with the parent and the parent is going to send me a copy of the IEP. That's my first log. When I get that IEP, I will go in again and log that I have received the IEP, and then contact other personnel like counselors or administrators that need to set up related services. Now, what next? If the conversation with the parent was, "My child needs extra time," then I might follow up with his teachers after I get the paperwork to make sure that they are prepared to provide this extra time. (Interview with teacher, April 2014)

This administrator shows us that helping students with special needs is a matter of finding out relevant information, and letting others know what they need to know, when they need to know it.

A teacher cannot discern who needs to know what information about a student with a disability and at what time if they do not have relationship building skills or an interest in acquiring them. Attending professional development, even when it is not required, is one way to see (in person or online) the other teachers with whom you need good relationships in order to meet your professional obligations to children. Colleagues, learners, and parents are not going to live close to another; they may not even all live in the same state. Finding common ground has the potential to make teaching and learning experiences vastly more pleasant.

Conclusion

In this chapter, we have discussed key questions that teachers of learners with disabilities may have as they transition from a brick-and-mortar school to an online learning environment. Answers to these questions are derived from studies that we have conducted with various online learning environments. Readers might have noticed that the most helpful thing for teachers to do as they transition to K–12 online environments is to attend as fully as possible to needs of the learners and their families (Carter and Rice 2015). Doing so provides the best chance for teachers to be sustained in the complex work of providing instruction in online learning environments.

We intentionally avoided framing this chapter as a set of definitive directives for educating learners with disabilities in online settings. Instead, efforts were made to illustrate the challenges in-service online teachers have described to us. Using information from experienced teachers, we have presented strategies that teachers new to the profession and new to online teaching and learning can use as starting points to meet the needs of students and their families as they engage with online coursework. We hope that this information helps teachers in practical ways and moves beyond merely retaining teachers to truly sustaining them.

References

Archambault, Leanna. "The Practitioner's Perspective on Teacher Education: Preparing for the K–12 Online Classroom." *Journal of Technology and Teacher Education* 19, no. 1 (2011): 73-91.

Artemeva, Natasha. "Toward a Unified Social Theory of Genre Learning." *Journal of Business and Technical Communication* 22, no. 2 (2008): 160-85.

Basham, James D. "UDL in the Instructional Planning Process." UDL-IRN, 2011. http://udl-irn.org/instructional-process/.

Basham, James D., and Matthew T. Marino. "Understanding STEM Education and Supporting Students Through Universal Design for Learning." *Teaching Exceptional Children* 45, no. 4 (2013): 8-15.

boyd, danah. "Social Network Sites as Networked Publics: Affordances, Dynamics, and Implications" In *A Networked Self: Identity, Community, and Culture on Social Network Sites*, ed. Zizi Papacharissi, 39-58. New York: Routledge, 2010.

Buber, Martin. *I and Thou.* New York: Scribner, 1970.

Carter, Richard A., Jr., and Mary Frances Rice. 2015. Understanding online teachers' work with students with disabilities, narratively. Paper presented at the annual meeting of the American Educational Research Association, Chicago, IL, April.

Center for Applied Special Technology. "Universal Design for Learning Guidelines Version 2.0," 2011. Wakefield, MA: Author. http://www.udlcenter.org/aboutudl/udlguidelines.

Deshler, Don, and Mary Frances Rice. 2015. Exploring the nature of vocabulary support in online earth science courses for secondary students with reading disabilities. Paper presented at the annual meeting of the American Educational Research Association. Chicago, IL, April.

Freire, Paulo. *Education for Critical Consciousness (Bloomsbury Revelations)*, Vol. 1. New York: Shead & Ward, 1973.

Garrison, D. Randy, and J. Ben Arbaugh. "Researching the Community of Inquiry Framework: Review, Issues, and Future Directions." *The Internet and Higher Education* 10, no. 3 (2007): 157-72.

Greer, Diana, Mary Frances Rice, and Richard A. Carter, Jr. 2015. "Like they're the only ones": Online educators providing special education services. Paper presented at the annual meeting of the American Educational Research Association, Chicago, IL, April.

Greer, Diana, Mary Frances Rice, and Donald Deshler. "Applying Principles of Text Complexity to Online Learning Environments." *Perspectives on Language and Literacy*, 2014. http://www.onlinedigeditions.com/article/Applying+Principles+of+Text+Complexity+to+Online+Learning+Environments/1653374/0/article.html

Greer, Diana, Mary Frances Rice, and Bryan Dykman. "Reviewing a Decade (2004-2014) of Research at the Intersection of Online Learning Coursework and Disability." In *Handbook of Research on K–12 Online and Blended Learning*, ed. Richard E. Ferdig and Kathryn Kennedy, 135-59. Pittsburg: ETC Press, 2014.

The Iowa Legislature. 2009. *IAC Rule 281.41.907: Program Costs*. https://www.legis.iowa.gov/docs/ACO/IAC/LINC/10-10-2007.Rule.281.41.907.pdf.

Rice, Mary Frances, and Richard Allen Carter, Jr. "With New Eyes: Online Teachers' Sacred Stories of Students With Disabilities" In *Exploring Pedagogies for Diverse Online Learners*, ed. Mary Frances Rice, 209-30. Bingley, UK: Emerald Group Publishing, 2015.

Rice, Mary Frances, and Cathy Coulter. "Exploring Four Chronotopic Shifts Between Known and Unknown in our Teacher Education Identity Narratives." In *Narrative Inquirers in the Midst of Meaning-Making: Interpretive Acts of Teacher Educators* (Advances in Research on Teaching, Volume 16), ed. Elaine Chan, Dixie Keyes, and Vicki Ross, 77-108. Bingley, UK: Emerald Group Publishing Limited, 2012.

Rice, Mary Frances, and Diana Greer. "Reading Online: Comprehension has New Meaning for Students With Disabilities." *Teaching Exceptional Children* 46, no. 5 (2014): 93-101.

Schwab, Joseph J. "The Practical: A Language for Curriculum." *The School Review* (1969): 1-23.

Shim, Seung Hwan. "A Philosophical Investigation of the Role of Teachers: A Synthesis of Plato, Confucius, Buber, and Freire." *Teaching and Teacher Education* 24, no. 3 (2008): 515-35.

Shogren, Karrie A., Michael L. Wehmeyer, Susan B. Palmer, Graham G. Rifenbark, and Todd D. Little. "Relationships Between Self-Determination and Postschool Outcomes for Youth With Disabilities." *The Journal of Special Education* (2013): 1-12.

Smith, Sean J., and James D. Basham. "Designing Online Learning Opportunities for Students With Disabilities." *Teaching Exceptional Children* 46, no. 5 (2014): 127-37.

van Deursen, Alexander, and Jan Van Dijk. "The Digital Divide Shifts to Differences in Usage." *New Media & Society* 16, no. 3 (2014): 507-26.

Zabala, Joy, Gayl Bowser, and Jane Korsten. "SETT and ReSETT: Concepts for AT Implementation." *Closing the Gap* 23, no. 5 (2004): 1-4.

CHAPTER 12

Assistive Technology in the 21st Century Online Classroom

Jacqueline Knight

Abstract

Although many teachers believe that they already use technology to its fullest degree in the classroom, they may not know that there is a difference between using technology for all students and specific technology geared for students with special needs. Teachers may also not understand why students with special needs must use the technology dictated by their administrator or their special education colleagues. This chapter discusses the definition of assistive technology (AT), student identification for services, low tech versus high tech devices, fairness of use of AT in the school setting, resources and programs available, and the use of AT for teaching online.

Introduction

Assistive technology (AT) is briefly defined as a device and a service given to students with disabilities that provides technology and training (for students and families) that, when needed, can be used to help students with disabilities succeed in school (Individuals with Disabilities Education Improvement Act [IDEA] 2004). In order to implement AT successfully in a child's day, it is important for the program, teacher, or special education team to initiate the appropriate AT needs assessment. AT is different than other technology implementations in that it is mandated for students with disabilities who qualify for AT services through their individualized education program (IEP) under the 2004 Individual with Disabilities Education Improvement Act (IDEA), an act created to help ensure equal access in the school environment to help students with disabilities make academic gains and eventually become productive citizens. The IDEA clearly states in Section 601(c)(5)(H) the education of children with disabilities can be made more effective with "supporting the development and use of technology, including AT devices and AT services, to maximize accessibility for children with disabilities." Additionally, the Assistive Technology Act (2004) was also passed by the 108th Congress in 2004, which provides funds through grants to states for AT use by K–12 students and students who were graduating and ready to begin their postsecondary life.

AT not only is a service, but also provides for the devices needed for the service. Section 602 (1) of the IDEA (2004) states: "In general, [t]he term 'assistive technology device' means any item, piece of equipment, or product system, whether acquired commercially off the shelf, modified, or customized, that is used to increase, maintain, or improve functional capabilities of a child with a disability." However, this does not include devices that need to be surgically implanted or the maintenance of such a device. When working with students online, one needs to not only think of the service aspect, but also consider which devices, software, applications, and equipment would be most appropriate for each individual learner.

One of the interesting aspects of AT is that it does not necessarily need to be computer-based and it should be noted that online learners may need low tech as well as (or instead of) high tech AT. From a post-it note to a high powered wheelchair, ATs vary in expense and size as well as are individualized to match student need. AT falls into two broad categories: low tech and high tech. For example, a slant board, a pencil grip, and a magnifying glass are examples of low tech, while computer software, a tablet, or an electric wheelchair are examples of high tech. A very simplified way of remembering the difference between the two is that low tech does not need a form of energy to run (such as batteries/electricity), while high tech does.

An aspect of AT that can be confusing for new and veteran teachers alike is the concept of *fairness*. Some teachers have illegitimately gone as far as to say that the use of some ATs in the classroom is *cheating*. Think about it: Is wearing glasses cheating? Glasses are a form of technology created to allow people to see well. As a society, we no longer perceive glasses as technology because glasses have become so universally used. AT is geared towards leveling the playing field for students with disabilities, just as glasses provide vision equivalency to those who do not need glasses. It is important to remember that not all students who have disabilities need

AT. However, students who have assistive technologies listed in their IEPs all have disabilities that warrant their need.

Dave L. Edyburn (2006) refers to such a need-based ratio that he calls the "Remediation vs. Compensation Equation." A child succeeding in school does not need remediation, while a child who is not succeeding may benefit from remediation. Each child has his or her own individual ratio where compensation (e.g., AT) helps the child to be successful in school.

> The R vs. C Equation requires the team to consider the compatible issues of challenge vs. frustration and instructional skill building vs. performance support. The allocation of time and effort (e.g., R=30%, C=70%) can be adjusted over time as the IEP determines whether the compensatory uses of technology are producing the desired level of successful performance. (Edyburn 2006, p. 22)

The desired goal is for the child to become independent within his or her own learning; looking at the value of both remediation and the use of technology to help with compensatory skills only benefits the student.

As the world of technology changes and allows all users to have greater accessibility, students with disabilities can benefit as well. For example, a decade ago, speech dictation software was expensive and cumbersome to use. Today, the universal design (UD) features of tablets and cell phones allow all users to use voice-to-text, text-to-voice, and word prediction optical character recognition (OCR). This UD accessibility has helped to level the playing field for adults and children with disabilities, as all end users (those who use the technology on their devices) have access to these features. However, AT is different than universal design for learning (UDL), which focuses on bringing technology and multi-modal ways of learning to classrooms. One difference between AT and UDL, other than its mandate under IDEA, is that UDL is focused on creating a learning environment, lesson, and routine for all students, while an AT plan is a service combined with a device (low tech or high tech) specifically designed with one student in mind.

What Does AT Have to Do With My Online Teaching and Learning Classroom?

According to the United States Census Bureau, in 2010, 19 percent of the population had a disability (Brault 2011). Of school-aged children (ages 5–17), 5 percent of children living in metropolitan areas and 6.3 percent living outside of metropolitan areas have been diagnosed with disabilities (Brault 2011). Additionally, current mandates indicate that students should be placed within the least restrictive environment (LRE) as much as possible. In regards to the continuum of special education, the LRE is within a general education classroom. Thus, if you are a teacher with either a multisubject or single-subject credential, then the likelihood of having a child with a disability in your online classroom is quite high. A study was released by Connections Academy in June 2014 relating to just this. Connections Academy is a large online school that surveyed their parents to find out why they chose online learning. The third-party survey was completed by over 18,000 parents of students enrolled in Connections Academy programs, and indicated factors leading parents to enroll students in the fully online schools (MarketWatch 2014). This survey did not take into consideration students with special needs; however, it did reveal the following:

- 14 percent of the parent/guardians responding indicated student health issues.

- 10 percent indicated their child was bullied in his/her previous school.

- 18 percent indicated that their child was academically behind compared to same-aged peers.

The Connections Academy survey was general in nature and not specifically designed to collect data relating solely to students with special needs. However, a separate study by Paula Burdette and Diana Greer (2014) queried parents of online students with special needs in online programs across the country. All of the 119 parent-respondents had children enrolled in online programs, and it was found that a variety of disabilities were supported:

> Of the 119 qualified responses, the primary disability most often reported for students in an online learning environment was specific learning disability (29 percent). Autism (13 percent) and other health impaired (13 percent) were the second and third most frequently reported disability conditions. Parents also reported their child's primary disability as speech or language impairment (9 percent), intellectual and multiple disabilities (both 8 percent), and emotional disturbance (7 percent). Very few parents reported their child's primary disability as hearing impaired (<3 percent), orthopedic impaired (<1 percent),

traumatic brain injury (<1 percent), and or visually impaired (<1 percent). No parents reported that their child's primary disability was deaf blindness or deafness, and 8 percent reported not knowing their child's primary disability. (p. 69–70)

When it came to services, Burdette and Greer found that parents were "pleased with the outcomes their children were experiencing in online learning, but some issues still exist for educating students with disabilities within this environment" (p. 67).

How Are Children Identified With a Disability?

Under the IDEA (2004), the "Child Find" mandate requires that all states (and their school districts) identify *all* children with disabilities, even if they do not attend public school, and now each state in the United States has a system in place for identifying students with special needs. This is where it gets a little complicated, though. If the online school is attached to a public school district or local education agency (LEA), then the Child Find mandate becomes easier as there is regulation to streamline the identification process. However, if a child has only attended private schools her entire life, it makes it harder for the school district to find that child. Nevertheless, it is still the LEA's responsibility to find and serve that child. The law does not change for private or charter schools: "Charters are required to follow all federal laws relating to students with disabilities, including that they ensure equal access and availability of special education and related services to students with identified needs" (Cortiella and Horowitz 2014, p. 38).

Once a child has been identified as potentially having special needs, it is up to the LEA to assess and decide whether or not he qualifies for special education under one of the 13 categories of special education. For online programs that are funded through a school district or LEA, this means that the school district would complete the assessment and hold the IEP meeting with the student's family (Rhim and Kowal 2009, p. 13). However, for privately funded online programs, it has yet to be determined if it is the district in which the program resides or if it is the student's district of residence that is responsible, as the law regarding who is responsible for special education services is unclear at this time since students can attend online private schools across district, county, and state lines. However, many online programs have become part of the charter school movement. In that case, the charter school or the LEA in which it resides is responsible for the Child Find mandate and providing services to students with special needs. Nevertheless, there have recently been questions about whether children within charter schools are being underidentified or excluded from programs because of their disabilities. Data are needed to indicate whether or not students with disabilities are being served appropriately by charter (virtual as well as brick-and-mortar) schools.

For the purpose of this chapter, one must assume that the online program is related to the student's LEA. In that case, a referral is made to a special education department connected with the student's school district. A school psychologist will do a formal evaluation of the child. If the parent, teacher, or any other professional working with the student believes that the student may need AT, then a specialist assesses the student. All of this information is brought to an IEP team (which includes the family, disability specialists, special education teachers, general education teachers, and district representatives). Regardless of the assessment, it is important to remember the following:

> The parents of the student are an important part of the team. The language of the law is very strong regarding the participation of the parents in the IEP process. Parents know the child better than anyone. A parent can be the most supportive person for an educator, and educators should value their input as such. Parents provide support for their children across all environments. They continue at home what is often introduced in the school environment. If AT is important to the success of the child in meeting his or her annual goals, it is vital that parents and representatives of the school system work collaboratively. Such collaboration also lessens the likelihood of AT abandonment if the child is working with the AT device across all environments. (Beard, Carpenter, and Johnston 2011, p. 80)

There are numerous ways that students are categorized for special education; one of the classifications is *incidence*. According to The National Center on Accessible Instructional Materials (2014), incidence refers to "how many students with any particular disability or combination of disabilities reside in a community." High incidence disabilities include specific learning disabilities (SLDs), communication disorders, emotional behavioral disturbance, and mild to moderate intellectual ability. Low incidence indicates disabilities such as blindness, visually impaired, deafness, hard of hearing, deaf-blindness, autism, multiple disabilities, and orthopedic impairment: "Under such a system, students with the most commonly seen disabilities may be more appropriately served by local public schools while students with relatively rare disabilities may not find adequate resources or highly qualified personnel" (The National Center on Accessible Instructional Materials 2014).

Once it is determined that a child needs AT services, a specialist works with the family and school to ensure that the devices and training related to the devices are provided, which includes fixing or replacing a device if it is broken along with training for all adults who work with the child (parents included). Additionally, if a specific device or software program is not working for a child, then the AT specialist identifies an alternative device or software to try. Sometimes the device is required at home and other times it is not. If a child needs a device in order to access curriculum (e.g., do homework), then the device may go home with him. Not all ATs fit every child; there is definitely a trial and error period and it is the AT specialist's job to check in with student, teachers, and parents to see how the technology is working for the learner.

In regards to funding, all schools must have access to an AT specialist for students who need AT. With many of the budget cuts that have occurred across the nation, school districts often hire AT specialists, and then the personnel are shared by numerous school sites. There are funds dedicated specifically for special education, and the salary for the AT specialist can come out of those funds.

A child who qualifies for an IEP should (by law) have an annual meeting to look at current present level of performance and to propose goals for the coming year. Each year, AT services are looked at as well. For students who are 16 years or older, their individual transition plan (ITP) portion of the IEP should also include the AT needed for the students to be successful in postsecondary life. For example, if a student needs OCR in order to access textbooks and other forms of print, then it should be included within the body of the ITP. Although colleges and universities do not have IEPs for students, they are required under the Americans with Disabilities Act to offer reasonable accommodations that are requested by the student. Some examples of reasonable accommodations could be extended time, a sign language interpreter, note taker, and priority registration. Thus, it is very important to clearly document student needs prior to their graduating from high school in order for them to receive services at the college level (Dell, Newton, and Petroff 2012). It is also important for a student to learn, while in their K–12 schools, how to self-advocate for their services and to learn which AT helps them the most. They should be taught directly (e.g., role play) how to ask for the AT and other services that they need in order to be successful. Although students at the K–12 level are guaranteed their services, teaching them to practice disclosure and self-advocacy could be pivotal to their success as an adult (Goldberg et al. 2003).

What Programs Are Available to Assist Teachers?

There are many online sites to help new and veteran teachers maneuver through this system. One program is the National Center on Accessible Educational Materials that "provides resources for educators, parents, students, publishers, conversion houses, accessible media producers, and others interested in learning more about AEM and implementing AEM and NIMAS" (2015b). Accessible educational materials (AEM) and National Instructional Materials Accessibility Standard (NIMAS) are materials that give students equal access to educational materials. For example, a textbook could be downloaded onto a computer or tablet as a PDF or daisy file, then software could then read the text to the student.

The federal government also has put together a website whose mission is to disseminate "information on disability programs and services nationwide" (Disability.gov), and it is a wonderful resource in that you can look for programs and services based by state and disability. One other program worth mentioning is a nonprofit called the Center for Applied Special Technology, or CAST, whose mission and vision states, "CAST pledges to work tirelessly to understand the full extent of human learner variability and to find transformative approaches that make education more effective for all" (2015). Although CAST's focus is UDL, much of its research and many of its recommendations can be useful to students who need AT services.

Finally, Understood.org (2015), created for parents of students with SLDs, desires "to give parents a direct path to the support they need most to make them feel more confident and capable, less frustrated and alone." That being said, it is a wonderful site to visit as a teacher in order to get ideas of what AT students are currently using, and to help teachers problem solve so that the technology can work for their students.

Types of AT

The following is an example of a scenario in which an online student needed help accessing curriculum due to a vision impairment:

Scenario: Valerie

> Although born with sight, as Valerie aged into adolescence her sight began to deteriorate. Despite her love of reading, her vision impairments impacted her ability to see text. Valerie desperately wanted to be able to keep up with her studies. Her parents were also concerned that she would not be able to graduate from high school with her sight worsening each year. An AT assessment was done to look at how much she could see with the use of support. Although a page-sized magnifying glass was helpful, it made Valerie feel different and uncomfortable. She refused to use it. Valerie qualified for services through Bookshare.org. On a tablet, with enlarged, bolded text (24 font), increased contrast, but a lower light setting, Valerie was able to access her textbooks via Bookshare and pass her classes successfully. Additionally, with the use of Bookshare as well as Learning Ally, she was once again able to enjoy literature and reading.

For this particular online student, many of the assistive technologies are literally at a finger's reach. Many students in today's early 21st century, in fact, are using the UD features on tablets (such as the iPad or numerous Android devices) as well as on their PC or Mac to help them access their curriculum. Apple has been historically at the head of the learning curve for UD-accessible features within its operating system. For example, if a student is on an iMac or other Apple product to access their online curriculum, then the built-in features can be beneficial to their learning. Under system preferences, there is a universal access icon. However, Microsoft and other PC/Android platform creators are now also including UD features within their operating systems.

Within the universal access features, the end user (online student) can choose between many options for seeing, hearing, keyboard action, and mouse operation. Options within the section *Seeing* include flipping colors (white on black versus black on white), voice over, zoom, and enhancing contrast. Voice over in itself has many options including verbosity, speech, navigation, web, sound, commanders, braille, and activities. The verbosity setting includes speech, braille, texts, announcements, and hints. Both web browsers Safari and Chrome have extensions that allow the user to remove advertisements, pop-ups, and other clutter, so that students can focus more on the text that should be read instead of getting distracted by other things on the webpage.

For students who have limited fine motor control (use of fingers on the keyboard, for example), switches can be inserted for the mouse as well as speech-to-text controls. Some students may use eye gazers or other types of pointers to help to get their messages across.

Setting up the right controls for each individual student is quite important on the end user side, and many families will need assistance in this regard. Sometimes, a specialist will visit the home to help set up the AT; other times, parents are walked through via video chats, informational videos, or telephone calls. That being said, as a teacher, the best thing one can do to help online students who need AT is to design the virtual classroom to be AT-friendly. However, oftentimes, teachers have little to no training on how to do so. One way of receiving training (or professional development) is to go to annual conferences held by organizations such as Council for Exceptional Children (CEC), ISTE, and CUE that regularly schedule speakers and panels specifically addressing AT in the classroom (please see the list of organizations at the end of this chapter.)

As with other types of access guarantees, "students with disabilities can't be denied access to online education because of their disability. It puts a burden on the program designers to ensure students with disabilities can easily access the online course content" (Rose and Blowmeyer 2015, p. 8). For example, when placing graphics within a text, it is important to make sure that the graphic is labeled so that the voice over software can read what the graphic states (for those who are visually impaired). Or, if highlighted text is being used, then it needs to be revealed in order for the AT software to be able to see it. When using videos or screencasting to demonstrate information, it is important to make sure that there are subtitles as well as a transcript available for students (CANnect 2015a). Additionally, it is important to remember that if there are too many graphics, an online text page that needs a mouse to navigate may be too difficult for an alternative navigator, such as an eye gazer or switch. The International Association for K12 Online Learning (iNACOL) recommends the following:

> Video resources should be captioned (see MAGpie under Appendix B: Resources) or have a transcript available. Text transcripts should be available for audio resources. Alternative presentations need to be identified for graphic presentations

of instructional content. The use of graphics as eye-candy—graphics to make a page pretty—should be minimized. Course and web page navigation needs to be designed to facilitate alternative navigation tools. Web resources outside the class environment need to be evaluated specifically for accessibility. (Rose and Blowmeyer 2015, p. 10–11)

Owing to the fact that online learning is done through a computer format, Lauren Rhim and Julie Kowal (2009) indicate the following as a list of ATs that online/virtual schools may need to offer: on-screen keyboards, grammatical support tools, braille embossers with text-to-braille conversion, animated signing characters (signing avatars), switches, alternative mouse systems, word prediction tools, accessible online learning tools, alternative keyboards, display-based personal data assistants, and voice recognition systems.

Other than universal access features, there are many programs and applications (apps) available to help students. According to Burdette and Greer's (2014) study, the majority of students who have disabilities and are using online learning have mild to moderate disabilities and been diagnosed with an SLD indicating that the child has the ability to learn but has not responded to research-based instructional models. Further, through valid assessment, a discrepancy the child's ability to learn in one or more of eight areas has been identified:

1. oral expression
2. listening comprehension
3. written expression
4. basic reading skills
5. reading fluency skills
6. reading comprehension
7. mathematics calculation
8. mathematics problem-solving (Burdette and Greer 2014)

According to the National Center for Learning Disabilities ([NCLD] 2014), "Learning disabilities are not caused by visual, hearing or motor disabilities, intellectual disabilities (formerly referred to as mental retardation), emotional disturbance, cultural factors, limited English proficiency, environmental or economic disadvantages, or inadequate instruction" (p. 3).

Additionally, it is interesting to note in the NCLD's (2014) report that more than 50 percent of educators believe that learning disabilities are due to laziness and home environment. It is important to understand that students with learning disabilities truly have a cognitive deficit that is impacting their ability to learn. One type of reading disability often spoken of is dyslexia—a language-based disability where words are difficult to understand (e.g., substituting b for d, q for g, etc.). However, other typical learning disabilities are dyscalculia (mathematics) and dysgraphia (writing). Dyslexia, dyscalculia, and dysgraphia are medical terms that fall under the DSM IV, so in an IEP they would fall under the category SLD and not be named so specifically. Another statistic worth mentioning from the report is that 42 percent of all students with special needs in 2001 had SLDs (approximately 5 percent of the nation's school-aged population), so the possibility of having a student with an SLD in your classroom is high (NCLD 2014).

Assistive technology resources are available for a range of needs. These include reading, mathematics, writing, listening, and speaking. Often the resources are free to the school and online student, making them practical considerations for online programs.

Reading

For students who have vision impairments or other disabilities that impact their ability to read, there are wonderful resources based on NIMAS, a part of AEM:

> Accessible educational materials, or AEM, are print- and technology-based educational materials, including printed and electronic textbooks and related core materials that are designed or converted in a way that makes them usable across the widest range of student variability regardless of format (print, digital, graphical, audio, video). IDEA (Individuals with Disabilities Education Act) specifically focuses on accessible formats of print educational materials. (National Center on Accessible Educational Materials 2015a)

Online teachers can incorporate links to specific AEM resources based on the curriculum at hand and can also provide the searchable website as a resource for online students and their parents.

Bookshare.org and the National Library Service for the Blind and Physically Handicapped (NLS) are two federally funded organizations that are specifically designed to help students with access to reading material. NLS is sponsored by the Library of Congress, while Bookshare is sponsored through a grant through the Office of Special Education Programs (OSEP) in the United States Department of Education. The NLS offers material in braille, ebraille, and audio. Bookshare offers text-to-voice recognition read by a digital voice in which words are highlighted as they are read, enlarged fonts are available, both physical and digital braille are available, and the material can be read directly from a web browser (e.g., Google Chrome). Another program that has long had funding for helping students is Learning Ally (2015), formerly known as Reading for the Blind and Dyslexic, which offers human-narrated audio textbooks and literature. All three programs offer their services for free to students who qualify.

There are also many software programs and apps that work fantastically to help students be able to read web content as well, such as Don Johnston's Read:OutLoud, ReadQ, JAWS and Browse Aloud (please see the Resources section in Appendix). It would behoove a teacher who is helping to implement AT to be trained in the program that the student is using. The AT specialist should be able to do that. However, having the basic understanding of these programs will help the teacher (and thus the student) move through the learning curve at a faster rate.

Mathematics

Lawrence Beard, Laura Carpenter, and Linda Johnston (2011) state that AT can play a primary role in assisting the student in mathematics to access the general education curriculum and be a successful learner. For students who need access to help with mathematics, there are many accommodations that can be made, including use of manipulatives, times tables charts, drawing pictures, and more. The most common support for students historically has been a calculator. After all, most high school math classes encourage students to use calculators. Not only can a student purchase a handheld calculator, but also they are more often than not included within the operating system of a computer, tablet, or smartphone. Talking calculators and big button calculators have also been found to be useful for students who cannot read the numbers (due to a disability like dyscalculia) or who have low vision (e.g., vision impairment). However, in regards to AT, it has not been until the last five or so years that technology has really become accessible and easy to use, likely due in part to the success of smart devices' overall ease of use as well as greater access to them. Today, many students have a smart phone, and many applications and included programs can be used to help with math. The calculator included on an iPhone or Android phone can be used for basic mathematical computation as well as for higher-level math. One app that can be downloaded, for example, is My Script Calculator that offers a calculator with handwriting recognition. For students who have difficulty punching in the numbers on the calculator, this is an amazing alternative.

Writing

Students who have difficulty with writing could have difficulties for many different reasons, such as grapho-motor coordination, expressive language disorder, dyslexia, or visual motor integration. Today, there are many tools to help students with their writing that come as part of a computer's operating system. Some of these features can be universally used. For example, the OCR software built into smart phones, tablets, and many computer operating systems can take words said orally and put them into text (voice-to-text OCR). An example is the microphone feature that is built into cell phones. Additionally, word prediction universally known as autocorrect is also commonly used, and some platforms offer a choice of words to choose from before autocorrect makes its choice. There are software programs and apps available that hone into these features. For example, Co:Writer by Don Johnston, Speak Q/WriteQ, and Kurzweil 3000 both have features where drop-down menus are given where a student can click on a word in the drop-down menu to make sure it is the correct one prior to inserting it. Dragon Naturally Speaking by Nuance is software (also available as an app) specifically for dictation. Students who have challenges with keyboarding or spelling can often have improved results writing papers using Dragon Naturally Speaking. There are also many typing programs that teach students appropriate fingering for a keyboard. One such program is Typing.com by Teaching.com that offers free services to teachers. Other students may not have a difficult time writing or typing, but may instead have difficulty organizing their ideas. Graphic organizers are a type of AT to help students organize their thoughts. There are many apps, such as Popplet by Notion Inc. and Tools4Students by Mobile Learning Services, which can help students composing on a tablet. Popplet also offers free web-based concept-mapping tools as does Webspiration and Bubbl.us. Other programs, such as Inspiration by Inspiration Software Inc. or Draft:Builder by Don Johnston, are similar concept-mapping software programs that need to be downloaded to the computer. Another less expensive option is to email students a formatted and fillable PDF or word processing document. Google Forms can also be beneficial if used with organization of thought in mind.

Listening and Speaking

Two other areas to keep in mind when working with students who have SLDs are listening and speaking. Although online learning happens asynchronously through the use of technology, there are times when a teacher communicates directly with students and have synchronous online hangouts or meetings. Additionally, teachers may want to give a lecture on a topic or create a screen cast. In such cases, it is important to keep students' IEPs in mind.

Auditory comprehension is an important part of literacy. It helps students learn to decode, allowing for a richer understanding of the world in which they live. Fortunately for children and adults with auditory comprehension difficulties, there are numerous types of strategies and technologies to help them: "Computers can both compensate for and provide drill and practice for activities to improve the comprehension of words, directions, and conversations" (Green 2011, p. 69). When working with students with auditory processing deficits, both low and high tech may be warranted as well as the use of non-AT strategies.

For many students with auditory comprehension deficits, listening and comprehending is difficult. Repeated instructions and the use of visual tools (such as graphics and graphic organizers) can be helpful. One way to help navigate this as a teacher is to provide lecture content in a variety of formats, including the provision of outlines or transcripts. This way, the student can focus on what is being said instead of trying to listen and write notes. Furthermore, repetition is very useful to students with special needs. Giving directions or highlighting important information multiple times is a nontechnology-based strategy that can be used within a lecture.

For students who are deaf or hard of hearing, there is a multitude of high tech solutions that may be recommended by a student's doctor or a deaf and hard of hearing specialist. Devices can include cochlear implants, hearing aids, voice amplification system, and an FM system for voice amplification, among others.

It is important to add that if a teacher is uploading a video for the students to watch (such as a screencast or a lecture), closed captioning should be enabled, as the "multisensory experience of watching captioned TV has been shown to significantly improve the reading skills of children" (Green 2011, p. 76). For students who have difficulty understanding the spoken word, having the text paired with the video directly allows them to access their curriculum.

Verbal expression (speaking) is another area of literacy that should not be overlooked. Students with communication disabilities may not be able to verbally state or share answers that they know, their thought process, how they feel, or why they know something to be true (Dell, Newton, and Petroff 2012, p. 139). Nontech strategies that can be used in the classroom are "providing additional response time, loading the environment with resources with which refer when communication, and accepting shortened or alternative types of responses" (Green 2011, p. 25).

Additionally, the use of graphic organizers is a low tech solution for helping students to sequence what they want to say. There are also high tech devices to help students who do have significant verbal expression delays communicate. These types of devices fall under the categories of augmentative and alternative communication (AAC) and voice output communication aids (VOCA). There are many apps that are labeled as picture exchange communication systems (PECS) that support communication by allowing the individual to draw from a library of picture symbols to communicate. While these are often delivered using an iPad or other digital device, teachers and speech pathologists can also help students and their families create a PECS system with the use of a three-ring binder. While PECS supports low communication, it has been deemed highly effective for teaching children with autism (Flippin, Reszka, and Watson 2010). It is possible that PECS, speech generation devices (SGDs), and other AAC or AT tools will evolve to meet the expanding needs of learners in the online classroom environment.

Conclusion

AT has taken a deeper hold within the educational system. Nevertheless, it is important to remember that no matter how good a product is, it will not be useful if the student is not willing to use it. Such is the biggest caveat to AT. If a child does not feel good using it, then the product is not doing for the child what it should, or if the child just refuses to use it, then it is time to go back to the drawing board. Technology is only as good as those who use it and those who train others to use it. Fortunately, teachers working in both on-ground or online formats have access to many related service professionals. There are AT specialists, speech pathologists, and occupational therapists who form part of the IEP or special education team. Teachers in today's world not only need to feel competent when it comes to computer literacy, but also have to be flexible in how students with disabilities access their curriculum and not get disappointed when the first thing tried does not work. In all actuality, the old saying *if at first you do not succeed, try and try again* really proves to be true in the world of AT. If it is not working for a student, then find out why, make adjustments, try something different, speak to other professionals in your field, attend conferences, and, most importantly, do not give up. Your students are counting on you.

References

Assistive Technology Act of 2004. Public Law 108-364. 108th Congress. Accessed April 20, 2015, http://www.resnaprojects.org/statewide/essentialdocs/pl108-364.pdf.

Beard, Lawrence, Laura Carpenter, and Linda Johnston. *Assistive Technology: Access for all Students*. 2nd ed. Upper Saddle River, NJ: Pearson Education, 2011.

Bookshare.org. Accessed April 21, 2015, https://www.bookshare.org/cms.

Brault, Matthew. "School-Aged Children With Disabilities in U.S. Metropolitan Statistical Areas: American Community Survey Briefs." Last updated November 2011, http://www.census.gov/prod/2011pubs/acsbr10-12.pdf.

Burdette, Paula, and Diana Greer. "Online Learning and Students With Disabilities: Parent Perspectives." *Journal of Interactive Online Learning* 13, no. 2 (2014). www.ncolr.org/jiol.

CANnect. "Accessibility of Learning Management Systems," 2015a. http://projectone.cannect.org/online-education/lms-accessibility.php.

—. "How-To Guide for Creating Accessible Online Learning Content," 2015b. Accessed April 15, 2015, http://projectone.cannect.org.

The Center for Applied Special Technology. About CAST. Accessed April 18, 2015, http://www.cast.org/about#.VXeoDxFFDrc.

Cortiella, Candace, and Sheldon H. Horowitz. *The State of Learning Disabilities: Facts, Trends and Emerging Issues*. New York: National Center for Learning Disabilities, 2014. Accessed April 19, 2015, http://www.ncld.org/wp-content/uploads/2014/11/2014-State-of-LD.pdf.

Council for Exceptional Children. "Public Policy Update: CEC's Summary and Update of PL 108-364, The Assistive Technology Reauthorization Act of 2004." Accessed April 2015, http://www.cec.sped.org/~/media/Files/Policy/Archives/Assistive%20Technology/Summary%20of%20Assistive%20Technology%20Law.pdf.

Dell, Amy G., Deborah A. Newton, and Jerry G. Petroff. *Assistive Technology in the Classroom: Enhancing the School Experiences of Students With Disabilities*. 2nd ed. Upper Saddle River, NJ: Pearson, 2012.

Disability.gov. Home Page, 2015. www.disability.gov.

Edyburn, Dave L. "Assistive Technology and Mild Disabilities." *Special Education Technology Practice* 8, no. 4 (2006): 18-28.

Flippin, Michelle, Stephanie Reszka, and Linda Watson. "Effectiveness of the Picture Exchange Communication System (PECS) on Communication and Speech for Children With Autism Spectrum Disorders: A Meta-Analysis. *American Journal of Speech-Language Pathology* 19 (2010): 178-95.

Goldberg, Roberta, Elenor Higgins, Marshall Raskind, and Ken Herman. "Predictors of Success in Individuals With Learning Disabilities: A Qualitative Analysis of a 20-Year Longitudinal Study." *Learning Disabilities Research and Practice* 18, no. 4 (2003): 222-36.

Green, Joan. *The Ultimate Guide to Assistive Technology in Special Education: Resources for Education, Intervention, and Rehabilitation.* Waco, TX: Prufrock Press, 2011.

Individuals with Disabilities Education Improvement Act of 2004. Public Law 108-446. 108th Congress. http://idea.ed.gov/explore/home.

International Association for K–12 Online Learning. Home Page. http://www.inacol.org.

Learning Ally. Bringing Parents and Teachers Together to Help Students With Learning Disabilities Like Dyslexia Succeed. Last modified 2015, https://www.learningally.org.

MarketWatch. "New Parent Survey Reveals Why K–12 Students Attend Online Schools Full Time." June 24, 2014, http://www.marketwatch.com/story/new-parent-survey -reveals-why-K–12 -students-attend-online-schools-full-time-2014-06-24.

National Center for Learning Disabilities. "The State of Learning Disabilities," 3rd ed., 2014. http://www.ncld.org/wp-content/uploads/2014/11/2014-State-of-LD.pdf.

National Center on Accessible Educational Materials. "About AEM," 2015a. http://aem .cast.org/about#.VXEI4qZ8uUM.

—. "Access for Learning," 2015b. http://aem.cast.org.

—. "Assistive Technology," 2015c. http://aem.cast.org/supporting/assistive-technology .html#.VbzDTvlViko.

—. Home Page. Last modified 2014, http://aim.cast.org/.

Materials Access Center. Welcome to the National Instructional Materials Access Center. Last modified August 1, 2015, http://www.nimac.us.

National Library Service for the Blind and Physically Handicapped. That All May Read .... Last modified July 29, 2015, http://www.loc.gov/nls/.

Rhim, Lauren Morando, and Julie Kowal. "Demystifying Special Education in Virtual Charter Schools," 2009. www.uscharterschools.org/specialedprimers.

Rose, Raymond M., and Robert L. Blowmeyer. "Research Committee Issues Brief: Access and Equity in Online Classes and Virtual Schools." Accessed April 2015, http://files.eric.ed.gov/fulltext/ED509623.pdf.

Understood.org. Assistive Technology, 2015. https://www.understood.org/en/school -learning/assistive-technology.

U.S. Census Bureau. "Nearly 1 in 5 People Have a Disability in the U.S., Census Bureau Reports," 2012. http://www.census.gov/newsroom/releases/archives/miscellaneous /cb12-134.html.

U.S. Department of Education. "Building The Legacy: IDEA 2004." Last modified May 2014, http://idea.ed.gov/explore/view/p/%2Croot%2Cregs%2C300%2C.

Appendix—Resources and Organizations

Resources

- Atomic Learning. www.atomiclearning.com/
- Browse Aloud. www.browsealoud.com/uk/
- Don Johnston Products: Read: Out Loud, Write: Out Loud, Co: Writer, Draft:Builder, and Snap and Read. donjohnston.com/
- Dragon Naturally Speaking. www.nuance.com/dragon/index .htm
- Enablemart. https://www.enablemart.com/
- The Geometer's Sketchpad by Key Curriculum. www.keycurriculum.com/products/sketchpad-explorer-for-ipad
- Go Q Software: Write Q/Speak Q. www.goqsoftware.com /wordQspeakQ.php
- Independent living aids, talking calculators, big button calculators (including scientific calculators), and amplification systems. www.independentliving.com
- JAWS Screen Reader. www.freedomscientific.com/Products /Blindness/JAWS
- Kurzweil Education and Kurzweil 3000. https://www.kurzweiledu .com
- LiveScribe, LiveScribe 3Smartpen, Sky Wifi Smartpen, and Echo Smartpen. www.livescribe.com/en-us/
- Mathtalk.com speech recognition mathematics program. www .mathtalk.com
- Maxiaids.com, including products for independent living such as computers and accessories, low vision products, and products for students that are deaf/hard of hearing. www.maxiaids.com
- My Script: My Script Calculator. https://itunes.apple.com/us/app /myscript-calculator-handwriting/id578979413?mt=8
- Read&Write extension for Google by Text Help.
- https://chrome.google.com/webstore/detail/readwrite-forgoogle /inoeonmfapjbbkmdafoankkfajkcphgd
- Tobii Dynavox augmentative and alternative communication devices. www.tobii.com/assistive-technology/north-america/
- Typing.com, notably online typing tutorials and practice. www .typing.com/

Organizations

- American Occupational Therapy Association. www.aota.org
- American Speech-Language-Hearing Association. www.asha.org
- Bookshare. bookshare.org
- CANnect. Web Accessibility for Online Learning. projectone.cannect.org
- Center for Applied Special Technology. www.cast.org
- Center on Disabilities, California State University at Northridge. www.csun.edu/cod
- Council for Exceptional Children. https://www.cec.sped.org
- CUE. www.cue.org
- International Society for Technology in Education. www.iste.org
- Learning Ally. https://www.learningally.org
- Learning Disability Association of America. ldaamerica.org
- National Center on Accessible Educational Materials. aem.cast.org
- National Center for Learning Disabilities. www.ncld.org
- National Center for Special Education in Charter Schools. www.ncsecs.org
- National Library Service for the Blind and Physically Handicapped. www.loc.gov/nls
- Rehabilitation Engineering and Assistive Technology Society of North America. www.resna.org
- Understood. understood.org
- Web Accessibility in Mind. www.webaim.org

PART 3

Implementation Strategies

Teacher-Created Online Content: Two Teachers' Tech Tales

Christopher Rozitis and Heidi Weber

Abstract

Teachers can easily and successfully create online content for students at all grade levels. Content can support curriculum goals and develop technological skills and understanding at the same time. In this chapter, we reflect on our combined 20 years of experience teaching online and share innovative and practical ways virtual classroom environments and digital discussions can be used with students. We also discuss how to successfully build content for online teaching at elementary-and high-school grade levels.

Introduction

As teachers, we are preparing students for futures we have not yet imagined. Technology permeates every aspect of our lives, so it is essential that we expose and train our children to be as competent with technology as we can. Judith Harris, Punya Mishra, and Matthew Koehler (2009) argue:

> The flexible use of tools becomes particularly important because most popular software programs are not designed for educational purposes...effective teaching requires developing an understanding of the manner in which subject matter... can be changed by the use of different technologies. Teachers must understand which technologies are best suited for addressing which types of subject-matter, and how content dictates or shapes specific educational technological uses, and vice versa. (p. 399–400)

Technology enables us to be more efficient and productive in our lives. Embracing technology as a tool for learning is therefore critical; the more we know, the more we impart on our students. Teachers can easily and successfully create online content for students at all grade levels including content that supports curriculum goals while, at the same time, developing technological skills. In this chapter, we discuss how teachers can create and utilize content for younger learners and how to successfully build content for online teaching.

Elementary Online Content

Virtual Classroom Environments

Rena M. Palloff and Keith Pratt (2007) state, "Students participating regularly in an online course cannot help but improve their ability to use technology" (p. 195). Young learners are simply drawn to technology. For this reason, elementary teachers can motivate students with online learning content while teaching technology skills simultaneously. Many assignments and tasks in which elementary teachers engage students can be set up in virtual classroom environments for easy, independent access, completion, and submission. Technology may not always transform the learning, but replacing pencil and paper tasks with digital tools creates many benefits. For example, by using a virtual classroom environment, elementary teachers can give students practice with entering a username and password, and teach safety in a digital community. Simply typing in characters correctly and accurately requires students to become familiar with location and use of specific function keys. Elementary teachers know these tasks are painfully tedious for young learners; however, the tasks are critical to building fluency and automaticity.

Reading and following directions in a virtual classroom also builds independence. An assignment in a virtual classroom requires scrolling through and visually scanning text in order to locate the directions. Most online classroom environments arrange content with recent assignments first so students must learn to scroll to the bottom for the earliest assignments. Working through a webpage and digital text is a skill that must be practiced for proficiency.

Another benefit for students who use digital tools is that virtual classroom environments provide training in basic internet navigation. Following hyperlinks and using browser tools such as back arrows are skills students need to learn and become proficient using. Also, increased communication opportunities abound with virtual classrooms. Students can post or send questions to teachers immediately, before they are forgotten. Teachers can even adjust settings so that students can read one another's posts and respond to each other to enhance their peer-to-peer communication skills.

Finally, teachers who use virtual classroom environments are able to teach students about digital citizenship through real-life application (Ribble and Bailey 2007). Teachers explicitly teach students how to be citizens of our local communities, so we must explicitly teach them what it means to be a citizen in the digital community. Digital citizenship addresses safety considerations, morals, norms, and expectations. In order to be a good digital citizen, students should know how to behave appropriately and accordingly online.

Basic computer knowledge, internet navigation, and citizenship skills are a bonus when combined with lessons that build and extend written communication abilities. From writing letters to words to sentences to paragraphs, students develop proficiency with transferring ideas into their own text. Communicating in print is a big part of the elementary curriculum and is embedded heavily in classroom lessons with paper and pencil assignments. Elementary teachers can build these skills simultaneously with digital tools.

Traditional classroom practices such as daily oral language (DOL) exercises or responses to reading can easily be integrated with a learning management system (LMS) as virtual classroom assignments. Creating practice activities is quick, and many platforms offer the option of uploading content you already use. School districts today may already have LMSs in place such as Google Classroom, Schoology, or Blackboard. If not, there are free options to explore such as Edmodo, which allows teachers to create a virtual classroom for real-time or asynchronous use.

As an elementary reading teacher, I (Heidi) have my third and fourth grade students look at illustrations and artwork to examine details and infer meaning. Using Edmodo, I post an image by uploading a PDF file and students respond to it using the site's assignment tool with simple text. Another example of using Edmodo occurs when I have my students read the book *Wonder* by R.J. Palacio (2012). To give all students an opportunity to explore deeper thinking, I post precepts for students to respond and interact with and provide feedback to their submissions.

Regardless of which LMS is used, introducing elementary students to a virtual learning environment allows teachers of young learners to use, integrate, and incorporate content they are already using. Keep in mind, of course, that elementary students may need face-to-face (f2f) interaction, guidance, and support that will assist them with 21st century technology skills.

Digital Discussions

Traditional methods and print materials, answering questions on paper, and holding in-class discussions continue to be important and necessary; however, blending learning opportunities like online questionnaires or surveys, comment boxes, and chat rooms/online message boards give students the best of both worlds. Harvey Singh (2003) points out that, at the simplest level, a blended learning experience combines offline and online forms of learning where the online learning usually means over the internet or intranet and offline learning happens in a more traditional classroom setting. Young children still need f2f interaction and traditional pencil and paper asks to develop foundational skills. Nevertheless, starting students at a young age with digital engagement is equally important. The key is keeping the learning objective the primary focus.

When students are working on an assignment and learning technology skills concurrently, teachers are maximizing learning time. Practicing skills with technology in isolation, such as keyboarding practice, can be beneficial, but why not let students build these skills with authentic learning tasks? Drill and practice software frequently focuses on isolated technology skills. Asking a student to type a response or compose original text doubles as both keyboarding practice and meets other curricular goals. Teachers should not feel a student has to master keyboarding skills first. It is like practicing reading fluency with only phrases in isolation or building math skills by only memorizing tables. Students build skills with authentic practice and opportunities. Opportunities that meet both technology and content objectives at the same time help students understand real-world applications.

The technology skills a teacher wants to instill emerge when instructional objectives come first; for example, consider writing progression. Before students can write essays, they need to learn how to construct paragraphs. Before paragraphs come basic sentences. Typing a sentence provides reinforcement with skills such as spacing between words, proper use of capital letters, and use of punctuation, in addition to spelling high-frequency words. A simple activity such as a DOL prompt where editing errors is the focus allows students to locate keys more automatically. Using online content created by the teacher focuses on the learning task, one in which the tech skills students learn and practice can be easily embedded.

Once these basic foundations are established, multiple learning goals can be met by setting up opportunities for interacting with text. Kathy A. Mills (2009) emphasizes that "[t]eachers need to rediscover the transforming potential of talk for developing students' reading comprehension" (p. 327–328). Teachers can create opportunities for students to talk digitally. Any prompts or questions used with a lesson can be put into an online learning tool for students to have conversations with others. Children love to talk, so digital discussions let them "talk," practice typing, and allow for conversations that are not limited by time; discussions can extend over several days or class periods.

Digital discussions can be started and facilitated with many different digital tools, but one extraordinary and free web-based resource is www.NowComment.com. Teacher-uploaded content is displayed on the left of the screen; student comments about the general document or specific paragraphs and sentences show in-context on the right of the screen. The document becomes a private chat room environment, one monitored and controlled by the teacher. NowComment also allows teachers to invite other classes or guests to join the discussion, enabling distance collaboration as well.

Digital discussions are excellent for teacher-created online content. An advantage of digital discussions is asynchronous talk; that is, conversations are not limited by time. Discourse can take place over several days or be revisited again in the future. Another advantage is the opportunity to connect with others across the digital community. Students can communicate with peers in other classrooms, buildings, or even other points around the world. However, an important reason to integrate digital discussions in an elementary classroom is to provide students with experience using technology in responsible ways. Mike S. Ribble, Gerald D. Bailey, and Tweed W. Ross (2004) remind us, "When students see adults using technologies inappropriately, they can assume it is the norm. This leads to inappropriate technology behavior on the part of students" (p. 7). Elementary teachers know the importance of modeling. When we teach young learners about the digital footprint they leave with every keystroke, we are instilling a lifelong lesson. Setting up, facilitating, and monitoring a digital discussion with young learners allows teachers to build literacy skills while reinforcing what it means to be a citizen of a globally connected world.

Linking Content for Easy Student Access

Definitions of blended learning vary, but basically when we blend, we are combining f2f instruction with virtual components. Charles R. Graham

(2006) describes the convergence of f2f environments and distributed learning environments as an integration of teacher-directed and self-directed learning. Young learners still need teacher support and guidance, yet they often find anything put onto a screen motivating and engaging. Elementary teachers are in the best position to blend these worlds together because student needs fluctuate between the two continuously; however, finding online content for young students to consume can be tricky. Reading level, age appropriateness, student safety, and security all need to be considered. For this reason, teachers of young students typically should control the content accessed in the online classroom carefully.

A simple, effective, and student-friendly way to direct students to online content is through the use of quick response (QR) codes. QR codes are barcodes that students can scan to be directed to specific online destinations. When teachers find a great content source, such as an article from www.timeforkids.com, they can link that source using a free QR code generator. Once scanned, students can read the article online and teachers can use a traditional method such as response or discussion. Code generators are easy to find online, and free apps for smartphones, tablets, and other camera-equipped devices are available. Creating online content then becomes as simple as finding a resource that works for young students and generating a code that provides quick and engaging access.

Generating QR codes from web sources already available is only one way to use QR codes for content. When teachers have specific needs, they can generate codes to direct students to their own original teacher-created content such as blogs, Google Forms, or websites. Beverly B. Ray and Martha M. Hocutt (2006) outline the effective and appropriate use of teacher blogs to collaborate and interact with peers as well as express/display creativity. Blogs are also great for setting up content to direct students to interactive reading/writing experiences. When looking for interesting ways to have students work with vocabulary, teachers can enter definitions into blog pages (such as on a free Wordpress.com account) and then generate QR codes for students to scan to access individual posts/pages. Math teachers can use QR codes for students to self-check answers to problems. What matters when using a QR code is putting content into a digital format that engages, interests, and motivates students.

Teachers can use QR codes for more than just directing students to content. QR codes can also be used to guide students to areas where they input information. A Google Form provides an excellent tool for students to locate questions where they enter responses or answers. From something as simple as solving a math equation to an open-ended question about a story, teachers can quickly create a form, link the form to a code, share the code with students, and let the students scan the code and respond. Even better, answers can be generated into a spreadsheet for easy teacher review and evaluation. Google Forms can also be used without QR codes.

One example of using a Google Form with students is when I incorporated it into a literacy lesson with my fourth grade students who read *Van Gogh Cafe* by Cynthia Rylant (1995). I taped a QR code at the end of every chapter that led students to a digital form of reading comprehension with questions to answer based on the chapter. Students used iPods or iPads to scan and access the codes in the classroom. Students who accessed the codes at home used their own mobile devices.

Teachers can also set up their own websites. There are many free website builders available, such as weebly.com. My students and I enjoy examining song lyrics as poetry for deeper thinking. After discovering that music videos enhance and augment the learning experience and provide windows into one's past, I started collecting songs and posted them to a website I created entitled *Loving Language with Lyrics* (lovinglanguagewithlyrics. weebly.com/). Through linking files, video and audio clips, my own reflections, teaching points, and mini lessons, I created a website with resources that help my students build literacy. We practice and reinforce elements of poetry like rhythm and cadence when we read lyrics collected on the website. Reading fluency is built and sustained through repeated reading of the lyrics. Literary devices such as figurative language can also be identified and analyzed in many songs, so a section is devoted to audio samples for instruction with corresponding mini-lesson videos to guide students as they construct their own print resource notebook. Through the curation of resources on a teacher-created website, students can be directed to specific content for instruction, skill development, and mastery of learning objectives. For additional examples of elementary online content, check out my Google Doc at tinyurl.com/ElemContent.

Elementary teachers are instrumental in providing a solid foundation for future learning. In the early grades, students learn how to learn. We teach them how to read, how to work with numbers, and how to cooperate and communicate in verbal and written formats. Elementary teachers instill lifelong learning habits. The same is true with technology usage. Prerequisite skills such as logging on or navigation of online resources are built early in a student's academic career. Elementary teachers also guide students to use online content safely and responsibly. When elementary teachers create content online, they have a dual purpose. They intend to teach content while ensuring that students know how to use digital tools as well as learn to be respectful digital citizens.

By the time a student enters high school, teachers assume that learners are quite proficient with accessing and using teacher-created content. High school teachers expect students to know and understand how to use online resources; the foundation should be in place. This is the point where teachers shift from helping students learn how to locate, interact with, and utilize content to using technology as a tool for presenting and delivering content. High school teachers may use technology that is new to a student, but the learning curve is much faster because the prerequisite skills are in place. Just as the student learning goals transition, the teacher-created content and methods transition. We now shift from creative ways to motivate and engage elementary students with teacher-created online content to our next tech tale where highly effective methods of organizing and structuring teacher-created online content for older students are detailed.

High School—10 Years of Online Teaching Experience

I (Christopher) began teaching online 10 years ago, that after 10 years of teaching in the classroom. It was an exciting time for me to be on the cutting edge of online learning, even though students in British Columbia and other parts of the world had been completing K–12 courses via correspondence for more than 100 years. I started with two online classes. One had only PDF files, while the other had poorly formatted HTML files with inadequately made graphics and no videos. Neither one of these classes motivated or engaged the learners, thus completion rates were generally low. In what follows, I share with you the tools I have used to transform my online classes into an engaging space for learners, where completion rates are much higher.

Course Tour Video

The first digital artifact that I offer in my classes is a course tour video (CTV), which has reduced dramatically the number of questions from learners about the course structure. The CTV gives an idea of how the course is run and where to find course materials. It is helpful to create a checklist of things you wish to cover in the CTV, including where content and quizzes can be found, how to complete the assignments, how to complete a discussion, how to sign up for exams, and how grades are calculated. Including information about yourself as the teacher for the course personalizes the CTV and humanizes the learner's experience. The length of the CTV should be no more than 10 to 15 minutes. Having a timeline of topics covered in the CTV will be helpful when a learner asks a question regarding the course, allowing you to reply, for example, "Your question will be addressed at time 2:20 of the course tour video."

Using screen capturing software is an efficient way to create a CTV for online courses. Screen capturing software allows you to record screen activity into a movie format. There are a number of different screen capture video programs available, many of which are free to try before purchasing (e.g., QuickTime, Screenr, Jing, Snagit, or Screencastify). Once you have made your screen capture video, you can then import it into a program such as Camtasia that allows you to add annotations, transitions, animations, media, and special effects.

To ensure learners watch the CTV, some teachers have opted to include a mandatory online quiz following the CTV. To be able to view the rest of the course, for example, students must receive 100 percent on the quiz. Questions on the quiz should reflect information that has been covered in the CTV, such as course structure, where to find assignments, and how to contact the teacher.

Learning Objectives and Assessment

Though it may seem obvious, prior to creating course structure, content, or assessments, one must consider the learning objectives for the course. The learning objectives not only help you streamline your course content and assessment, but also tell learners what they will be able to do by the end of each lesson. They should be written in a format that is observable and measurable. In order for your assessment to align with your assignments, Eleanor Dougherty (2012) suggests you should strive to do the following with your learning objectives:

- teach literacy skills in all content areas
- teach students to comprehend and critique a variety of texts and ideas
- write prompts that ask students to write or orally explain in response to reading
- include speaking and listening as a means of comprehending and communicating

- expect that students will use and write language to communicate appropriately for an audience and a purpose
- require evidence from texts and credible sources
- create opportunities for students to use and manage technology to learn and produce their own products
- write instructional plans that document and plot the teaching that transforms an assignment into learning

The simple step of clarifying objectives at the outset can help focus student effort and can also guide the effective development of online content and assessment.

Mapping Course Content

Using a course map or table can facilitate your organization of learning objectives, assessments, and content or learning activities (Pollock 2013). This table should have four columns: (1) module or unit number, (2) learning outcomes, (3) assessments, and (4) content or learning activities.

Discussions or Forums

Discussions or forums contribute significantly in an online course where there are three types of interactions: student-student, student-teacher, and student-content (Moore 1989). Discussions and forums can be used for these three types of interactions, enabling enrichment and a place for learners to increase their knowledge, prepare them for online learning activities, and create opportunities for student collaboration. The following are some suggestions I found useful when setting up discussions:

- Remind learners that forums are a cooperative group effort and an essential part of the class.
- The subject line in a discussion is important. Ask the learner to put something that is appropriate and catchy. This will attract other learners to read the post.
- When appropriate, restrict the learners from viewing other learners' posting until they post their own.

Using online discussions, the teacher has an opportunity to promote authentic writing skills and to help students make connections with the content and with one another.

Rita-Marie Conrad and J. Ana Donaldson (2012) have developed a Phases of Engagement model that provides teachers with a strategy for increasing collaborative engagement. The following are examples from each of the phases.

1. Phase 1. Connection—This activity should be fun and nonthreatening. An example would be a social icebreaker. The icebreaker should require creativity and foster openness. Here is an example of a Phase 1 activity:

   Introduce Yourself:

   One of the most important aspects of an online course is the interaction between learners. Online discussion provides a great opportunity for you and your fellow learners to get to know each other. Ask learners to write and post their self-introductions, including their educational backgrounds, as relating to the topics of the course. Also, have them include a response to *all* of the following:

   - draft one or two specific goals you want to accomplish by the end of the course
   - consider and describe how this course can contribute to your career goals
   - discuss your excitement, challenges, or apprehensions as you begin this course

   Ask the learners to respond to at least two other postings with thoughtful, insightful, and helpful responses.

2. Phase 2. Communicate—Learners are put into pairs to facilitate a structured interaction that requires critical thinking, reflection, and sharing of ideas. Here is an example of a Phase 2 activity:

   News of the Week:

   Learners work with a partner to acquire a course-related news item. You should have different pairs post a news item each week. Do not allow the same news items to occur more than once, as doing so ensures that students read previous news items. This partner activity contributes to the overall course environment by getting new ideas flowing among learners. (Conrad and Donaldson 2004).

3. Phase 3. Collaborate—The teacher creates small groups by combining pairs from the previous activity. An example would be a progressive project, one where other learners critique their partner's work. Here is an example of a Phase 3 activity:

Progressive Project:

Each learner is given a different topic. Learners post their projects in the discussion area where other members of a group provide a critique. The critiques should include: (1) I like the fact…(a compliment), (2) I wonder if…(a constructive criticism), (3) a good next step might be… (a recommendation). The learner then uses the critiques to make changes to the project prior to submitting the project for marking by the teacher. Conrad and Donaldson (2004) note that this activity works well in an asynchronous online environment.

4. Phase 4. Cofacilitate—These group projects transfer learners to the responsibility of enabling their own learning. The activities are learner designed and led. An example would be student-driven generated course content. Here is an example of a Phase 4 activity:

Course Vocabulary Bank:

The objective of this activity is to summarize the course content terms while encouraging learners to use their thinking, interpretation, and creativity. Learners sign up for terms they wish to develop. The definitions should include text, image, and video. Posting the definitions in the discussion/forum area allows for critique from other learners. Conrad and Donaldson (2012) indicate that these types of activities strengthen the understanding of the course concepts. Learners are giving back to the course and not just receiving.

The preceding examples are just a few that can be incorporated into your online classroom. I find most of the learning in my classes occurs within the discussions area. Leonard Williams and Mary Lahman (2011) have shown that online discussions foster active learning behaviors and increase learner outcomes. Another tool that increases learner outcomes is multimedia. The following section considers what you should and not include in each piece of multimedia.

Multimedia In Your Classes

Images, animations, videos, and audio files are important components within an online classroom. These multimedia items can be found across the content, quiz, and forum areas of the LMS. Richard Mayer's (2009) book *Multimedia Learning* outlines 12 principles for creating multimedia that improves learning. The first five deal with reducing the amount of irrelevant processing in multimedia learning:

1. *Coherence Principle*: Learning is improved when irrelevant or unneeded words, pictures, sounds, music, and symbols are excluded from a multimedia presentation.

2. *Signaling Principle*: Learning is improved "when cues that highlight the organization of the essential material is added" (p. 108). For example, during the CTV, a list of topics to be discussed are presented at the beginning of the movie.

3. *Redundancy Principle*: Learning is improved more "from graphics and narration than from graphics, narration, and printed text" (p. 118). See the section on *Students Creating Learning Objects* (LOs) for an example of my process, in which my students are taking graphics and making them into movies with accompanying narration.

4. *Spatial Contiguity Principle*: Learning is improved when matching words and pictures are presented near to each other. For example, when creating closed captioning for movies, it is better to have the closed captioning on the movie rather than in a separate text file.

5. *Temporal Contiguity Principle*: Learning is improved "when corresponding words and pictures are presented simultaneously" (p. 153). When I first started teaching online physics 10 years ago, the online course had images with separate audio files. Now these same pictures have been changed to animations with the audio presented simultaneously.

The next three principles are for managing critical processing in multimedia learning:

6. *Segmenting Principle*: Learning is improved "when multimedia is presented in user-paced segments" (p. 175). If you are creating complex content such as fractions, then learning is improved when there are multiple animations versus one large animation. For example, separate animations should be made for addition, subtraction, division, and multiplication.

7. *Pre-Training Principle*: Learning is improved when the names and characteristics of the main concepts are previously known. For example, knowing the names and functions of each part of the heart would precede a lesson on how the heart plays an important function in the circulatory system.

8. *Modality Principle*: Learning is improved when a picture has spoken words. Going back to my first physics class, many of the images included text to explain the concept; however, changing the image to an animation with narration improves learning.

The next four principles foster generative processing in multimedia learning. Mayer (2009) defines generative processing as "cognitive processing aimed at making sense of the material and includes organizing the incoming material into coherent structures and integrating these structures with each other and with prior knowledge" (p. 221). The principles are the following:

9. *Multimedia Principle*: Learning is improved when pictures are added to words. For example, when students are struggling with locating an item in the online course, I create a screen capture image and add captions (text) with the proper steps in finding the content.

10. *Personalization Principle*: Learning is improved when multimedia includes conversational words. For example, when explaining the circulatory system, use words such as *your* heart, instead of *the* heart.

11. *Voice Principle*: Learning is improved when narration is provided by a human voice. Some people do not like the sound of their voice when they hear a recording of it; therefore, they decide to use the computer- or machine-generated voice. However, if others are going to use the multimedia with narration, then it should have a human voice.

12. *Image Principle*: Learning is not necessarily improved with the teacher's image on the screen.

Course Automation

Online high school teachers prefer to automate when they can, which allows more time for student-teacher interaction. The following are some of the items that I automate in my course:

- a welcoming email explaining the course and offering a personal introduction

- self-marked quizzes
- reminders for those that have not logged into the course recently
- notifications of submitted work, including the time frame for grading along with instructions on what students should do next
- reminders that students score at least 80 percent on an online quiz before the next one is made available
- cautions that students may not submit an assignment until the previous one is scored in order to prevent students from submitting all their course work at once or from making repeated mistakes

The next section looks at a project that I have been revising for the last seven years. The project has students participate in creating LOs that are then embedded into the course.

Students Creating Learning Objects

When you are hired to teach an online course, it is likely that you will be given a course with existing content, which may or may not be current. Some schools have instructional designers and others do not. The school that I am working at does not have instructional designers, so I built an assignment where students help create the LOs. Daniel Churchill (2007) describes an LO as being (1) an instruction or presentation object, (2) a practice object, (3) a conceptual model, (4) anything digital or nondigital. Students can help redo images, change images to movies, add to the course glossary, and even help create practice questions. The following are the steps I follow when students are creating LOs that are going to be used in a course:

1. The teacher decides which LOs need to be created and makes a list. Also, the teacher provide his expectations for the LOs.
2. The teacher provides a different LO for each learner to create. I suggest giving the LO task to the learner after they have completed approximately half of course. I find that students at the halfway point of the course tend to complete the entire course; therefore, you will not have to continually edit your list of LOs.
3. Learners create and then submit the LOs into the course Discussion/Forum area. I suggest that learners give feedback to

at least two other classmates. I ask learners to use the following format for feedback:

- "I like the fact that…" (compliment—one comment of admiration about something you found useful)
- "I wonder if…" (constructive criticism—one question about an item that was unclear)
- "A good next step might be…" ("go big"—one recommendation that you think would enhance the assignment)

4. Based on feedback, learners revise their LO.
5. Depending on the LO, I then ask the learners to present their project live via a web conferencing tool.
6. Learners revise their LO for a third time and submit their work for grading.
7. Teachers put the LO into the course for other learners to use.

I have found that students take great pride in their work, especially when others are going to view it. Daniel Mochon and Michael I. Norton (2012) attribute this to the Ikea effect. The Ikea effect has learners attribute more value to an LO they have created.

Conclusion

Online K–12 courses have been available in the United States since 1990 (Barbour 2010) and in Canada since 1994 (Barker, Wendel, and Richmond 1999). A key role of the online educator is to edit and create content, assignments, and LOs. To ensure instruction is efficiently delivered and targeted to online learners (Morrison et al. 2011), online teachers must be flexible, dynamic, and organic in both their design and delivery of course materials (Irlbeck et al. 2006). This chapter described strategies from two online teachers experienced in creating effective content for the online K–12 environment. As we saw, creating content for learners can be as simple as uploading or typing in material already being used in regular f2f classrooms. For young learners, online content doubles as a training ground for even the most basic skills such as logging in, using passwords, and keyboarding practice. Teacher-created content at the elementary level also allows teachers to introduce students to digital citizenship, setting a foundation for life. At the high school level, creating effective content and assessments depends on having a clear set of learning objectives and a clear sense of how the online learning environment affects student learning. If you add a drop of water to a cup of tea, then does it make a difference? It does. This concept transfers to creating online content. Every little piece of content counts, whether it be useful or distracting.

References

Barbour, Michael. "Researching K–12 Online Learning: What Do We Know and What Should We Examine?" *Distance Learning* 7, no. 2 (2010): 6-12. http://www.infoagepub.com/index.php?id=89&i=52.

Barker, Kathryn, Terrence Wendel, and Murray Richmond. "Linking the Literature: School Effectiveness and Virtual Schools," 1999. http://www.futured.com/pdf/Virtual.pdf.

Churchill, Daniel. Towards a Useful Classification of Learning Objects. *Educational Technology, Research and Development* 55, no. 5 (2007): 479-598.

Conrad, Rita-Marie, and J. Ana Donaldson. *Continuing to Engage the Online Learner: More Activities and Resources for Creative Instruction.* San Francisco: Wiley, 2012.

—. *Engaging the Online Learner: Activities and Resources for Creative Instruction.* San Francisco: Wiley, 2004.

Dougherty, Eleanor. *Assignments Matter: Making the Connections That Help Students Meet Standards.* Alexandria, VA: Association for Supervision & Curriculum Development, 2012.

Graham, Charles R. "Blended Learning Systems." In *The Handbook of Blended Learning: Global Perspectives, Local Designs,* ed. C. J. Bonk and C. R. Graham. New York: Wiley, 2006.

Harris, Judith, Punya Mishra, and Matthew Koehler. "Teachers' Technological Pedagogical Content Knowledge and Learning Activity Types: Curriculum-Based Technology Integration Reframed." *Journal of Research on Technology in Education* 41, no. 4 (2009): 393-416.

Irlbeck, Sonja, Elena Kays, Deborah Jones, and Rod Sims. "The Phoenix Rising: Emergent Models of Instructional Design." *Distance Education* 27, no. 2 (2006): 171-85. doi:10.1080/01587910600789514.

Mayer, Richard. *Multimedia Learning.* 2nd ed. New York: Cambridge University Press, 2009.

Mills, Kathy A. "Floating on a Sea of Talk: Reading Comprehension Through Speaking and Listening." *The Reading Teacher* 63, no. 4 (2009): 325-29.

Mochon, Daniel, and Michael I. Norton. "The IKEA effect: When Labor Leads to Love." *Journal of Consumer Psychology* 22, no. 3 (2012): 453-60. doi:10.1016/j.jcps.2011.08.002.

Moore, Michael. "Three Types of Interaction." *American Journal of Distance Education* 3, no. 2 (1989): 1-7. doi:10.1080/08923648909526659.

Morrison, Gary, Steven Ross, Howard Kalman, and Jerrold Kemp. *Designing Effective Instruction.* 6th ed. Hoboken, NJ: Wiley, 2011.

Palacio, R. J. *Wonder*. New York: Alfred A. Knopf, 2012.

Palloff, Rena M., and Keith Pratt. *Building Online Learning Communities: Effective Strategies for the Virtual Classroom*. New York: Wiley, 2007.

Pollock, David. "Designing and Teaching Online Courses," 2013. http://fsweb.bain bridge.edu/QEP/Docs/DesigningandTeachingOnlineCourses.pdf.

Ray, Beverly B., and Martha M. Hocutt. "Teacher-Created, Teacher-Centered Weblogs: Perceptions and Practices." *Journal of Computing in Teacher Education* 23, no. 1 (2006): 11-18.

Ribble, Mike, and Gerald Bailey. *Digital Citizenship in Schools*. Arlington, VA: International Society for Technology in Education, 2007.

Ribble, Mike S., Gerald D. Bailey, and Tweed W. Ross. "Digital Citizenship: Addressing Appropriate Technology Behavior." *Learning & Leading with Technology* 32, no. 1 (2004): 6.

Rylant, Cynthia. *The Van Gogh Cafe*. San Diego: Harcourt Brace, 1995.

Singh, Harvey. "Building Effective Blended Learning Programs." *Educational Technology* 43, no. 6 (2003): 51-54.

Williams, L., and M. Lahman. "Online Discussion, Student Engagement, and Critical Thinking." *Journal of Political Science Education* 7, no. 2 (2011): 143-62. doi:10.1080/15512169.2011.564919.

Student-Centered Digital Learning Through Project-Based Learning

Andrew Miller

Abstract

Project-based learning (PBL) is a model of instruction that creates a student-centered environment where students take control over their own learning. Through PBL, students learn content and skills at the heart of the curriculum, and the teacher serves as resource and facilitator of the learning. PBL has essential components such as voice and choice, a public audience, a driving question to promote inquiry, and ongoing feedback and revision. This chapter reviews the difference between projects and PBL, and also how teachers and students can develop effective PBL units in an online environment. It provides specific considerations for using online instructional resources, assessing student learning, and the role of the teacher in an online PBL unit.

Introduction

With online learning, teachers and administrators of such programs and classes have the opportunity and the space to transform student learning to a place of empowerment. Many students are familiar with the traditional *sit and get* instruction, but prefer a different approach in which they are in the driver's seat of their own learning. Online courses can provide such a space where students are more in control and teachers act more as guides or coaches of their learning. In such environments, project-based learning (PBL) can be an engaging way of teaching and learning for students of all grade levels (Guthrie et al. 2004). This chapter discusses how online teachers working across all grade levels can implement a more student-centered, PBL approach.

Projects Versus Project-Based Learning

Projects where students produce work to show their learning are nothing new to education. Often, after a unit of instruction, students develop a project to demonstrate what they learned. For example, after a unit on persuasive or argumentative writing, students might choose a research topic and engage in a debate on a controversial topic. This example of a performance assessment moves learning beyond a traditional exam or test. However, this is not quite PBL.

One of the key components of a PBL project is that students learn content through engagement in the project, not learning material before they complete an assignment or assessment. The latter is sometimes referred to as a "dessert" project (Larmer and Mergendoller 2010, p. 2). A PBL project incorporates the engagement and relevance of the project along with the rigor and strength of assessment to make the project the "main course" of the learning (p. 1). Rather than have a student learn the material and then (re)produce the content in a project, a PBL approach presents the student with a project before learning a majority of the content. With PBL, a student is given an authentic task or challenge to investigate and explore, which leads to inquiry and questions directly related to the learning content. In terms of online learning, a project could include multiple modules with different content or even a project that spans the course of multiple modules. Students still learn the material, but they are learning it through the project rather than only creating a project after they have learned the material. Here, the project challenges students to engage with and create new content rather than simply to demonstrate understanding based on content provided by the teacher.

In understanding how students become creators of content, here is an example of PBL with persuasive writing. In order for students to develop persuasive writing skills and also learn new content on the topic of government, a teacher presents a question to students, such as "How do we convince people to vote a certain way on an issue?" then asks students to create campaign ads, speeches and letters, or presentations that demonstrate their skills and knowledge of the content (Miller 2014). Instead of waiting to complete an authentic challenge *after* a unit of instruction, the teacher uses PBL to create inquiry and engagement to learn the content.

Students are motivated by interest in the content and an authentic need to answer questions, develop solutions, and produce work. In an online environment, students are able to show what they learn through a variety of digital tools, publishing opportunities, and assessments.

An Effective Model for Learning

Engagement online occurs when students are actively involved in problem or project-based collaborative approaches where students generate new knowledge (Conrad and Donaldson 2012), and PBL combines a variety of instructional methods to do just that. A PBL project might include lecture-style videos, digital simulations, and readings of important texts. Teachers can also leverage a variety of digital tools to support students, including video libraries, resource lists of hyperlinks, webquests, and digital games to provide timely instruction that is easily accessible through the internet. When students engage in a PBL project, studies have shown that they retain the content longer and move towards deeper understanding rather than simple rote recall of the information (Penuel and Means 2000).

In one such study, researchers (Parker et al. 2011) examined students in an advanced placement (AP) U.S. government and politics course who utilized a traditional approach to instruction and students in an AP economics class who utilized PBL as the primary approach to instruction. Students in both AP courses were given five projects over the course of the year aligned to the major content of the course and then completed the AP exam. Students in the PBL AP classes performed better on the more complex scenario tests that required more critical thinking than the non-PBL AP class. In addition to content, students improved their critical thinking, collaboration, and communication skills.

In *Project-Based Second and Foreign Language Education: Past, Present, and Future*, Gulbahar H. Beckett and Paul C. Miller (2006) report that by working collaboratively with classmates, students specifically improve conflict resolution skills (Beckett and Miller 2006). PBL projects are not only effective for teaching important content and skills, but also teach students to be more self-directed and to improve their ability to collaborate and resolve conflict.

Evidence of PBL Success in the Online Classroom

Technology has always been a critical component to PBL and has demonstrated that it can open doors for more diverse learning and student agency. Although PBL in the online environment is a newer approach to teaching and learning, other researchers have also documented the effective use of PBL with online students. For example, students at A.C.E. Leadership Academy in Albuquerque, New Mexico worked with a local bank to develop a more sustainable branch of the bank (Schachter 2013). Students used 3D modeling software, SketchUp, to create 3D models of the bank and presented the designs to bank officials. Students at Yountville Elementary School in Napa, California used Skype to connect with experts in the field of medicine as well as iPads to research and learn about human body systems to help make recommendations for sick people.

As this research suggests, online PBL has been successful in having students find relevance and build collaboration and critical thinking skills, all the while learning content. Susan M. Bridges, Michael G. Botelho, and Peter C. S. Tsang (2010) found that students enrolled in college-level dental courses in a blended PBL format were more engaged in collaboration that stemmed from working in teams to solve problems. In initial parts of the course, student talk was more "discursive," but gradually moved to more evidence-based conversations (Bridges, Botelho, and Tsang 2010). Also, students enrolled in an online college-level PBL computer science course showed more evidence of critical thinking skills than their counterparts in a more traditional format (Sendag and Odabasi 2009).

Ayfer Y. Alper (2003), who studied thirty high school students enrolled in a fully online PBL course, reported increased retention rates in the course and argues that all students learned course content despite different levels of cognitive flexibility. Similarly, a study of high school students enrolled in an online virtual reality course showed more interactions of collaboration and collaborative "play," and the student-to-student interactions helped them deepen their understanding of content knowledge (Morales, Bang, and Andre 2013).

Selecting Learning Objectives and Standards

PBL projects should engage students not just for the sake of fun, but also for the sake of learning. This is done through the selection of key learning objectives and content standards that students learn and share during the project. PBL teaches students content standards, concepts, and in-depth understandings that are fundamental to school subject areas and academic disciplines (Larmer and Mergendoller 2015). When planning a project, there should be careful and deliberate attention given to the content and skills students learn. Teachers can do this by examining their overall course objectives or content standards and unpacking them into learning targets. For example, if a course objective is for students to gain knowledge of world religions, then teachers need to construct or select specific learning targets and key understandings under this umbrella. These might include specific skills, facts, or connections students must master as they learn the content.

Teachers can also be creative in the area of curriculum integration. They can select learning from a variety of subjects or perhaps one of two disciplines. Keep in mind that PBL may not work for every learning objective in a course, however. As explained later, one key component of a PBL project is authenticity and connection to a real-world problem. Some content can more easily lend itself to an authentic challenge than other content. As teachers design the projects with their students, they need to be selective and critical in the selection of the content standards and skills.

In addition to key content at the heart of the course, PBL provides a context to teach and assess competencies that one might consider outside of the mainstream curriculum. These competencies or "success skills" might include collaboration, critical thinking, presentation skills, and self-management (Larmer and Mergendoller 2015). In addition to traditional content such as linear equations in high school math or ecosystems in elementary or middle school science, PBL projects must be designed where success skills are taught and assessed alongside the traditional content. Just like a traditional unit of instruction does not teach and assess all content or skills in a curriculum year, a PBL project should focus on specific content and skills. One project, for example, might focus on collaboration and civics content, while another project might focus on global citizenship and world religions. PBL projects are very deliberately designed to address a specific set of selected learning outcomes. Projects associated with PBL are designed with these learning outcomes in mind and often emphasize curriculum and content standards, which ensures that a project is truly focused on learning and not just a fun activity.

Designing the Challenge and Authentic Work

Once content and skills have been selected in the design of a PBL project, teachers need to design the overall challenge that requires students to learn and show what they have learned. Sometimes, a challenge can be a design project, such as designing a new bridge in order to learn physics or math skills. Other projects can explore philosophical issues or historical contexts. Often projects are more problem-based, such as students looking at possible solutions for environmental problems. The key is to have this challenge connected to relevant, real-world issues and contexts, and these connections might be local or global. When designing a PBL project for online learners, teachers and students can choose the scope of the project based on the flexibility in places and locations where students learn, and this challenge should be presented to students before they have learned the project. At the same time, the teacher should ensure that students already have the needed basics in terms of background knowledge to ensure they have something to draw from as they engage in the process of inquiry.

Projects can be authentic in a variety of ways, and some projects are more authentic than others depending on the content selected. A historical-based project might include a scenario of an actual or fictitious event that occurred in the past or an event that could occur in the future. For example, if students learn about a variety of forms of government, then they might be tasked as governmental officials to reform or even start the government of a new country. While this challenge is not real per se, the challenge offers authentic and practical experience that someone in the real world might experience. Projects become authentic when students do work, engage in processes, or use real-world tools used by experts or practitioners (Larmer 2012). With a combination of authentic tools, challenges, and audiences, projects can create ideal, deeper learning experiences.

Another example of PBL might involve students learning about physics and the use of the scientific process to understand why one falls off a skateboard. The scientific method is a process used by scientists and therefore makes this project authentic. A project might also connect to real-world topics such as community, war, or religion, or require students to learn content and skills that lead to products and presentations designed to meet real-world needs. Here, students might learn about various world religions and why people have misunderstandings or stereotypes about them and then work to inform people about the truth in order to create tolerance and understanding of these beliefs.

Further, a highly authentic project might involve more than one of these components. Teachers should do their best to increase the authenticity for the purposes of student engagement. PBL—especially when situated in an online or technology-rich teaching and learning environment—provides an opportunity for students to be the creators of new content, where they are not just consumers of information, but innovators. As teachers brainstorm challenges, they can ask themselves, "When do people in the real world learn and need to know the content and skills I have selected?" and "How and when do adults use this content and skills in the real world?"

Selecting Summative Assessments & Voice and Choice

Online K–12 students of all levels are poised to benefit from PBL experiences that are situated on the internet. Rather than passive observers, students become active participants in selecting products that demonstrate their learning. Once the content and the challenge have been selected and designed, teachers and students must select appropriate summative assessments and products to demonstrate the intended learning outcomes as well as assess students in authentic ways that transcend the traditional exam. Instead of an essay, students might write letters or blogs using Google Docs or Blogger. Instead of a multiple-choice exam on math skills, students might create presentations or even design posters to demonstrate math skills using Prezi and Glogster. There might be one major product or a selected few for students to create—it depends on the content and skills that the project intends to teach and assess. For example, if a teacher wants to assess speaking skills, then students might create a YouTube video or a podcast using free, open source software like Audacity to record and edit audio. If a teacher wants to assess poetry terminology and knowledge, then students might create a poetry book using Lulu, a website that allows users to create and self-publish their writing.

One key component in the selection and design of student products is "voice and choice" (Larmer and Mergendoller 2015). Since a goal of PBL is to be more student-centered, students need to have some control in the products they produce and the voice they have in creating these products. Teachers should allow for options that are appropriate to the students as well as the content selected. If a teacher is assessing writing skills, then the product might have options only in the form of writing, from blogs to speeches to brochures. If the project assesses knowledge of the water cycle, the product might take a variety of forms, as options may or may not require writing skills. Here, students might create a poster, model, brochure, or presentation. Sometimes, these products are done collaboratively, but it is important to provide opportunities for students to produce individual products so teachers can assess individual student learning as well.

Planning Assessments and Instruction

Once the overall project, the content learning, and the products have been established in the design process, teachers need to plan the instruction and assessments that will occur throughout the project. Assessment is not a surprise in PBL. It is incorporated into the project during the initial planning process and can take place as soon as the objectives and the overall project have been determined. Assessment tools should be used to ensure not only high quality products, but also high quality learning. Teachers can create rubrics and checklists aligned to learning goals, or they can work with students to coconstruct assessment tools.

Students along with the teacher can set the benchmarks and establish formative assessments. Many lessons for online learners may have digital quizzes, journals, and online discussion boards that teachers can use to check for understanding. Teachers can also use polling tools such as Socrative or Poll Everywhere, or online mindmapping tools such as Bubbl. Us, Webspiration, or mindmeister to gauge student learning. These formative assessments can also be used for teachers to plan instruction. Based on error analysis, teachers can look for global and targeted errors (Fisher and Frey 2012). Targeted errors can allow the teacher to give differentiated instruction through other online and digital resources or use a virtual meeting for individual tutoring.

As is the case with assessment planning, teachers need to align their instruction to the content and skills students will need to successfully complete the project in the context of the overall course. Some of this content learning will come from the digital lessons and activities. If there are no digital resources available for a specific skill or piece of content, then teachers will need to create that content or find it online, which might include another video, reading, or direct instruction lesson. Before launching the project, teachers should make the online assessment and instructional tools available to students.

Launching the Project, Inquiry, and Questioning

While the project itself should engage students, it is still important to launch the project with an entry event to hook them. There are many ways to launch a project. If a teacher wants students to learn about the Cold War, then she might show some propaganda clips to pique student interest and give them a preview of the topic. Or, if students are engaged in designing a bridge, then the teacher might present students with a fictitious or original letter from an architectural firm to ask students for their help. If students were exploring controversial topics, then they might engage in a short debate on the topic to learn more about the content needed for the project. A doctor could engage students in learning about systems of the body and illnesses by serving as a guest speaker on how they do their job. Other entry events include digital simulations, intriguing statistics, and interesting articles or readings. The key component of the entry event is that it emphasizes questioning and inquiry as opposed to resolution or the provision of information. It needs to create a *need to know* for the project (Larmer and Mergendoller 2012). An entry event should give hints, not answers. The answers come from inquiry.

Many teachers design a driving question that is engaging, captures the focus of the project, and gives student the overall purpose for learning. Presented at the launch of the project in a synchronous meeting, in a discussion board thread, or perhaps in a web conference or phone call with students, this question, which can be created by the teacher or cocreated with students, might be open-ended such as "How can we make sure our water is safe to drink?" or "Should we stop the construction of the oil pipeline?" It can also focus on an intriguing topic such as "Is it really safe with all the chemicals in our kitchen?" The intent is to use the question to launch the project and use it as a reflective tool throughout, as teachers and students use the driving question to check for student understanding and to set goals for new learning.

Once students are presented with a driving question and the project is launched, teachers must solicit additional questions from students. These might focus on the overall process and products or the simply the process of the project, and they should align to content. For example, if the overall driving question is "How do we get rid of the stereotypes of world religions?" then a student might ask, "What are some of the stereotypes of Judaism and what do Jewish people really believe?" If the driving question and overall project was designed effectively and aligned to content, the teacher will then be able to direct students to the online lessons, resources, and tools that support students in answering their questions. As students generate questions and inquire further, they create a malleable list that can be used as a progress meter and reflective element of their learning. While teachers may be able to ask students what their questions are, they may also need to scaffold the learning. Teachers can use sentence starters or stems presented in a synchronous meeting or discussion board, or use a process where students generate and refine the questions and then use the new questions to develop next steps for the project.

Giving Effective Feedback and Coaching

Once students start their project, it is crucial that the teacher coaches students and gives meaningful feedback. Teachers outside of the virtual world struggle to do this in a timely basis, mainly because creating and delivering instruction takes a lot of time. In the online environment, the teacher's role shifts to the role of a coach and time is freed up for the primary role of coaching and providing feedback.

It is crucial that teachers give feedback that is goal-referenced, actionable, clear, and timely (Wiggins 2012). When teachers see a student making errors in learning or struggling to complete work, they need to provide immediate support. Teachers should inform students what they need to do to change the behavior or correct the error as well as let students know what they are doing well. Teachers often forget to affirm the positive behavior and learning, which is just as valuable as the critique. Teachers should commit to providing feedback on major benchmarks and formative assessments as well as regular weekly emails in order to let students know how they are doing. Whether through voice calls or different forms of written communication, ongoing feedback and support can be key to pushing students towards success in an online PBL project.

Synchronous Learning and Collaboration

Synchronous learning, where students and teachers all meet at the same time, is an optional support for PBL approaches and can be used for both differentiated lessons and digital collaboration. Teachers can use synchronous, online class meetings to monitor student progress and ensure high quality learning and high quality products. Instead of using virtual class time to present content, teachers can use online meetings as an opportunity to support and promote a culture of collaboration online. Most online schools offer web meeting software for basic administrative and communication uses and some teachers use it to support student interaction and learning. Although not always practical, the opportunity to host synchronous meetings can promote communication, student engagement, and success. As an addition to asynchronous discussion boards and other group features to be found in the LMS, the option for students to meet, talk, work, and make presentations in real time is an option to consider.

Final Presentations of Learning and Reflection

Near or at the end of the project, students should consider making presentations of their work to an authentic audience. There are many ways to make a project public. In an online learning environment, technology can allow a variety of audience members to view students' final projects. A simple way to make student work public is to post it on a website or portal so that parents, teachers, and other students can view it. Another key way to make the work public is through the use of a virtual synchronous classroom. Students might take turns presenting their work in a synchronous session or record it for viewing later to curate the learning.

While parents and other students can serve as effective audience members, teachers and students should also reach out to a larger audience that authentically connects to the project. If students are designing a bridge, for example, they might try connecting with governmental officials who approve such bridges or architects with relevant expertise. Not only can this raise the stakes for students, but these audience members are in a position to provide particularly insightful feedback.

Instead of simply sharing their work, students are encouraged to respond to questions from the audience. Experts are encouraged to ask questions and confirm student understanding of the content and skills they have shared in their final presentations and products. For example, audience members can comment on a Google Document, or record videos with feedback and questions.

After the final presentation of learning, there is an opportunity for students to reflect on not only the content and skills they have learned from the project, but also the process and project. Many teachers ask students to reflect on their challenges, how they worked with others and received feedback, and the content they thought was most interesting. Teachers and students can also use this time to reflect on how the project might be improved the next time it is implemented. In essence, not only are students creating the products of learning that show proficiency in skills and content, but also providing feedback to create or recreate the project for later implementation. This reflection might occur through a video log, written interview, ongoing journal writing, feedback to professional mentors and partners, or discussion board posts.

Advocating for PBL in the Online Classroom

Depending on the individual school or program, there may be policies, procedures, or components of online learning to consider and address when implementing online PBL. One of these components is a lack of students' and teachers' voice with an established curriculum. Online modules or units are sometimes prescribed, with few choices in terms of final products or summative assessments. Online teachers may need to advocate for flexibility in the assessments or in terms of how the online modules or lessons are organized. Regardless, teachers will want to work within the overall scope and sequence of the course and build PBL experiences aligned to related course modules.

This is a time of change and opportunity in education, and early experiences with PBL in the fully online setting emphasize its promise. Teachers with a creative vision for project based approaches can take courage from the successes of those pioneering this approach in online K–12 programs. They also add to a growing body of research and literature that will help guide and uplift the evolving world of teaching and learning in the 21st century.

Conclusion

Online PBL honors the tenets of personalization, where students have control not only over the time and place of their learning but also *how* they are learning. More importantly, PBL is student-centered and puts the individual in the driver's seat of their online learning. Teachers become designers of the experience. They become guides to course content, rather than purveyors of it. Students own the content through action, exploration, inquiry, presentation, and publication. The PBL project becomes the launching point for student-centered learning. While there may be roadblocks for implementation of PBL projects, teachers can and should do their best to design these meaningful projects for students to create an innovative approach to online learning.

References

Alper, Ayfer Y. 2003. The effect of cognitive flexibility on students' achievement and attitudes in web mediated problem based learning. Unpublished PhD diss., Ankara, Turkey: Ankara University Graduate School of Educational Sciences.

Beckett, Gulbahar H., and Paul C. Miller. *Project-Based Second and Foreign Language Education: Past, Present, and Future*. Charlotte, NC: Information Age, 2006.

Bridges, Susan M., Michael G. Botelho, and Peter C. S. Tsang. "PBL2.0: Blended Learning for an Interactive, Problem-Based Pedagogy." *Medical Education* no. 44 (2010): 1117-47.

Conrad, Rita-Marie, and J. Ana Donaldson. *Continuing to Engage the Online Learner: More Activities and Resources for Creative Instruction*. San Francisco: Wiley, 2012.

—. *Engaging the Online Learner: Activities and Resources for Creative Instruction*. San Francisco: Wiley, 2004.

Fisher, Douglas, and Nancy Frey. *Better Learning Through Structured Teaching*. Alexandria, VA: ASCD, 2014.

—. "Making Time for Feedback." *ASCD Educational Leadership* 70, no 1 (2012): 42-46.

Guthrie, John T., Allan Wigfield, Pedro Barbosa, Kathleen C. Perencevich, Ana Taboada, Marcia H. Davis, Nicole T. Scafiddi, and Stephen Tonks. "Increasing Reading Comprehension and Engagement Through Concept-Oriented Reading Instruction." *Journal of Educational Psychology* 96, no. 3 (2004): 403-23.

Larmer, John. "What Does it Take for a Project to be Authentic?" *Buck Institute for Education* blog, 2012. http://bie.org/blog/what_does_it_take_for_a_project_to _be_authentic.

Larmer, John, and John R. Mergendoller. "Gold Standard PBL: Essential Project Design Elements." Buck Institute for Education blog, 2015. http://bie.org/blog /gold_standard_pbl_essential_project_design_elements.

—. "The Main Course, Not Dessert." *Buck Institute for Education,* 2010. http://bie .org/object/document/main_course_not_dessert.

—. "Seven Essentials for Project-Based Learning." *ASCD Educational Leadership* 68, no. 1 (2012): 34-37.

Miller, Andrew. "Designing PBL Projects to Increase Student Literacy." *International Reading Association IRA E-ssentials*, 2014. http://www.reading.org/general /Publications/e-ssentials/e8060.

Morales, Teresa M., EunJin Bang, and Thomas Andre. "A One-Year Case Study: Understanding the Rich Potential of Project-Based Learning in a Virtual Reality Class for High School Students." *Journal of Science Education and Technology,* no. 22 (2013): 791-806.

Parker, Walter C., Susan Mosberg, John D. Bransford, Nancy J. Vye, John Wilkerson, and Robert Abbott. "Rethinking Advanced High School Coursework: Tackling the Depth/Breadth Tension in the AP US Government and Politics Course." *Journal of Curriculum Studies* 43, no. 4 (2011): 533-59.

Penuel, William R., and Barbara Means. 2000. Designing a performance assessment to measure students' communication skills in multi-media-supported, project-based learning. Paper presented at the annual meeting of the American Educational Research Association, New Orleans, LA, April.

Schachter, Ron. "Project-Based Learning 2.0: Technology Pushes PBL into Fifth Gear in K12," 60-64. *District Administration*. Professional Media Group, 2013.

Sendag, Serkan, and H. Ferhan Odabasi (2009). "Effects of an Online Problem-Based Learning Course on Content Knowledge Acquisition and Critical Thinking Skills." *Computers and Education,* no. 53 (2009): 132-41.

Wiggins, Grant. "Seven Keys to Effective Feedback." *ASCD Educational Leadership* 70, no. 1 (2012): 10-16.

Open and Free Educational Resources for K–12 Online and Face-to-Face Classrooms

John Elwood Romig, Wendy J. Rodgers, Kat D. Alves, and Michael J. Kennedy

Abstract

Open educational resources (OERs) reside in the public domain and have been licensed for reuse. OERs hold great potential for increasing access to high-quality educational materials and can be used to enrich K–12 education in online as well as face-to-face (f2f) formats. However, OERs and other free resources do not automatically undergo the same quality control procedures of commercial or publisher-created materials. As a result, it is often up to teachers to evaluate and screen OERs and other free resources. Additionally, teachers may be underprepared for the demands of creating and curating engaging content in an online setting. In an effort to help teachers address these challenges, this chapter provides guidance and support for locating, using, and creating OERs in online courses.

Introduction

Most stakeholders in the field of education today consider technology skills vital to preparing students for future careers. Accordingly, schools spend billions of dollars on technology at the federal, state, and local levels (Grunwald and Associates 2010). However, significant questions remain about how technology is used in the classroom and online, how effectively school districts use technology to meet their objectives, and what resources are available to teachers. Reasonable answers to these questions are necessary to formulate if school districts want to spend technology resources wisely and if teachers want to effectively incorporate technology in the classroom and/or in an online course environment. This chapter describes and defines open educational resources (OERs) and explains how OERs compare to other free resources on the internet. It also shares approaches for locating open and free resources in three key areas: (1) podcasts, (2) open books, and (3) open courses and other tutorial-type resources. Additionally, the chapter provides a brief review of theory to assist teachers in technology decision-making, and it describes a specific example (along with instructions) of an OER that can be used to teach vocabulary to students.

Perceptions of Technology Use

Leanna Archambault and Kent Crippen (2009) conducted a descriptive survey of online teachers to identify their needs. The survey found that teachers may be underprepared for teaching in an online setting, and it suggested the technology demands of teachers working in an online setting are much greater than those in the face-to-face (f2f) classroom. Archambault and Crippen (2009) noted that many of today's teacher preparation programs require only one stand-alone technology course for teachers. Therefore, preparation of online teachers often falls upon the teachers themselves and/or the training/resources offered by the K–12 online schools that hire them. A key aspect of technology integration—especially in fully online schools and courses—often relies on the teacher's ability to locate and share quality content and/or quality learning experiences. To that end, the ability to locate, evaluate, and leverage OERs is a valuable skill to be addressed in this chapter.

Open Educational Resources

OERs reside in the public domain or licensed for open use, meaning the creator or copyright holder has given permission for the user to download, store, modify, and remix the resource to fit the user's needs, and "Open Educational Resources include full courses, course materials, modules, textbooks, streaming videos, tests, software, and any other tools, materials, or techniques used to support access to knowledge" (The William and Flora Hewlett Foundation 2015, p. 1). In contrast, numerous resources are offered freely online that are not necessarily licensed for open use.

Free resources are provided at no charge to the user, but the creator of the resource does not give permission for the resource to be downloaded, stored, or modified by the user.

Music is an area that some readers may be familiar with and may help clarify the distinction between free and open education resources. Musicians often put music videos online on a website such as YouTube. These videos are free resources to the extent that they are available for the user to listen to and enjoy at no cost. However, typically the artist does not give express permission for music to be downloaded from YouTube and stored on the user's computer. On the other hand, some musicians do use a Creative Commons license to make their music available for open use. This music can be downloaded, modified, and used in whatever ways the artist has authorized. This music may be considered an open educational resource.

Technology and the internet open the possibility of providing high-quality materials to populations, both in the United States and internationally, that historically have not had access to high-quality materials. Teachers making effective use of these free and open resources are seizing the opportunity to enrich their online courses and impact student learning in positive ways.

In a review of OERs, Daniel E. Atkins, John Seely Brown, and Allen L. Hammond (2007) found that at the internet's inception, "The available materials neither promoted enhanced learning nor incorporated the latest technological and pedagogical advances" (p. 1). The need for high-quality OERs was the impetus for several contributors, including the Hewlett Foundation, the Bill and Melinda Gates Foundation, the Andrew W. Mellon Foundation, and the Alfred P. Sloan Foundation, investing in their development. These groups and others were largely successful at increasing production, access, use, and evaluation of OERs (Casserly and Smith 2007).

The quality of OERs is inconsistent, however, and locating useful resources often requires knowledge, time, and effort on the part of the teacher. David Wiley (2011) argues that OERs are like toothbrushes. Simply distributing them does not necessarily mean they are doing the good that was intended. Just because people download OERs does not mean that they are using them in the classroom and using them effectively. Like toothbrushes, OERs require a certain amount of training (Wiley 2011).

Getting Started with OERs

While there is a wide degree of variability in OERs, they are defined by some common features. They are free online resources that can be distributed, edited, and remixed to fit a teacher's purpose. This section provides essential information on three areas of OERs: (1) podcasts, (2) open books, and (3) open courses and other tutorial-type resources. While not an exhaustive list, these resources are some common OERs used in K–12 contexts.

Podcasts

Podcasts are audio or video recordings. Khe Foom Hew (2008) listed the defining characteristics of podcasts as "[f]ile-based downloads… syndicated and used with the Really simple syndication (RSS)…consumed on the user's personal computers or portable devices" (p. 334). Common providers of podcasts include regularly broadcasted radio programs that place recorded episodes online, performers or film studios promoting material, individuals sharing information, and educational institutions and teachers providing content to learners. Podcasts have two major benefits: (1) providing access to authentic material, and (2) customizing information for the intended audience (Rosell-Aguilar 2007). Content acquisition podcasts (CAPs), discussed later in this chapter, are a specific type of teacher-created podcast designed to teach content such as vocabulary to students.

When locating pre-existing podcasts, teachers can use many of the same strategies used in locating high-quality sources for a research paper. Teachers should look for podcasts that come from a reputable source or have been vetted by a professional organization. *The Princeton Review Vocab Minute*, for example, is more trustworthy than a podcast found on someone's personal blog. Animal Planet, CNN Student News, BBC, and Sesame Street all have educational podcasts intended for young students. These podcasts and others can be found at kids.learnoutloud.com/Kids-Free-Stuff.

Another podcast database is podbay.fm, which offers many podcasts organized by content categories. While most of the podcasts are intended for older audiences, the site does offer some podcasts for young students in the *Kids and Family* section. A similar resource, www.podcastcharts.com, also provides users with the ability to search podcasts by category. Likewise, the podcast directories for iTunes and iTunes U include some highly-rated podcasts appropriate for K–12 students. Podcasters registering their podcasts with iTunes are also able to specifically identify their podcasts as *clean*, meaning the language and content are considered appropriate for a general audience.

Podcasts support students who learn best through auditory approaches, and—because they can be enjoyed away from the confines of computer screen and keyboard—podcasts can complement the online classroom in the context of integrated mobile learning approaches. Another advantage of podcasts is the ability to expose students to primary audio sources. For example, *Great Speeches in History* (www.learnoutloud.com) provides users the ability to listen to recordings and renditions of actual speeches from history, including speeches ranging from Dr. Martin Luther King Jr.'s *I Have a Dream* speech to President George Washington's farewell address. Variants on the traditional audio podcast include audiobooks such as those available on iTunes or Podiobooks.com, enhanced podcasts that can incorporate links or images, and video podcasts or vodcasts. While some of these resources are fee-based, many free offerings can be located simply by using the filter or search term *free* when searching a podcast directory.

Open Books

An open textbook or OER book typically involves a departure from the traditional layout and look of a traditional print book. An open book generally incorporates some text, but it may also include videos, images, interactive graphics, note-taking features, and social features. Some open books can remain online or be printed to create a hard copy.

Sites like OpenCulture.com, Google Book Search, BookFinder, and ReadPrint are just a few searchable sources that can be used to locate free books and open textbooks that are compatible with various devices including Kindle and iPad/iPhone. In situations in which online students do not commonly have access to a tablet or other mobile device, it is possible to locate free books or open textbooks available for download in PDF format and/or that can be read online in HTML format. Online schools that issue iPads to students can search the iTunes Store to locate free multimedia books. For example, a search for free nonfiction turned up a series of high-quality animal books for students aged 9–12. There are also several repositories of open books of interest to K–12 teachers. While not an exhaustive list of OERs options for books, the following three resources are a great place for teachers to start their search for open books.

First, Wikibooks (www.wikibooks.org) has nearly 3,000 open books available in English. These books can be filtered by subject area to ease the search process for teachers. Wikijunior provides access to nonfiction books for students under 12 years old. However, other than the general Wikibooks section and the Wikijunior section, this resource does not assign a reading level to the content. As with any open resource, teachers should make sure the content is engaging, robust, and appropriate, and that students are able to comprehend the material on these sites before assigning it. Some online schools include staff who serve as distance education librarians or media specialists, and they can often help locate appropriate resources.

Another collection of open books can be accessed at www.ck12.org. This site offers a wide variety of open textbooks, including student and teacher editions. The books on this site are divided across grade levels, meaning that teachers can reasonably assume that the reading levels of the books correspond to the grade level.

Finally, Project Gutenberg (www.gutenberg.org) offers more than 49,000 free eBooks. A strength of this resource is the number of fiction titles available. Several popular K–12 titles are offered through this site including *Adventures of Huckleberry Finn, A Tale of Two Cities,* and *Alice's Adventures in Wonderland.* This site, however, does not offer much in terms of search filters. Users can search popular downloads and the latest releases, or they can enter a title into the search bar. This site also does not assign a reading level to each book.

Open Courses and Other Tutorial-Type Resources

Open courses and other tutorial-type resources are rapidly increasing in popularity in K–12 settings. Khan Academy (www.khanacademy.org) is one of the most popular tutorial websites with around 580 million lessons delivered to students. Khan Academy provides free (but not open) tutorials in math, science, finance, arts and humanities, computing, and test preparation. The site also offers content from partner websites such as museums, universities, and institutes.

Hippocampus (www.HippoCampus.org) is a nonprofit website that teachers may find useful. This site provides free but not open resources for math, natural science, social science, and humanities. The site offers more than 5,000 videos from twenty reputable collections including NASA, the NROC project, and several colleges. Teachers can create an account to customize playlists for students, though teachers should be thoughtful about how they use these types of websites. Both websites offer instruction at a certain instructional level and rely on certain instructional methodologies, both of which may or may not be appropriate for all students. Therefore, teachers should consider the learning strengths and challenges of individual students and make decisions about these resources accordingly. In the case of Khan Academy's Early Math, for example, students registering with the site have the option to complete diagnostics that ensure they are placed in tutorials that are appropriate for their individual needs and readiness level. Such diagnostics are not available on Hippocampus.

A related term, massive open online courses (MOOCs), refers to free online courses available to anyone with internet access. They can include video or audio lectures, assigned readings, homework assignments, and discussion features; and they can cover a wide variety of content. These courses allow students to learn material at an individualized pace. They provide expanded access to quality education for populations that historically have had limited access, such as residents of rural areas. MOOCs may also be helpful for providing richer and deeper learning experiences for advanced students and provide access to professional development for teachers who do not have access to it elsewhere.

Teachers may find www.moocs.com helpful when searching for and selecting MOOCs. Not all MOOCs listed on the website are free. This database allows teachers to filter and discover websites offering MOOCs. It also provides a basic description of each resource in the database. For additional links to podcasts, books, open courses, and other tutorial-type resources, consider using Open Culture.com along with some of the other repositories and search engines listed.

Selecting OERs

With hundreds of thousands of options available, teachers can easily get overwhelmed trying to select high-quality material. Much like knowing how to select high-quality sources for a research paper, teachers need to be able to recognize high-quality OERs. The process of selecting OERs begins with knowing where to find them.

Teachers can begin by taking advantage of organizations devoted to distributing quality OERs. In addition to websites already referenced in this chapter, Creative Commons (www.creativecommons.org), OERs Commons (www.oercommons.org), Merlot (www.merlot.org), Openstax College (openstaxcollege.org), K12 Open Ed (www.k12opened.com), Curriki (www.curriki.org), and ipl2 (www.ipl.org) all offer varying services to assist K–12 teachers in selecting high-quality OERs. These websites are some of the most common databases and search engines for OERs, and, typically, OERs found on these websites are licensed for open use and, in some cases, are professionally screened or peer-reviewed making them more reliable than those that may be found through a simple Google search. Table 15.1 summarizes the features offered through each of these websites.

Table 15.1   OERs Databases and Search Engines

Name of Resource	Website	Description
Creative Commons	www.creativecommons.org	Search engine that delivers open content from a variety of sources
OER Commons	www.oercommons.org	Hosts thousands of free resources available for download; filtered by subject area and grade level
Merlot	www.merlot.org	Hosts thousands of free resources available for download; resources have peer reviews and user ratings available
Openstax College	www.openstaxcollege.org	Provides free peer-reviewed textbooks for students. Typically a resource for college settings
K12 Open Ed	www.k12opened.com	Listing of websites offering OERs
Curriki	www.curriki.org	Large quantity and variety of resources available for teachers
ipl2	www.ipl.org	Listing of websites offering OERs filtered by content area

Still, many teachers will continue to use search engines such as Google and YouTube in an attempt to identify OERs, despite the fact that returns provided by such search tools are not controlled or curated for specific educational purposes. Teachers can find content that is licensed for open use by using the advanced search features on Google and YouTube. However, just because a resource is licensed for open use does not guarantee any level of quality.

School media specialists can be a valuable resource for helping teachers identify OERs that are of high quality both technologically and educationally. Many media specialists hold training sessions or technology overviews that would be helpful for teachers. They can also be a resource during lesson planning by collaborating with teachers on how best to incorporate technology into a given lesson. Some media specialists will even offer to coteach a lesson or a unit, which allows the teacher to collaborate on the creation and delivery of technology-infused content and learning activities. Presentations by the media specialist can even be made available in real time and simultaneously recorded for future reference via web meeting software such as Adobe Connect, Collaborate, WebEx, or GoToMeeting. For schools not equipped to offer live online meetings or presentations, these types of demonstrations can be prerecorded and linked for student access within the online course. After the initial presentation, a dialogue can then be continued in the online discussion area, where students can interact with the media specialist and get answers to their questions relating to search strategies, citation style, content, or related topics.

Teachers working in the f2f or online school environment should take advantage of resources available through media specialists as these professionals have expertise in areas that a classroom teacher may not. Some online programs include additional staff members who can assist teachers in the actual online setting, while others may simply provide consultant services to provide advice and resources in support of specific online projects and teachers. Instructional designers can be very helpful by working with content experts (teachers) to curate and/or create online media and structure content and activities for student learning.

Mayer's Cognitive Theory of Multimedia Learning

Selecting OERs can be very difficult for a classroom teacher whether she teaches f2f or online, as the options often seem endless and quality remains a constant concern. Richard E. Mayer's (2009) cognitive theory of multimedia learning (CTML) is one theory that can guide teachers in their selection and use of OERs. Mayer's (2009) theory and its twelve accompanying principles have been empirically tested and demonstrate the ability to reduce cognitive load of the learner when used in multimedia settings. The principles and a description for each are listed in Table 15.2.

The CTML is grounded in three key learning theories that helped Mayer apply the science of how people learn (HPL) to inform the design of multimedia instruction: (1) Paul Chandler and John Sweller's (1991) cognitive load theory; (2) Allan Paivio's (1986) dual processing principle; and (3) Alan Baddeley's (1986) concept of the phonological loop, visuospatial sketchpad, and connected central executive. Mayer applied concepts

Table 15.2   Mayer's Design Principles and Brief Descriptions

Research-Based Instructional Design Principles (Mayer 2009)	Brief Description of Mayer's Instructional Design Principles (Mayer 2008, 2009)
Coherence Principle	Instructional materials are enhanced when irrelevant or extraneous information is excluded.
Signaling Principle	Learning is enhanced when explicit cues are provided that signal the beginning of major headings or elements of the material being covered.
Redundancy Principle	Inclusion of extensive text (transcription) on screen along with spoken words and pictures hinders learning. Carefully selected words or short phrases, however, augment retention (Mayer & Johnson, 2008).
Spatial Contiguity Principle	Onscreen text and pictures should be presented in close proximity to one another to limit eye shifting during instructional presentations.
Temporal Contiguity Principle	Pictures and text shown on screen should correspond to the audio presentation.
Modality Principle	People learn better from spoken words and pictures than they do from pictures and text alone.
Segmenting Principle	People learn better when multimedia presentations are divided into short bursts as opposed to longer modules.
Multimedia Principle	People learn better from pictures and spoken words than from words alone.
Personalization Principle	Narration presented in a conversational style results in better engagement and learning than more formal audio presentations.
Voice Principle	People learn better when narration is clearly spoken with respect to rate and accent.
Image Principle	People learn better when images are nonabstract and clearly represent the content being presented.

from these scholars to develop his CTML, one which explains that people learn best when visual and auditory modes of instruction complement each other. The principles of the CTML have helped instructional designers create high-quality multimedia. A video that incorporates Mayer's principles while explaining each principle can be found at this site: https://vimeo.com/89716786.

Contributing to OERs

The quality of open materials on the internet can be unpredictable. The OER community has many high-quality resources that can enhance a classroom or lesson, but teachers cannot thoughtlessly accept all open or free resources. Teachers can help the OER community in two ways. First, teachers can participate in social communities that encourage open peer review. On websites like merlot.org, teachers can rate materials using a five-star system and comment on materials, and teachers should do what they can to reduce the use of low-quality technology by promoting high-quality OERs and helping other teachers find them. A second way teachers can give back to the OER community is by creating OERs and making them available for other teachers to use. As mentioned earlier in this chapter, CAPs are one example of teacher-created OERs, The following section uses CAPs to illustrate how teachers can contribute to the OER community by creating high-quality resources.

Content Acquisition Podcasts

CAPs are designed by collaborative teams that include special education teachers and content area teachers (Kennedy, Deshler, and Lloyd 2015). CAPs have been developed for teachers (CAP-T) and students (CAP-S). They are not podcasts in the technical sense because they do not rely on RSS feeds for distribution, but they are similar to podcasts in that they are short (1 to 3 minutes for CAP-S) multimedia vignettes that combine still images and audio recordings to teach content such as vocabulary in an explicit manner. They are designed using a combination of Mayer's (2009) CTML and principles of explicit instruction (Archer and Hughes 2011). CAPs have great potential for online teachers. First, CAP-T is a free and open online tool that teachers can use to improve teaching practice regardless of setting. Second, CAP-S is a free and open online tool that online teachers can use to provide students relevant background knowledge, review of essential information, or tiered support for struggling learners.

While the look and sound of CAPs are developed based on Mayer's (2009) CTML, the content of CAPs is drawn in this case from a menu of evidence-based practices (EBPs) for vocabulary instruction depending on the term being taught. Some of the EBPs currently included in CAPs are semantic feature analysis, explicit instruction with examples and non-examples, student-friendly definitions, morphemic analysis, and graphic organizers. Figure 15.1 shows a CAP that was developed to support students in their study of vocabulary. An example of a CAP teaching the word *photosynthesis* can be found at www.qmediaplayer.com/?186, and a CAP teaching *planets* can be found at www.qmediaplayer.com/?231.

CAPs are OERs licensed for reuse under Creative Commons for non-commercial purposes and are part of an ever-growing library of resources for teachers available online. Currently, CAPs primarily address sixth to eighth grade science, social studies, and math terms, and readers can review existing CAPs by visiting vimeo.com/mjk.

CAPs have a strong record of empirical support for use in teacher education and secondary education, and they are one example of how teachers can contribute to the OER community and increase the quality of available materials (Ely et al. 2014; Kennedy, Deshler, and Lloyd 2015). The teams of teachers that develop CAPs also benefit from the collective expertise and perspective of different fields of education that are a part of the CAP development process. This collaboration and Mayer's (2009) underlying theoretical framework produce a high-quality resource

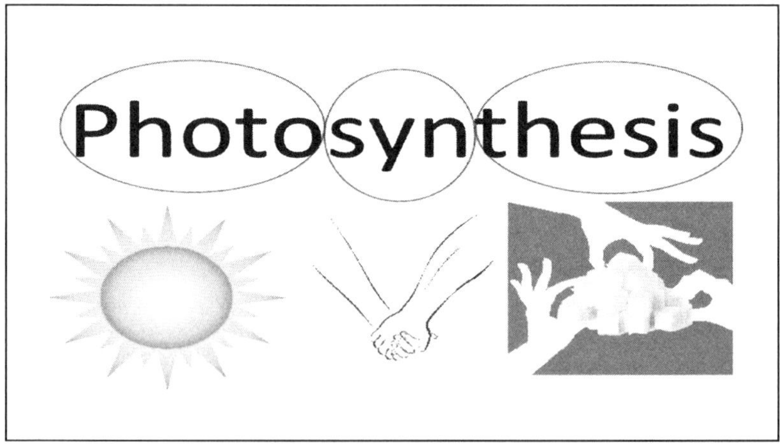

Figure 15.1 CAP used for vocabulary instruction

that has improved student academic performance (Kennedy, Deshler, and Lloyd 2015).

Further, CAPs have the potential to be both OERs and an option for teacher-created technology. As teacher-created resources, CAPs are powerful, yet easy to create with standard technology available on almost any computer. Teachers can create these tools at no cost and with no additional technology. A two-part CAP detailing the steps of making a CAP is available at https://vimeo.com/24179998 and https://vimeo.com/24182724. Step-by-step instructions are also provided in the Appendix to this chapter.

Conclusion

Technology has great potential for revolutionizing education, and online courses can make optimal use of OERs to enrich course content through multimedia approaches. Access to educational resources is greater than ever before. Students in remote parts of the country and the world can now access a vast assortment of educational books, courses, videos, and other resources. However, quantity of resources does not equal quality of resources. Teachers need to be thoughtful about choosing materials that have a sound instructional framework and that are also technologically reliable. Mayer's (2009) CTML is a valuable framework for choosing resources to include in a lesson. CAPs were presented as an example of OERs and/or a technology that was designed based on CTML. Teachers can begin use of OERs by using one of the websites provided for locating high-quality OERs, and, as they become more comfortable with OERs, can begin creating open content and distributing it to students and fellow teachers.

References

Archambault, Leanna, and Kent Crippen. "K–12 Distance Educators at Work: Who's Teaching Online Across the United States." *Journal of Research on Technology in Education* 41 (2009): 363-91.

Archer, Anita L., and Charles A. Hughes. *Explicit Instruction: Effective and Efficient Teaching.* New York: Guilford Press, 2011.

Atkins, Daniel E., John Seely Brown, and Allen L. Hammond. 2007. "A Review of the Open Educational Resources (OER) Movement: Achievements, Challenges, and New Opportunities," 2007. http://www.hewlett.org/uploads/files/ReviewoftheOERMovement.pdf.

Baddeley, Alan. *Working Memory.* Oxford, UK: Oxford Press, 1986.

Casserly, Catherine M., and Marshall S. Smith. "Revolutionizing Education Through Innovation: Can Openness Transform Teaching and Learning." In *Opening Up*

Education: The Collective Advancement of Education Through Open Technology, Open Content, and Open Knowledge, ed. Toru Iiyoshi and M. S. Vijay Kumar, 261-76. Cambridge, MA: The MIT Press, 2007.

Chandler, Paul, and John Sweller. "Cognitive Load Theory and the Format of Instruction." *Cognition and Instruction* 8 (1991): 293-332.

Ely, Emily, Michael J. Kennedy, Paige C. Pullen, Mira C. Williams, and Shanna E. Hirsch. "Improving Instruction of Future Teachers: A Multimedia Approach That Supports Implementation of Evidence-Based Vocabulary Practices." *Teaching and Teacher Education* 44 (2014): 35-43.

Grunwald and Associates. *Educators, Technology and 21st Century Skills: Dispelling Five Myths*. Minneapolis, MN: Richard W. Riley College of Education, Walden University, 2010. www.WaldenU.edu/fivemyths.

Hew, Khe Foon. "Use of Audio Podcast in K–12 and Higher Education: A Review of Research Topics and Methodologies." *Educational Technology Research and Development* 57 (2008): 333-57.

The William and Flora Hewlett Foundation. "Open Educational Resources," 2015. Accessed June 9, 2015, http://www.hewlett.org/programs/education/open-educational-resources.

Kennedy, Michael J., Donald D. Deshler, and John Wills Lloyd. "Effects of Multimedia Vocabulary Instruction on Adolescents With Learning Disabilities." *Journal of Learning Disabilities* 48 (2015): 22-38.

Mayer, Richard E. *Multimedia Learning*. 2nd ed. New York: Cambridge University Press, 2009.

Paivio, Allan. *Mental Representations: A Dual Coding Approach*. Oxford, UK: Oxford University Press, 1986.

Rosell-Aguilar, Fernando. "Top of the Pods - In Search of a Podcasting 'Podagogy' for Language Learning." *Computer Assisted Language Learning* 20 (2007): 471-92.

Wiley, David. "OER, Toothbrushes, and Value," 2011. Accessed June 10, 2015, http://opencontent.org/blog/archives/1780.

Appendix. CAP Production Steps

Phase 1: Preparation

Step 1.0 Identify ONE clear topic or concept to be taught in each CAP. *For example: What are the characteristics of planets?*

1.1 Brainstorm the most important information to include in your CAP.

Step 2.0: Create standard PowerPoint slides (heading and bulleted supporting points) for your topic.

2.1 Create a clear PowerPoint title page slide.

2.2 Put only one detail or piece of information on each slide.

2.3 Make sure you have a slide at the beginning and end that gives the exact definition you want people to remember. Provide at least one clear example that illustrates the meaning of the term.

2.4 Type speaker notes for each slide (under the slide, where it reads "Notes" or "click to add notes"), then print a copy of your slides and speaker notes to use when recording narration later on.

2.5 Remember to keep it simple—eliminate extra content from slides and your planned comments.

Phase 2: Production

Step 3.0 Replace most of the slides you created in step 2 with images that represent your topic as closely as possible (keep the title slide). *For example: A slide that introduces the concept of alliteration might contain a picture showing that "Bill Bounced a Ball."*

3.1 Select one eye-catching image per key idea. Use search.creativecommons. org, google.com/images, bing.com/images, or another internet search engine to find copyright-free photos or other images. Save the image to a folder you create for this project. Store all of your saved pictures in the same folder.

3.2 Select medium to large images that fill most of the available slide space, but do not let the images get fuzzy or distorted.

3.3 The pictures you select should have a central focal point that limits the need for viewers to move their eyes across the screen.

3.4 Avoid cluttering images with words or distracting details. For slides where you plan to insert text over a picture to emphasize key terms or ideas, make three copies of that slide.

Step 4.0: Insert text over images by using "insert text box" on the second of the three slides. The first and third slide should be free of text.

4.1 Select one word or a short phrase (three to four words) that demonstrates the key idea for the slide and type it into the text box. Using full sentences is not advised. Be clear and concise.

4.2 Use 40-point or larger font size; select text color that is easy to read given the contrast with the background images and colors. [NOTE: The text box "fill color" tool can be used to ensure good contrast between images and text.]

4.3 Place text boxes either in the middle of the slide or near a major part of the picture without covering it up.

Step 5.0: Prepare and time your slide narration so it coincides with any on-screen text. *For example, when recording a presentation about making pizza:*

5.1 Create three identical slides using the steps above. Insert a text box (see steps 3.0–4.3 above) in the second of three identical slides that has the words "add cheese."

5.2 Begin narrating these slides (see step 6.0). With slide 1 of 3 on the screen say, "The next step in making pizza is" then hit "Enter" to advance to the second slide which is already prepared with the text box and say "add cheese" (narration will match text on the screen). Hit "Enter" and finish narration on this part of making a pizza while slide 3 (without any text, but same picture) is on screen.

5.3 Repeat this process for every key piece of information to be addressed in the CAP.

IMPORTANT: Not every picture needs additional text—reserve use of text for the most essential concepts/pieces of information within your CAP.

Step 6.0: Finalize slides and familiarize yourself with the written narrative before recording narration. Save your file.

6.1 Under the PowerPoint pull-down menu, click "Slide Show" and then "Rehearse Timings."

6.2 Rehearse narration using your printed slides and speaker notes—they are your "script"; hit enter to advance through the slides. Note the total length of your narration when done.

6.3 PowerPoint will ask if you want it to automatically link the amount of time you spent on each slide for later use. Click YES.

6.4 Practice recording the podcast several times until comfortable and confident. If it is longer than three minutes (shorter is fine), or if more than three to five concepts are presented, divide the CAP content into two or more podcasts (part I, part II).

6.5 Save the file as a movie. Select the quality of playback (highest quality is recommended).

Step 7.0: Import saved .ppt movie file into your choice of iMovie (MAC) or Windows MovieMaker (PC). Note: Depending on your version of PPT, you may be able to save the recorded presentation directly as an MPEG-4 or as a Windows Media Video. Either format can be uploaded to YouTube or Vimeo without the need to use the moviemaking software described in Step 7.

7.1 There are several options for recording narration and linking to your movie—there is no correct way. Recording narration within PowerPoint is possible, but this can be unreliable (based on experience with Office 2011 or previous versions). An easy way for novices to record narration following the preceding steps is to use Apple's iMovie or Window's Movie Maker programs.

7.2 Drag the file into the video production timeline (at bottom of screen in both iMovie and Movie Maker).

7.3 Ensure your computer's built in microphone or external mic is functioning properly and at an appropriate volume. Record a test statement to confirm audio level prior to narration.

7.4 Record narration in a room free from background noise or other distractions. Preview your recording. If sound is distorted or otherwise imperfect, diagnose the problem (you were too close to microphone, etc.) and rerecord.

7.5 Speak in a clear, engaging voice; record in front of a mirror or with another person to create a more natural-sounding recording. Good posture, smiling, and hand gestures can also improve the quality of vocal recordings.

7.6 Listen to your recording for unnecessary pauses (vocal fills such as "um" or "like" or other dead air). If they are noticeable/distracting, rerecord your CAP.

7.7 Save/Export your finished video as a Quicktime, MPEG-4, or Windows Media file.

Phase 3: Publishing

Step 8.0 Upload your saved video to the web.

8.1 Upload your CAP to the learning management system (e.g., Blackboard, Canvas, and D2L) or other site (e.g., www.vimeo.com; www.youtube.com).

Tools and Strategies for Assessment in an Online Environment

Kim Livengood and Lesley Casarez

Abstract

Assessment of online student learning often involves free and commercially available technology tools and applications as well as technology tools and applications that are built into the learning management system (LMS). However, given the vast array of options, it can be a challenge for online teachers to know when, where, and how to develop engaging and effective assessments. Various types of assessments including formative, summative, peer, and self-assessments can be designed using a number of different technology tools. Teachers can also use these tools to provide personalized and specific feedback, including opportunities for peer-review among students. This chapter discusses various types of online assessments, free or low-cost tools that save time and promote learning, and the industry standards from nationally recognized organizations that influence technology integration and online learning.

Introduction

The rapid availability of new technologies for use in the learning process and environment can overwhelm teachers. When integrating new technology, the challenge quickly becomes how to effectively assess learning and learning outcomes using new programs, apps, and tools available online. Online learning environments, in particular, hold the potential to create opportunities for novel forms of assessment and better support learning with the introduction of new technologies (Thille et al. 2014).

The assessment process involves an interactive feedback loop: students provide feedback via the assessment and teachers provide feedback on learning progress to the students (University of Tasmania 2011). This cycle enhances the students' content knowledge and skills as well as provides teachers valuable insight into instructional methods (Thille et al. 2014). Since an assessment is about students demonstrating mastery of an objective by presenting the information and skills they have learned, many of the same tools that teachers use to present content can be used by students to demonstrate mastery.

Assessment is an integral part of online courses, as outlined by Quality Matters (QM), an organization that promotes and improves the quality of online education and student learning. As part of the standards for K–12, QM (2014) describes key assessment points:

- 3.1. The types of assessments selected measure the stated learning objectives and are consistent with course activities and resources.

- 3.2. Assessment strategies and student expectations for successfully completing the course are clearly defined.

- 3.3. Specific and descriptive criteria of assessment strategies are provided for the evaluation of students' work and assist the teacher in determining the level of achievement of course outcomes and competencies.

- 3.4. Assessment strategies and tools allow the student to reflect on his or her progress towards mastering learning objectives and course requirements.

- 3.5. Multiple methods of assessment strategies are selected based on the specified learning objectives and student need. (p. 1)

Although QM is typically implemented on a schoolwide basis, the key points remain valid for online teachers. Other organizations, such as the International Association for K12 Online Learning (iNACOL), support student access to education and quality blended and online learning opportunities. In the "National Standards for Quality Online Courses" (2011), iNACOL outlines the use of multiple strategies and activities to assess student readiness for and progress in course content and provides students with feedback on their progress.

The International Society for Technology in Education (ISTE) in 2008 described the importance of assessment in online education in Standard 2 for teachers: "Teachers design, develop, and evaluate authentic learning experiences and assessments incorporating contemporary tools and resources to maximize content learning in context and to develop the knowledge, skills, and attitudes identified in the standards" (p. 1). One of the sub standards addresses the focus more specifically: "Provide students with multiple and varied formative and summative assessments aligned with content and technology standards, and use resulting data to inform learning and teaching" (p. 1).

Assessment is a critical component of the learning process. By focusing on various types of assessment and utilizing tools for implementation, teachers can integrate technology into the assessment portion of the learning process. However, it is important that teachers keep in mind that new tools and technology available for assessment purposes change frequently. The options provided in this chapter are just a sample of the numerous tools available.

Types of Assessments

Formative Assessment

Formative assessment is an ongoing way to monitor student progress and adjust instruction when necessary. According to Kyena E. Cornelius (2014), "Formative assessment occurs during instruction to inform teachers of student understanding and guide additional instructional strategy decisions" (p. 112). These assessments should be used for producing data relating to measurable objectives of learning within a unit, data on the performance achieved by students on that objective, and data that allow the teacher to identify gaps in knowledge and skills (Missett et al. 2014). Data collected from this type of assessment guide instruction by gauging student understanding of lesson objectives. Formative assessments also provide data for planning decisions regarding pace, readiness, and scaffolding needs of students.

Providing feedback on formative assessments gives students the opportunity to improve their learning. Several technologies allow teachers manageability and constant access for monitoring. The variety of tools available also allows teachers to monitor different types of data collected addressing different learning objectives.

Multiple tools provide opportunities for the teacher to evaluate the progress of an entire class, small groups, or an individual student. These tools offer synchronous and asynchronous options. A poll-type tool could be used to assess the class as a whole at any point. In general, discussion boards, journals, or blogs could be used to facilitate the assessment of groups of students or individually throughout a course. However, formative assessment does not need to be limited to these tools. Any tool used for collaboration including the teacher as a group member allows for such progress checks.

Summative Assessment

Summative assessment evaluates student mastery of learning outcomes. Summative assessment is an activity usually conducted at the end of a term, chapter, semester, year, or similar for grading and evaluation purposes. Typically, summative assessment includes closed-ended questions, such as multiple-choice, true/false, and fill-in-the-blank questions (Glazer 2014). Assessments used to report student achievement or determine mastery of learning objectives, such as high stakes state assessments, end of topic, or end of unit assessments, fall under the category of summative assessment (Cornelius 2014).

End-of-course summative assessments give teachers important feedback to determine the effectiveness of the teaching strategies, but not necessarily to improve instruction for students currently enrolled. The overuse of summative assessment without student feedback has been criticized, and the practice of giving exams for the purpose of assessment without providing feedback on the examination material is denounced (Yu and Li 2014). As summative assessments typically take place at the end of a term or topic, teachers may move on to the next topic without giving feedback on how well a student performed on a summative assessment. By designing summative assessments to automatically give feedback, such as immediate answers, explanations, and scores for multiple-choice exams, students are able to understand performance with attention to areas of competence and areas of needed improvement.

Some of the same technologies previously described for formative assessment, such as discussions and blogs, may also be used for summative assessment. Additionally, some of the more comprehensive technology tools, such as presentations, podcasts, videos, and websites, can be incorporated in a different format for this type of assessment.

Peer Assessment

In peer assessment, students grade or evaluate classmates' work based on an identified standard or rubric assigned by the teacher. The feedback provided by students may include a score based on the teacher rubric or suggestions for improvement (Orsmond, Merry, and Callaghan 2004). A peer review completed prior to a final submission is a type of formative assessment.

With peer assessment, students benefit through evaluating others by improved metacognitive skills and increased awareness of issues within their own work. Assessing others' complex and simple projects by the use of technology gives students the opportunity to gauge the work of others and further interpret the standards established by the teacher. This process may also help students notice issues within their own work that may need to be addressed (Lee 2015).

In a traditional learning environment, the teacher often oversees peer assessment that may be incorporated to facilitate collaboration (Gielen et al. 2011), though the physical logistics of collecting materials and redistributing them to peers can be complicated for a traditional learning environment (Davis 2000). An online course environment introduces the need for a different approach to peer assessment. All types of assessments are capable of incorporating peer reviews including podcasts, videos, discussions, presentations, and blogs. However, without some strategy for teacher supervision and/or a tangible incentive, students may not invest in the peer assessment process enough to reap the benefits (Suen 2014).

A common challenge for the implementation of peer review strategies is participation. Students are more likely to participate in the review process if the teacher assigns a due date and creates peer pairs only after all assignment drafts are submitted. When students make the effort to submit a draft on time, they are more invested in the assignment so that all students submitting drafts review others' assignments as well as receive a review. Timing of a peer review within the course also influences effectiveness. It is also imperative that students understand the teacher's expectations. If the peer review assignment appears at the beginning of the course, then the students may not know how to interpret the instructions, rubrics, or standards. If, instead, the implementation of the peer review process is later in a course after first receiving teacher feedback, a student will have a better idea of how to evaluate another student's assignment. Any type of technology used for an assessment could also utilize peer review prior to a final submission.

Self-Assessment

Through reflection of their own work, students evaluate their own progress and make strides to improve learning. According to Regina Grantz and Robert Gruber (2014), a self-assessment component implemented in a course should help students "observe or become aware of their own performance, analyze their performance and make connections between their development over a series of course activities, judge their performance against predetermined criteria, and plan for future performance and development within and beyond the course" (p. 24).

Self-assessments also help students to become less dependent on their teachers, more responsible, and autonomous (Ćukušić, Garača, and Jadrić 2014). Rubrics are a helpful tool for self-assessment as they provide the predetermined criteria and the expectations for students to monitor their learning.

In addition to the original project, the self-reflection itself may incorporate different technologies. Dale H. Schunk (1996) identified three processes common to self-assessments. First, self-assessments give students an opportunity to make observations about specific aspects of learning. Second, self-assessments impact students to make judgments about achievement in relation to the learning objectives of the lesson or the course. Third, self-assessment forces students to make decisions about the steps they need to take to accomplish learning goals in a course. Students may self-assess at different points during longer, more complex projects, such as a video or website development, while a self-assessment may only be needed upon completion of a shorter assessment, such as a podcast.

Student Feedback

Feedback is fundamental to an assessment process designed to promote learning. Well-designed feedback presents the students' current state, along with sufficient information to make a determination about the appropriate next action (Thille et al. 2014). Feedback should be realistic and should include areas for improvement and positive response. Having clear criteria or guidelines provided to students before the assignment creates transparency and gives an understanding of the expectations required (Glazer 2014).

By providing detailed guidelines, students are able to focus, stay on track, and be more successful in their educational endeavors. Rubrics provide this guidance by outlining expectations and purposes of assignments. Various types of rubrics used depend upon the product to be assessed, and sometimes more than one type of rubric may provide a more comprehensive assessment. Written feedback tends to be common in online courses, but verbal and even video feedback provides more communication and interaction in the course.

Many LMSs integrate the use of online assessment tools that allow teachers to provide rich student feedback. For example, Turnitin, a web-based subscription service, helps teachers identify potential plagiarism within a written assignment. By using Turnitin to support academic integrity and provide feedback to improve student learning, students must learn the importance of original writing and are often challenged to think more independently and critically. Turnitin also offers teachers a range of feedback tools, including voice comments, drag-and-drop comments, and rubric-associated comments to engage students in the feedback process. Another assessment tool that can be integrated into an LMS is Crocodoc, which provides inline grading features on written assignments. Crocodoc has markup tools that not only allow teachers to add comments on students work but also allow teachers to highlight an etextbook or form. Crocodoc can also be used on mobile devices and integrated into web apps.

Some tools, such as Edmodo, that focus on the education market have options specifically for providing feedback. Other tools may have natural options such as responding to a discussion or blog entry. Verbal feedback can be provided through a podcast. Teachers can also use an edited screenshot of a static image and include notes to students or create a video using a screen capture tool, which provide students with a visual form of feedback.

Course Assessment

Feedback from the student to the teacher is equally important. Several professional organizations, such as QM and the United States Distance Learning Association, have established guidelines to help identify online courses that meet standards for quality. Established rubrics guide teachers on areas to consider when developing, maintaining, and reviewing courses. Numerous tools solicit student feedback to assess the effectiveness of the course content and the implementation of technology. Typically, the LMS also includes a survey tool that allows teachers to initiate their own midcourse or end-of-course survey. Additionally, a polling tool provides anonymous survey-type course feedback. Tools such as discussion boards and blogs also allow students to reflect on the effectiveness of the presentation of course content and implementation of strategies in relation to the learning objectives.

Rubrics for Assessment Strategies

A LMS allows teachers to create assignments and attach existing or new rubrics that are integrated in the LMS. A great advantage of these electronic rubrics is that they save time and promote objectivity, with the points tallied automatically as the instructor reviews the work and clicks on the appropriate level of competence for the various criteria. Constructing rubrics for projects and assessments helps teachers clarify learning objectives they aim to assess, which also supports identification of authentic performance tasks (Andrade 2005). Rubrics also help ensure fairness in grading and bring objectivity to the criteria considered for subjective grading (Kinne, Hasenbank, and Coffey 2014). The process of developing a rubric not only helps teachers clarify expectations for assessment, but also helps students understand expectations (Kinne, Hasenbank, and Coffey 2014).

Rubrics provided to the students in the beginning of a course can set the stage for the implementation of critical thinking skills. Each of the types of rubrics can be applied to an assessment at different points throughout the evaluation process. A primary rubric is used to determine student progress on completion of the components of larger projects (Rocco 2007). Possible rubric criteria include content information as well how the information is presented. For example, a student-created website may need to include two types of information, three additional links, and an image or video. A rubric, whether primary, analytical (which identifies and assesses components of a finished product), or holistic (which evaluates or assesses the whole process or product), is not limited to formative assessments; summative, peer, and self-assessments may also use primary, analytical, and holistic rubrics.

Student Authentication

One issue that has become a concern with the rise in online education is student authentication. How do teachers know that online students are who they say they are? One way to promote academic integrity is to utilize multiple assessment techniques in place of high stakes exams (Western Interstate Commission for Higher Education 2008). Teachers can instead rely on interactive discussions, writing assignments, quizzes, capstone projects, group work, and online exams (Western Interstate Commission for Higher Education 2008). Proctoring tools may also be utilized with examinations, as test security can be problematic. These tools allow the instructor to know for certain that the student is the actual enrolled student and ensure that the student is not using prohibited materials during the online exam.

If high-stakes testing situations are used in an online course, tools can be implemented to help with academic integrity. For instance, some schools may require that students go to a physical proctoring center to take the exam. Another option is utilization of proctoring devices or businesses that monitor students while they take exams, such as services provided through ProctorU, a live online proctoring service that allows the user to connect via webcam, monitors the user during the test, and authenticates the test taker's identity. ProctorFree is a similar program that does not require integration with an LMS. Browser lockdown services, such as Respondus LockDown Browser, disable all activities such as printing, copying, going to other websites, or accessing other applications. With the easy availability of smartphones or other digital devices, these lockdown services are best used in conjunction with some additional form of monitoring.

Tools for Assessment Strategies

The availability of tools and technology is constantly changing. The following section provides only a sample of tools useful for assessment. Tools specifically designed for the K–12 audience have been noted; however, the appropriate age level will vary depending on the how the teacher integrates the tool and/or how the students use the tool. Some tools may be too complex for younger students to use alone for a summative assessment, but with guidance the same tool may be useful for a formative assessment. It should be noted that many additional tools are available which contribute to the assessment process in similar ways, although the addition of technology as an assessment strategy is oftentimes an additional source of anxiety for the many students who suffer from test anxiety. The problem-solving required to effectively use new technology dictates the use of critical thinking skills and may add to student frustration with the assessment task. If actual use of the specific technology is not part of the learning objective, then providing less-complicated tools may ease student concerns, allow for more attention to mastery of objectives, and require less attention to mastery.

Several types of the tools discussed in this section may be available within specific LMSs. If those tools fail to meet needs, or if they are not available within the LMS, then options for free tools that meet a range of technology skills are available. When choosing an appropriate tool, both availability and effectiveness in meeting the needs of students should be considered.

Writing Tools

Tools that require students to write in order to demonstrate mastery of learning objectives, such as discussion boards and journals, may be familiar to teachers. Discussions are commonly used in a face-to-face (f2f) learning environment and are easily integrated in an online environment for a number of subjects. Using student journals may be commonly related to writing courses or science courses, but this strategy addresses learning objectives for a number of courses as do other writing-based tools common to the online course.

Discussion Boards

The discussion board is a common built-in LMS feature used by teachers to facilitate online teaching and learning. Monitored or evaluated asynchronous discussion boards often function as either a formative or summative assessment and facilitate peer assessment. A discussion focuses on one specific objective or lasts the entire length of the course, and the tool itself allows the teacher to break the class up into smaller and more collegial discussion groups. For each post, students need to analyze, evaluate, and synthesize information. The purpose, length, and criteria of the posts and discussion board determine how to evaluate an activity. To evaluate students' progress throughout the duration of a discussion board, teachers need to regularly monitor student posts. While discussion board posts tend to show how effectively students understand the content, responses to other students' posts on the discussion board add another level of evaluation as students support and/or question posts from their peers.

For a summative approach to assessing the discussion board, students' posts throughout a discussion could be evaluated holistically in order to determine if the students effectively integrated the content presented in the lessons. Another option could be to have the students summarize what they learned through their participation in the discussion board by having students present an analysis of the content learned and a summary on how well they connected the content to real world applications.

Teachers may also choose to create a participation rubric to assess students' performance on the discussion board. Criteria in the participation rubric may include participation timeline and participation rigor. With the participation timeline, students are assessed on meeting deadlines and/or other course expectations such as posting a set number of days per week. With participation rigor, students are assessed on their reflections, critical interactions with their peers, appropriate use of writing style, and overall completion of the assignment requirements. The assessment of online netiquette can be added to the participation rubric as well.

Common social media tools, such as Facebook and Twitter, operate as discussions. Discussions may be completely open to the public when using these tools, or privacy settings can be changed in Facebook to limit access. Some teachers may still be uncomfortable using these tools for class discussions, however, due to these privacy issues. For example, Twitter chats allow users to communicate on certain topics by using a chat hashtag on a predetermined date. Use of the common hashtag during the discussion allows the users to filter the Twitter feed so that only those messages are included. Live chats typically center on a predetermined topic and can include questions provided in advance. After the Twitter chat, users may be assessed either by the teacher or by peers according to outlined criteria, such as number of posts or thoughtfulness of posts. Users could also be required to write a summary of the Twitter chat that allows them to present an analysis of what they felt were the most important parts of the chat. The questions to facilitate the discussion would be similar to the open-ended questions that could be used to facilitate a discussion during an f2f class.

Twiducate

Another option for online discussions is Twiducate (www.twiducate.com), a social networking and media site created specifically for K–12 schools. Options are available to set privacy settings where only students with access to a class view the discussion. The teacher signs up the class and provides students with a code to log in to the class network.

Edmodo

Edmodo (www.edmodo.com), a K–12 network, requires that all participants have a free account so that access is controlled, so only students with accounts and enrolled in a course view the information in an Edmodo course. The screen view has a format similar to a Facebook screen with posts. A teacher posts on the class page, which then appears in each student's feed. Students need only to respond to the post, and this discussion will only be available to those who have permission to view the class. In addition to discussion capabilities, Edmodo has other tools that could be used for assessment, such as multiple choice quizzes and poll questions. Edmodo can be viewed in twelve different languages, and add-on options are available with a fee.

Neat Chat

Neat Chat (www.neatchat.com) is a free online synchronous discussion tool that does not require an account. Students only need the URL address to access the discussion. If more privacy is needed, then the administrator requires a password for access to the page. Students enter the discussion at any time and still access previous comments.

Chatzy

Chatzy (www.chatzy.com) is another online discussion tool. A quick discussion room can be set up even without an account. Access to the discussion will remain available for fourteen days after the last activity. The discussion does not actually need to be synchronous, but the structure of the page reflects a synchronous format. With a free account, links to each of the discussions are automatically saved.

Journals

Journals provide teachers the opportunity to focus on the progress of the individual students without feedback from other students. Whereas discussion boards and blogs may be open to at least the rest of a class if not the public, journals may be written just between the teacher and student. The teacher evaluates the progress of students based on their ability to synthesize the current content, and students may contribute to the journal periodically through the class or for just a part. Similar to the discussion board, an individual journal entry may be used to evaluate as a formative assessment or the collection of journal entries may be evaluated for a summative assessment. For example, in science, students typically record observations from experiments in journals or log books, while in a history class they may enter their thoughts about current events. Cooperative projects always create a grading challenge when trying to determine if each student completed their share of the work. In journals, students can document the work completed at each stage.

Blogs

Blogs function similarly to discussion boards when all of the students reply to the teacher's or others' posts. Students can summarize the information learned and/or ways to apply the information in a blog post at any point during a course. If each student has a different focus such as a different topic for a research project, then the conversation threads stay clearly separated when using a blog format. Comparable to individual journal entries, a single blog entry may be appropriate for a formative assessment while the collection of entries may be considered a summative assessment. The interactive aspect provides an opportunity for peer assessment when replying to an entry. In an English language arts class, for example, students could summarize and analyze the sections of a novel. With the interactive feature, students could then comment on their classmates' insights. As another example, math students could blog about how to solve word problems.

Edublogs

Edublogs (www.edublogs.org) has been designed for teachers of K–12 students. The free account will only allow for a teacher blog to which students respond. The user can control the language of the dashboard. For a fee, the teacher blog has additional tools such as privacy settings, email support, and student management tools. Also included within the fee are student accounts; students are not charged individually.

Blogger

Blogger (www.blogger.com) is a free tool associated with Google and Gmail. This tool includes a number of options such as layout customization, mobile app options, 62 different languages, and privacy settings. Each person blogging will need to have an individual free account. If the school uses Google Apps for Education, then students may already have access to a Blogger account.

Audio Tools

Several tools include sound as an option, but several tools only record sound without other options. When only using sound, the words chosen to meet the criteria of the assessment are critical. Specific criteria, such as a time limit, add to the students' need to analyze, evaluate, and synthesize to develop the content of a sound recording commonly known as a podcast. The criteria of a final audio recording may be extensive enough to be considered a summative assessment. For example, after completing a research project for any subject, students could present a summary of their paper orally using a podcast. However, a brief update recording may fit the need for a formative assessment, such as students practicing speeches. If the product is a self-recording, then a reflective self-assessment of the product may be appropriate.

Vocaroo

Vocaroo (www.vocaroo.com) has a simplified format and does not require an account. Rather, a single button with a red circle and the words *click to record* allow for quick recording. The ease of use typically negates the need for students to ask questions and allows them instead to focus on the criteria of the assignment. Upon completion, the final product can be shared using a unique URL address or downloaded in one of four different formats. Additionally, a quick response (QR) code can be generated and an app is available for both Apple OS and Android OS.

SoundCloud

SoundCloud (www.soundcloud.com) requires account registration, but the free account provides up to three hours of storage. The recording process requires several steps and the user has the option to change the background image. The final product is only shared through a web URL. However, nine different types of files can be uploaded to share through this site and 42 languages are available.

iPadio

Although iPadio (www.ipadio.com) requires a few more steps to set up a free account initially, it does offer an option that others do not have. Users record podcasts from a phone rather than a computer once registered. Recordings are then shared through different outlets including Sound-Cloud, YouTube, and iTunes.

Voki

Voki (www.voki.com) adds a dimension to sound recordings through animation. With a free account, users choose the avatar and characteristics to present information in one of 20 different languages. Information is presented using a computer-generated voice or recording the user's own voice. The free account allows for a 30-second recording.

Visual Tools

Students have different strengths; some students are comfortable writing while others may prefer showing information visually. When the objective focuses on the content rather than how the content is shared, visual options may be applicable. Adding visual characteristics to the written word adds another element of critical thinking. Students are required to analyze, evaluate, and synthesize visually. Visual tools may represent a formative assessment when the products are periodically checked while students continue to work to determine progress toward the final product. The draft of these final products may be involved in a peer review process, edited, and submitted as summative assessments. Mind-mapping tools, for example, allow students to synthesize information such as class notes or notes from a textbook that have been analyzed and evaluated. In a geometry class, students may use mind mapping to organize the characteristics of different polygons with images. These images may be collected online or photos taken by the student and uploaded.

Lightshot

Lightshot (https://app.prntscr.com) provides a download for both Mac and Windows operating systems and works with eleven different languages. This tool takes screen shots and has some limited editing capabilities that allow the user to highlight specific details for the audience. Students may emphasize information related to the objective or a teacher may emphasize points that affect an assignment score.

Popplet

Popplet (https://popplet.com), designed for K–12 schools, provides visual mind-mapping capabilities, either online or via an app. Popplet provides a way to organize thoughts and ideas in a visual manner. Students capture facts, thoughts, and images and learn to create relationships between them to demonstrate their understanding of the content.

Mind 42

Mind 42 (www.mind42.com) offers an online platform for users to develop a quick mindmap. Users may collaborate simultaneously to create mind maps that include images, web links, and color-coded text.

Trello

Trello (https://trello.com) allows users to organize information and show content relationships in a variety of formats for projects with the option to collaborate with others. This tool stores information in the cloud accessible via an app or website. In addition to organizing information, group members may communicate within the tool using four different languages.

Presentation and Portfolio Tools

Presentation tools offer a possible strategy for combining the written word with visual support. The combination of the two components adds to the critical thinking requirement. Students not only analyze, evaluate, and synthesize presentation products, but also illustrate relationships between the organization, words, and images. For example, students may research a specific topic such as a famous person in history or a scientist's achievements, then design a presentation to share the information with the rest of the class. In a manner similar to the visual tools, the products can periodically be checked to determine progress as a formative assessment. Final presentations may be peer-reviewed and then submitted as summative assessments.

Portfolios assess student progress over a period of time and may include evidence of specific skills. Typically, portfolios assess a common theme of learning. Portfolios have been described as a more authentic means of assessment than traditional exams. Rather than showing that the learner knows what has been taught, the portfolio demonstrates that the student can do what has been taught (Damiani 2004). Using a portfolio as an assessment tool is a process with several steps:

1. Decide on a purpose or theme.
2. Consider what work samples to include.
3. Determine how samples will be selected for inclusion.
4. Decide whether to assess the process and the product or the product only.
5. Develop a scoring system or rubric.
6. Share the scoring system with students.
7. Include the student in discussing the final product.

Many of the tools used for presentation can be used to present a portfolio in an online course. It will depend on the theme chosen and what the portfolio is meant to show that the student can do.

Haiku Deck

Haiku Deck (www.haikudeck.com) is a presentation tool that allows the user to provide an image-based presentation. The user inputs wording for the presentation and either selects or uploads a picture as the background for each slide. This program is simple and easy to use.

Glogster

Glogster (www.glogster.com) allows text, images, graphics, and animation to create an online poster presentation. Built-in resources are available, or users may find their own media. Users may either use the online version, or there are also apps.

Prezi

Prezi (https://prezi.com) has a free educational account that will allow for private presentations in nine languages. Presentations are organized in a visual manner, with the option to embed both images and videos. Users work on the presentation saved in the cloud or on their computer. Collaboration with multiple users on one presentation is also possible, and an app is available if preferred.

Present.me

Present.me (https://present.me) allows the user to include a split screen, with the user's *talking head* on one side and the presentation materials on the other side. The program allows the user to upload a document, record the accompanying video, and share the presentation.

Video Tools

Video enables students to combine a number of elements in an effort to demonstrate mastery of a learning objective. Due to the complexity of planning, recording, and editing videos, the final project is often appropriate for a summative assessment. Additionally, a final project could be shared for peer assessments. If the video records a student's demonstration of a skill, then viewing the completed video would offer an opportunity for self-assessment.

Vyclone

Vyclone (www.vyclone.com) is a video collaboration tool that allows multiple users to create a single video, based on the idea of crowdsourcing. This one video will automatically combine the various vantage points of all the users' recordings. Users may either upload videos via Android or IOS devices.

At any grade level, students may be conducting a science experiment as part of a class. If students filmed their experiments using the Vyclone app then uploaded their videos, then they could be used to show multiple viewpoints and multiple conclusions all in one video that could then be shared with the students in the class. This same tool could be used in any class that incorporated a role-play activity.

Screencast-O-Matic

Screencast-O-Matic (www.screencast-o-matic.com) allows an easy way for the user to capture a screen and create a video, simply by clicking one button. Up to 15 minutes of recording time is allowed, and there are several options for sharing the capture, such as YouTube, MP4, and AVI.

Online Polling Tools

Online polling tools may be used synchronously and asynchronously to provide formative feedback. Some of these tools integrate questions appropriate to assess factual information while other tools allow open-ended questions to quickly check for students' current perspectives. These tools can be used either synchronously or asynchronously.

ActivePrompt

ActivePrompt (www.activeprompt.org) is an image-based polling tool. The teacher uploads an image and students drag a red dot to the part of the image that they choose as their answer. Then, the teacher is able to view a heatmap of where the dots are located.

ActivePrompt can also be utilized asynchronously. For example, a picture poll can be shared in the LMS with students during a particular module. Students complete the poll as they work through the module and at the end of the module, the results can be shared to see if everyone was on the same page.

Poll Everywhere

Poll Everywhere (www.polleverywhere.com) is another polling tool, with the option of embedding polls into PowerPoint presentations. Students respond to polls with either mobile devices or online. This would be a good option for synchronous online sessions, although there are also possibilities for asynchronous use.

Poll Everywhere may be beneficial when students are involved in a synchronous discussion, and the teacher is interested in knowing if everyone *gets* the topic at hand. As it can be embedded into PowerPoint slides and students can use tablets, computers, or phones to answer questions, this tool allows for real-time assessment.

Quiz Tools

Timing during a course often determines or dictates if an online test or quiz should be used as a formative or summative assessment. If the test or quiz does not affect a grade, then it may be considered a self-assessment, which could be appropriate prior to content presentation. These results could give the students, as well as the teacher, an idea of the students' prior knowledge. As a formative assessment, this type of tool could be used to check progress as students move through the content. Students and/or teachers could use the results to determine when students are ready to move to the next step. Any quiz that requires brief answers such as multiple choice, true/false, or fill-in-the-blank could be presented using an online quiz tool.

JeopardyLabs

The JeopardyLabs tool (https://jeopardylabs.com) allows the teacher to input course content in an online Jeopardy template. The game is played online and does not require loading into presentation software. There is also the option of viewing games that others have created.

Zaption

Zaption (www.zaption.com), designed for K–12 audiences, allows the teacher to upload videos and image then add questions to make it more interactive. Data are tracked in order for the teacher to see what students understand and areas that need improvement. The site includes an option for creating questions in one of four different languages.

Website and Wiki Tools

Websites or wikis provide a number of criteria options for assessments depending on the objectives and guidelines. These tools may be used as standalone assignments or in combination with other tools. For an in-depth history project, for example, students could individually collect information about different aspects of a time period in history. The information is then analyzed, evaluated, and synthesized to share with others in the class. The solo projects could then be combined using a website or wiki to present a more complete picture of the era.

Wix

Wix (www.wix.com) will host a website free in one of 14 different languages. Users do not have to be familiar with any programming language, as a drag and drop method is used. A number of free templates and tools are also available.

Wikispaces

Wikispaces (www.wikispaces.com) offers a free education account. Users build their own wiki with resources or collaborate to build a group wiki. Settings can be changed so that access to a wiki is either available by invitation or link.

Conclusion

New technologies provide opportunities for various types of assessments that engage students. Different types of assessments require a clear understanding of the expectations that accompany the assessments. By providing students with expectations for learning outcomes, teachers are able to grade more efficiently, objectively, and consistently. Assessments can take on many forms, including online tests used in conjunction with a proctored testing system, electronic rubrics used to monitor and evaluate students' performance on the discussion board, or a variety of web assessment tools integrated in an LMS. Tools for implementation, with a focus on free or low-cost options, enable teachers from different environments to incorporate assessment tools that cater to a variety of student learning styles and allow students to use personal strengths to demonstrate mastery of content. Although only a sample of tools have been provided in this chapter, additional technology may also be incorporated to conduct assessment, making assessment within the online environment more dynamic, effective, and engaging.

References

Andrade, Heidi Goodrich. "Teaching with Rubrics: The Good, the Bad and the Ugly." *College Teaching* 53, no. 1 (2005): 27-30.

Cornelius, Kyena E. "Templates for Collecting Daily Data in Inclusive Classrooms." *Teaching Exceptional Children* 47, no. 2 (2014): 112-18.

Ćukušić, Maja, Željko Garača, and Mario Jadrić. "Online Self-Assessment and Students' Success in Higher Education Institutions." *Computers and Education* 72 (2014): 100-09.

Damiani, Victoria B. "Portfolio Assessment in the Classroom." In *Helping Children at Home and School II: Handouts for Families and Educators*. National Association for School Psychologists, 2004. http://www.nasponline.org/communications/spawareness/portfolioassess.pdf.

Davis, Elizabeth A. "Scaffolding Students' Knowledge Integration: Prompts for Reflection in KIE." *International Journal of Science Education* 22, no. 8 (2000): 819-37. doi:10.1080/095006900412293.

Gielen, Sarah, Filip Dochy, Patrick Onghena, Katrien Stuyven, and Stijin Smeets. "Goals of Peer Assessment and Their Associated Quality Concepts." *Studies in Higher Education* 36, no. 6 (2011): 719-35.

Glazer, Nirit. "Formative Plus Summative Assessment in Large Undergraduate Courses: Why Both?" *International Journal of Teaching and Learning in Higher Education* 26, no. 2 (2014): 276-86.

Grantz, Regina, and Robert Gruber. "How Well Did I Learn What I Learned? The Art of Self-Assessment." *Journal of the Academy of Business Education* 15 (2014): 23-40.

International Association for K–12 Online Learning. "National Standards for Quality Online Courses (v2)," 2011. http://www.inacol.org/wp-content/uploads/2015/02/national-standards-for-quality-online-courses-v2.pdf.

International Society for Technology in Education. "ISTE Standards for Teachers," 2008. http://www.iste.org/standards/iste-standards/standards-for-teachers.

Kinne, Lenore J., Jon F. Hasenbank, and David Coffey. "Are We There Yet? Using Rubrics to Support Progress Toward Proficiency and Model Formative Assessment." *Association of Independent Liberal Arts Colleges for Teacher Education* 11, no. 1 (2014): 109-28.

Lee, Chun-Yi. "The Effects of Online Peer Assessment and Family Entrepreneurial Experience of Students' Business Planning Performance." *The Turkish Online Journal of Educational Technology* 14, no. 1 (2015): 123-32.

Missett, Tracy C., Marguerite M. Brunner, Carolyn M. Callahan, Tonya R. Moon, and Amy Price Azano. "Exploring Teacher Beliefs and Use of Acceleration, Ability Grouping, and Formative Assessment." *Journal for the Education of the Gifted* 37, no. 3 (2014): 245-68.

Orsmond, Paul, Stephen Merry, and Arthur Callaghan. "Implementation of a Formative Assessment Model Incorporating Peer and Self-Assessment." *Innovations in Education and Teaching International* 41, no. 3 (2004): 273-90.

Quality Matters K–12 Program. "Standards from the QM K–12 Secondary Rubric," 2nd ed., 2014. https://www.qualitymatters.org/node/2722/download/StandardsfromtheQMK-12SecondaryRubric,Second%20Edition.pdf.

Rocco, Stevie. "Online Assessment and Evaluation." *New Directions for Adult & Continuing Education* 113 (2007): 75-86.

Schunk, Dale H. 1996. Self-evaluation and self-regulated learning. Paper presented at the Graduate School and University Center, City University of New York, October.

Suen, Hoi K. "Peer Assessment for Massive Open Online Courses (MOOCs)." *International Review of Research in Open and Distance Learning* 15, no. 3 (2014): 312-27.

Thille, Candace, Emily Schneider, Rene F. Kizilcec, Christopher Piech, Sherif A. Halawa, and Daniel K. Greene. "The Future of Data-Enriched Assessment." *Research and Practice in Assessment* 9 (2014): 5-16.

University of Tasmania. "Guidelines for Good Assessment Practice," 2011. http://www.teaching-learning.utas.edu.au/__data/assets/pdf_file/0004/158674/GAG_v16_webversion.pdf.

Western Interstate Commission for Higher Education. "Are Your Online Students Really the Ones Registered for the Course? Student Authentication Requirements for Distance Education Providers." *WICHE Cooperative for Educational Technologies,* 2008. http://wcet.wiche.edu/wcet/docs/publications/Briefing_Paper _Feb_2008.pdf.

Yu, Haishen, and Hongmei Li. "Group-based Formative Assessment: A Way to Make Summative Assessment Effective." *Theory and Practice in Language Studies* 4, no. 4 (2014): 839-44.

CHAPTER 17

Mobile Apps and Technology Integration for Virtual and Hybrid Learning Spaces

Gregory Shepherd

Abstract

Mobile technology offers many different applications to enhance project- and performance-based learning. These tools, free in most cases, transform mobile devices into knowledge-gathering and organizing instruments, allowing K–12 students to create and refine digital products. This chapter discusses how to deploy mobile learning (M-learning) for online learning environments. It also reveals strategies to help K–12 online learners develop 21st century skills, and it documents the student learning process through media production, interactivity, and collaborative problem-solving. Teachers and program administrators are encouraged to experiment with different mobile applications and are shown ways to repurpose such apps creatively for project development and management in the online K–12 environment.

Introduction

In education, we strive to use the technological tools that make communication, collaboration, and research easier. The challenges we face are how to weave the use of these tools with best methodological practices in order to create engaging and meaningful activities. Whether the context is K–12 or higher education, the hybrid classroom, purely online instruction, or mobile learning (M-learning), the primary concern remains the creation of pedagogically sound learning opportunities and strategies to monitor, guide, and measure student learning.

While research suggests that mobile technology has the potential to enhance and improve engagement and learning, teachers have yet to maximize the potential of M-learning tools (Buckner and Kim 2014, p. 101). There are many impediments and concerns that have slowed the integration of these tools into mainstream K–12 curricula. Among them are a lack of familiarity with mobile tools and their applications, professional development that fails to show how pedagogy drives the use of these tools, and the constantly evolving package of mobile apps. Policies limiting the use of mobile tools because of concerns over cyber safety, security, access, and costs of maintaining these rapidly changing technologies also create substantial obstacles to wholesale integration.

In spite of these issues, numerous teachers and researchers extoll the virtues of mobile technologies to enhance learning. Still, pragmatic and systematic explorations of techniques and strategies for repurposing and deploying mobile technology for skills development and deep learning are scarce. Elizabeth Buckner and Paul Kim (2014) note, "Virtually no pedagogical techniques have been designed to utilize numerous mobile phones to support learning" (p. 101). Teachers facing a new and, at times, unfamiliar technology paradigm would benefit by a step-by-step integration process that allows pedagogy to dictate the proper use of M-learning tools. This chapter scripts a number of practices useful for jumpstarting the use of mobile tools in K–12 online learning environments with particular emphasis on fostering creativity and innovation in the curriculum and activity design process. Successful M-learning models are outlined and specific examples of mobile-based activities and projects are offered to illustrate the benefits to learning and strategies for 21st century skills development.

Two models, the Stanford mobile inquiry-based learning environment (SMILE) and a tech-integration teacher education module, call for pedagogy to drive the choice and use of mobile tech tools (Shepherd 2014). The former relies on one specific mobile app designed to support inquiry-based learning, and the latter shows teachers how to repurpose existing apps for targeted skills development. Both of these models encourage teachers to use mobile tools in online settings in order to see and experience how to leverage their functionality.

SMILE and other approaches described in this chapter make use of ubiquitous mobile devices for collaboration and creativity. Content and problem-solving activities are relevant as they can be tailored to local issues and customs, as "Future innovations in educational technology must continue to not only leverage local content and practices, but also to nurture local creativity and entrepreneurship" (Buckner and Kim 2014, p. 116). Gregory Shepherd's (2014) teacher education model calls on teachers to use mobile apps for their intended purpose to become familiar with their functions and begin to visualize their use for specific tasks to enhance learning. Based on steps found in *The Innovator's DNA: Mastering the Five Skills of Disruptive Innovators* (Dyer, Gregersen, and Christensen 2013), future teachers are taught to repurpose apps to assist in the production of digital products that demonstrate learning (Shepherd 2014, p. 55). The benefit of such a process manifests in the development of specific pedagogical skills. By learning to innovate within the parameters of existing mobile tools, teachers need only become arbiters of good apps while creatively deploying them and evaluating how well they support and enrich learning.

Another modality that underlies the use of mobile technology is project-based learning (PBL), defined as a "systematic teaching method that engages students in learning essential knowledge and life-enhancing skills through an extended, student-influenced inquiry process that is structured around complex, authentic questions and carefully designed products and tasks" (Mergendoller et al. 2006, p. 587). Studies of K–12 and higher education environments continue to show that PBL favors long-term retention of knowledge, collaborative problem-solving, and critical media literacy skills more than traditional instructional methods. According to Jennifer Ray Pieratt (2011), the necessary components for setting up PBL opportunities include (1) use of significant content, (2) development of 21st century competencies, (3) in-depth inquiry, (4) focus on driving questions, (5) need to broaden knowledge, (6) voice and choice, (7) critique and revision, and (8) projects published to a public audience.

The step-by-step integration process that follows outlines a series of considerations for blending mobile tools and project and lesson design with online instruction. The following five sections sequence effective strategies for creating and managing tech-integrated learning opportunities using PBL: (1) preparation, (2) pedagogy-driven activity design, (3) instructional methods, (4) 21st century skills and standards alignment, and (5) measurement of skills development and learning.

Preparation

Clearly, preparation is about getting learners ready to accomplish the tasks and solve the problems associated with the project. Research, inquiry, data collection, fieldwork, proficiency with content knowledge, and an increasing ability to understand as well as analyze contexts and problems provide the groundwork. In addition, a thorough orientation to the functions of the mobile tools required is in order. This orientation should include a number of simple exercises using apps so that learners can practice and receive feedback prior to final project production. For example, if content is being delivered through mobile tools, then instructions on its use are paramount. However, simple skills checks during the introductory activities should attempt to confirm students' proficiency. If learners will be expected to produce a video for a final project, for instance, then short assignments immersing them in mobile video capture and editing should grant them the experience necessary to hone their skills.

Since preparation involves initial work with content, analytical skills, and mobile tool proficiency, teachers might consider using two apps—VoiceThread and Subtext—that invite interaction with preparatory digital content. VoiceThread allows users to upload asynchronous commentary around a video, text, or photo, which can be used to deploy interpretive, analytical, and problem-solving tasks that set the stage for project development. Subtext allows teachers to embed comprehension questions, surveys, videos, links, and discussion prompts into reading assignments. Both apps provide teachers the ability to exercise their students' inquiry skills and gain access to valuable content.

Pedagogy-Driven Activity Design

Since pedagogy tends to vary according to discipline, focus should be placed on general principles. However, practitioners are encouraged to align learning tasks with standards, methods, and practices called for by their discipline. In world languages, for example, the American Council for the Teaching of Foreign Languages (ACTFL) refers to a sequence of tasks (interpretive, interpersonal, and presentational) as an integrated performance assessment (IPA) since project/performance steps including preparation, inquiry, collaborative problem-solving, and project delivery call for different types of communication (Adair-Hauck et al. 2006, p. 359).

Listening tasks can enhance learning by combining the use of podcasts or YouTube video content with the mobile app Quizlet to assess understanding. Interactive and collaborative tasks are made easy through Tandem, Skype, and Slack, while presentations are improved through any number of mobile video apps including Touchcast and Haiku Deck. These tools generally offer a free/entry-level version as well as a paid version that offers a wider array of features.

Certainly, language arts and social sciences disciplines rely directly on this sequence of tasks, and the hard sciences follow a similar progression, yet the question of whether mobile tools serve a distinct pedagogical purpose remains central (de la Fuente 2014, p. 273). Summarizing how to maximize the benefits of distance learning, Robert J. Blake (2009) states, "The 'sage on the stage' should give way to the highly effective chat workgroups of three or four that often include a teacher who is always willing to help, prod, and encourage in ways that provide a degree of interactivity unattainable in the crowded traditional classroom" (p. 832). Similarly, placing an emphasis on interaction and teacher feedback, the Online Learning Consortium (OLC) calls for learner/teacher as well as learner/learner interaction (Moore 2005).

So, if interactive tasks, along with interpretive and presentational ones, can be made *highly effective* through mobile tool integration, online students in K–12 environments benefit by using their devices to access content and create digital media. Examples of criteria used to evaluate the potential effectiveness of specific apps fall into three categories: (1) pedagogy, (2) feedback, and (3) flexibility and functionality (Shepherd 2014, p. 51–52). The following questions guide the evaluation of mobile apps.

1. What type of communication or research does the app allow—data collection, primary research, and writing, speaking, reading, or listening?

2. Does it enhance online learning experiences by providing access to authentic contexts or publication to authentic audiences?

3. Does the tool allow for the type of student digital media production that draws from real-world resources and/or shows evidence of learning?

4. Does the app fit well within the context of a larger project/progression and/or does it assist in transitioning students from simple to complex tasks?

5. What targeted skills does the mobile technology develop or support in the course of the project—researching, reporting, collaborating, polling, speaking, writing?

The preceding set of questions allows teachers to measure the utility of technology tools with regard to specific tasks and reflect on pedagogical concerns related to their specific disciplines.

Activities may span a range of topics but are ideally structured to ease students into their use and integration of new technologies. In one example, students were asked to develop an awareness campaign supporting or condemning different political movements in Latin America. They were asked to produce a 2-minute public service announcement and a pamphlet to be used for fund raising purposes. Both digital products were distributed at a mock charity event where they solicited donations with public appeals for monetary support. The design of the activity was sound before technology integration commenced. However, pamphlet production was made easier with Pic Collage and Adobe Slate, videos with Flipagram and Clips were posted on the class website, and donation updates were broadcast live through Google Forms. Online learners posted their materials (pamphlet and video) to WordPress or Google Sites where classmates evaluated strength of arguments and rewarded compelling fundraising campaigns with mock donations tracked in Google Forms over a short period.

Not only were there substantial benefits for learners having engaged in peer assessment and created their own digital artifacts to convince potential donors, but the real-time calculation and graphing of donation tallies allowed the activity to flow more smoothly. In this sense, the soundness of the initial design made tech integration seamless: "The potential benefits of collaborative exchanges, whether set in the classroom or managed online, as always, depend more on sound pedagogical design of the tasks the participants are asked to perform rather than the actual locus of the learning event" (Blake 2009, p. 823).

Instructional Methods

As with pedagogy, methods adapt to disciplinary needs, though, in general, PBL advocates for an open-ended, student-centered, learning-by-doing approach. With regard to M-learning, Agnes Kukulska-Hulme (2009) acknowledges that the "key attributes of mobile learning are identified as the potential for learning to be personalized, situated, authentic, spontaneous and informal" (p. 162). She goes on to note that spontaneous and informal learning is more difficult to script but that, for the most part, M-learning "is an occasion to capture a moment of interest, for example through the action of annotation, with the goal of continuing to build on that interest in another place, at a later date" (p. 162).

Peggy A. Ertmer and Krista D. Simons (2005) remind us, "Teachers will need new tools or strategies that can support them as they adopt new roles, facilitate student inquiry, provide ongoing formative feedback, and implement new types of classroom management strategies" (p. 322). All of these methods emphasize interaction between teachers and other learners, accessing authentic content and learner accountability through project management.

Whether activities and projects address natural sciences, language arts, social sciences, or mathematics, the relationship between methods and technology is solidified in conversations about learner engagement and meaningful learning opportunities. "This means that the role of technology also needs to change from merely providing information access to providing opportunities for students to engage in inquiry practices that result in the production of artifacts that communicate their ideas and can be shared with an audience beyond the classroom" (King et al. 2014, p. 175).

If mobile tools and M-learning make it easier to communicate, collaborate, produce, and share these artifacts, then our students become active and engaged participants in their own learning process: "Teachers should redirect their energies away from notions of control toward learning objectives that ensure that the tasks and tools will motivate students to become active participants" (Blake 2013, p. 134). Gordon Bateson and Paul Daniels (2012) add that "[o]nce a successful methodology for a technology has been established, it encourages others to experiment and get involved. In this way, the grassroots introduction of technology may well prove more effective in the long term" (p. 145). Heather Toomey Zimmerman and Susan M. Land (2014) illustrate this mindset in their guidelines for facilitating informal and place-based learning: "(1) facilitate participation in disciplinary conversations and practices with personally relevant places, (2) amplify observations to see the disciplinary aspects of a place, and (3) extend experience through exploring new perspectives, representations, conversations or knowledge artifacts" (p. 82). The use of mobile apps and tools allows online K–12 teachers to construct learning experiences addressing all three of these guidelines in a dynamic and engaging manner.

M-learning and E-learning: A Synergistic Opportunity

Mobile devices can go far beyond the role of being a conduit for such standard or administrative tasks as reviewing content in learning management systems (LMSs), checking grades, or practicing drills prescribed by a teacher. Just about all the major LMSs offer access to online courses via mobile applications. In emerging nations, mobile devices are providing relatively low-cost entry into a vast realm of new resources and functionality. In a report on the use of mobile technology in emerging nations, the Pew Research Center (2014) reports cell phones are "almost omnipresent" (p. 1). However, when employed appropriately in conjunction with face-to-face (f2f), blended, or fully online instruction, these devices have the potential to go far beyond mere content delivery or rote administrative tasks.

Some fully online programs have started putting mobile devices in the hands of their online students. The mindset behind such actions may emerge from the simple intent to provide a device through which students can access online course content and online textbooks. However, great strides are to be had through this universal provision of mobile devices because the infrastructure is then in place to support teaching and learning that involves exciting and transformative opportunities for student research, creativity, and collaboration. The "No Bugs Were Harmed" example that follows illustrates strategic and complementary uses of M-learning and E-learning.

No Bugs Were Harmed

Liz Kolb is a teacher known for her innovative approaches to implementing M-learning at the K–12 level. She uses mobile devices to enrich teaching and learning experiences by having students use those devices in interviews, virtual tours, field work, and many other investigative activities (Kolb 2011). In one example, students engaging in a science lesson on ecosystems were asked to take photos of natural artifacts in the field, such as different kinds of plants or insects. Once those images or digital artifacts were captured and curated, it then became possible for her budding student/entomologists to upload and describe the best digital specimens in a collaborative wiki such as a virtual science lab or online zoo. As mobile apps and devices become available to entire classrooms of online students, the M-learning infrastructure is then in place to support new opportunities for online teaching and learning.

21st Century Skills and Standards Alignment

Mobile tool integration following the models previously described renders broad support to both 21st century skills and core content standards.

Information, media, and technology skills come into play during the research, writing, and presentation phases of any task. But when projects are live talk shows, video news programs, virtual museums, public service announcements, business proposals, how-to videos, marketing campaigns, and environmental impact reports, the use of mobile technologies not only enhance the learning process through doing, but also increase engagement. Learners create easily-publishable artifacts of learning while fostering 21st century project-management and tech skills. Their digital projects contribute to the same worldwide fabric from which they draw. Perhaps the greatest outcome of mobile tech integration in PBL is that these 21st century tasks and productions call for creativity, collaboration, flexibility, and technical skills—ones necessary for professionals and lifelong learners in our now digital world.

Another activity, a video newscast developing political, economic, social, and cultural content on specific countries through in-field interviews, editorials, and story reporting demonstrates broad standards coverage. Information and communications technology (ICT) and media literacy skills receive substantial attention in the production of the video. Certainly, the interdisciplinary themes of global awareness and literacy in financial, economic, civic, health, and environmental issues are central. Even life and career skills such as social, cross-cultural, and leadership proficiencies are woven throughout this project. Accountability for specific tasks has been directly addressed by adding a requirement that students add credits to the end of their videos, noting who was responsible for direction, research, editing, camerawork, writing, and graphics. Since students are more deeply engaged the sociopolitical realities and experienced the dynamic nature of media as both its consumers and its producers, they become participants rather than spectators. Using mobile devices to gather data, capture and edit video products, and conduct interviews in the field further motivates autonomous learning while engaging students in ICT skills development.

This video newscast activity can be retooled to accommodate nearly any project, grade-level, or discipline where the topic can be divided into segments. For example, science projects might examine the different aspects of a certain geography such as soil composition, vegetation, wildlife, or rainfall using short video segments. Likewise, social studies courses can evaluate the theory, practices, and policies of a given social problem. Using distributed approaches by which each student or student group contributes an element of content, online students using mobile devices can create and contribute, each taking an active role in their own learning and the learning of others.

Measurement of Skills Development and Learning

When it comes to student performance, what constitutes evidence of learning? The rubric for the newscast project previously mentioned frontloads the criteria associated with critical thinking and argument formation in order to emphasize the importance of using the video segments to make and support particular stances. Examining student analysis of the different contexts and the balance between description and argumentation can show to what extent the skills of persuasion and inquiry are exercised. Looking at the organization of the story tells us how well learners structure their segments, while the criteria evaluating the interviews show us how students use questions to extract supportive data. Overall, skills development in all of the following categories are expected: (1) critical inquiry in the interviews; (2) use of research, visuals, and interviews as supportive evidence; (3) organized video production; and (4) the informed interpretation of cultural texts.

Rubric generators in most LMSs (such as Canvas) give teachers the ability to publish learning markers and manage their assessment of student work where learners can follow their skills development using associated LMS mobile applications. The criteria provide students concrete examples of what constitutes critical thinking, referencing specific kinds of discourse including analysis, interpretation, comparison, synthesis, and evaluation. Applying this rubric shows where there is evidence of learning, measuring the depth of skills development and specifying where students can improve. Also, and perhaps most importantly, this is where the teacher can evaluate the strengths and weaknesses of the different steps of the project. For example, if the mobile tool does not help develop the skills expected, another may be considered. Likewise, if student text analysis leans towards the retelling of content rather than actual analysis, pedagogical adjustments can be made earlier in the activity sequence.

Lastly, the digital products and performances captured and created by mobile tools, such as video reports, surveys, podcasts, and websites can be vastly more efficient to share with stakeholders than scraps of paper and other traditional assessments. When projects are published to secure venues, students can examine their performances postevaluation to reflect on skills demonstrated, gaining a more precise vision of the relationship between their work and the assessment. Parents and administrators can perhaps better see evidence of learning along with skills and knowledge development. By examining online and mobile-based projects, curriculum planners can also more readily assess the value of tech integration and specific pedagogical decisions.

Tasks and Apps

As previously discussed, many examples of successful mobile tool integration show ways of thinking that foster innovative uses for free and ubiquitous applications for all types of learning contexts. Table 17.1 offers suggestions for different categories of tasks since mobile tool integration in curriculum design works best when learning tasks determine what application can enhance learning.

Table 17.1   Learning Tasks and Their Associated Mobile Applications

Learning Tasks	Mobile Applications
Collaboration and Project Management:	Wikis, Google Sites, Google Docs, Google Forms, Slack, and Trello
Video Capture, Editing, and Animation:	Videoshop, Fly, Explain Everything, Touchcast, Flipagram, Magisto, VideoCollage, Clips, Animoto, and YouTube Capture
Podcasting:	Garageband, Adobe Voice, and VoiceMemo
Reading for Comprehension:	Subtext and Quizlet
Synchronous Chat:	WeChat, TodaysMeet, Tandem, and Skype
Augmented Reality:	Aurasma, QR Code Readers and Creators, Sky Safari, and Google Earth
Virtual Reality:	Google Cardboard
Place-Based Learning:	LeafSnap, Woices, and Aris Games
Social Media:	Edmodo, Twitter, Facebook, Moodle, and Voicethread
Learning Management System:	Canvas, Google Classroom, Fidelis, and Coursmos,
Game-Based Knowledge and Skills:	QuizUp, TriviaCrack, Quizlet, Elevate, Google Forms, Aris Games, Math Evolve, and iBiome-Wetland
Polling:	SurveyMonkey, Google Forms, and Loop
Presentations:	PowerPoint, Haiku Deck, and Prezi
Content Knowledge:	Khan Academy, Earth Viewer, Sky Safari, Wikipedia, iTunes University, TED, YouTube, Fotopedia UNESCO Heritage, National Parks by National Geographic, Mathref, Elevated Math, Biome Series, and Napoleon Bone Apart

Several activities and projects that have successfully integrated mobile tools include digital storytelling through video editing or animation, fieldwork documentation and report generation, how-to videos, collaborative wiki building, ARIS games Quests, virtual museums, and mock events, including elections, trials, and awareness campaigns.

The creation of a virtual museum involves several steps. The interpretive phase places students into research groups requiring them to curate two or three objects from a given collection before compiling and organizing their data in a group wiki (Google Sites or Wikispaces). Teachers are able to call for different levels of exploration in the student wikis (description, comparison, analysis, function, significance, etc.) in the publication of any number of student-created media artifacts. After setting up images in online blog sites, Aurasma is another app that can be used to embellish the exhibits as it allows users to overlay student-produced videos as well as evaluate and analyze the objects in the collection. Student-produced surveys or quizzes using Quizlet, SurveyMonkey, or Google Forms can be deployed as follow-up activities to assess the quality of the wikis, or to assess why certain objects are popular and what meaningful interpretations emerge from the experience of interacting with virtual museum objects.

Consider asking students to engage in a mock political election. Current events or historical moments provide the context. Students are tasked with the challenge of (1) researching the issues facing candidates, (2) developing a campaign platform, (3) producing videos outlining the key components of the candidates' mission statement, (4) engaging in real-time debates, (5) carrying out the election with Google Forms, and finally (6) debriefing and evaluating the hows and whys of the results. All tasks in this project can be carried out through mobile devices, including the live debate administered with Google+ Hangouts. As with other activities, students can share a permanent presentation or exhibit using any combination of wikis, blogs, or other sites involving shared student authorship. The option of performing opinion polls at the different stages of the mock election is not only made easier through SurveyMonkey or Loop, but also increases interactivity and engagement with content.

Conclusion

The primary factor determining successful integration of mobile technology for all learning contexts is the ability of teachers to know and repurpose applications for specific tasks and evaluate their effectiveness in terms of disciplinary pedagogies and national standards:

> Teachers must renew their methodological training and be able to guide students toward methodologies that promote autonomous interaction and collaborative work. . . . Learning can be restructured and adapted from the principle of ubiquity, but for this challenge, institutions need to orientate methodologies toward the use of new mobile devises, from the possibilities offered primarily through open educational resources (OERs) distributed on wikis, blogs, mash-ups, podcasts, social software, virtual worlds, personal learning environments (PLEs), massive open online courses (MOOCs), and other emerging online practices. (Sevillano-García and Vázquez-Cano 2015, p. 107)

Along those same lines:

> As recently as 2007, a comprehensive review of mobile assisted language learning by Agnes Kukukska-Hulme and Lesley Shield found that for the most part uses of mobile devices were pedestrian, uncreative, and repetitive and did not take advantage of the mobility, peer connectivity, or advanced communication features of mobile devices. Most activities were teacher-led and scheduled, not leveraging the anytime, anyplace mobile environment. Oral interactions and learner collaboration were infrequently used. The problem is less one of hardware/software shortcomings and more in developers' conceptualization of how language learning could be enhanced in new, innovative ways with the assistance of mobile devices. (Godwin-Jones 2011, p. 7)

Teachers ought to invest thought and action by experimenting with solutions that leverage existing apps and their ability to gather data, create digital artifacts, and manage projects through file sharing and collaborative problem-solving in virtual spaces. The skill of repurposing apps for specific tasks and sequencing these tasks into larger projects becomes paramount for online and hybrid classrooms, not to mention f2f contexts. Finally, concrete actions that could help accelerate the adoption of M-learning methods in all classroom contexts would involve (1) celebrating and documenting models of excellent M-learning, (2) designing and implementing more academic courses dedicated to sound M-learning methods including teacher education offerings, and (3) professional development that goes beyond how to use mobile applications into hands-on explorations of how pedagogies across the disciplines can leverage M-learning for deeper and more authentic learning projects.

References

Adair-Hauck, B., E. W. Glisan, K. Koda, E. Swender, and P. Sandrock. "The Integrated Performance Assessment (IPA): Connecting Assessment to Instruction and Learning." *Foreign Language Annals* 39, no. 3 (2006): 359-82.

Bateson, Gordon, and Paul Daniels. "Diversity in Technologies." *Computer-Assisted Language Learning: Diversity in Research and Practice* (2012): 127-46.

Blake, Robert J. *Brave New Digital Classroom: Technology and Foreign Language Learning.* Washington, DC: Georgetown University Press, 2013.

—. "The Use of Technology for Second Language Distance Learning." *The Modern Language Journal* 93, no. s1 (2009): 822-35.

Buckner, Elizabeth, and Paul Kim. "Integrating Technology and Pedagogy for Inquiry-Based Learning: The Stanford Mobile Inquiry-Based Learning Environment (SMILE)." *Prospects* 44, no. 1 (2014): 99-118.

Dyer, Jeff, Hal Gregersen, and Clayton Christensen. *The Innovator's DNA: Mastering the Five Skills of Disruptive Innovators.* Boston: Harvard Business Press, 2013.

Ertmer, Peggy A., and Krista D. Simons. "Jumping the PBL Implementation Hurdle: Supporting the Efforts of K–12 Teachers." *Interdisciplinary Journal of Problem-Based Learning* 1, no. 1 (2006): 40-54.

—. "Scaffolding Teachers' Efforts to Implement Problem-Based Learning." *International Journal of Learning* 12, no. 4 (2005): 319-28.

de la Fuente, María José. "Learners' Attention to Input During Focus on Form Listening Tasks: The Role of Mobile Technology in the Second Language Classroom." *Computer Assisted Language Learning* 27, no. 3 (2014): 261-76.

Godwin-Jones, Robert. "Emerging Technologies: Mobile Apps for Language Learning." *Language Learning & Technology* 15, no. 2 (2011): 2-11.

King, LaGarrett J., Christina Gardner-McCune, Penelope Vargas, and Yerika Jimenez. "Re-discovering and Re-creating African American Historical Accounts Through Mobile Apps: The Role of Mobile Technology in History Education." *The Journal of Social Studies Research* 38, no. 3 (2014): 173-88.

Kolb, Liz. *Cell Phones in the Classroom: A Practical Guide for Educators.* Eugene, OR: International Society for Technology in Education, 2011.

Kukulska-Hulme, Agnes. "Will Mobile Learning Change Language Learning?" *ReCALL* 21, no. 02 (2009): 157-65.

Mergendoller, John R., Thom Markham, Jason Ravitz, and John Larmer. "Pervasive Management of Project Based Learning: Teachers as Guides and Facilitators."

In *Handbook of Classroom Management: Research, Practice, and Contemporary Issues*, ed. Carolyn M. Evertson and Carol S. Weinstein, 583-618. Mahwah, NJ: Erlbaum, 2006.

Moore, Janet C. "The Sloan Consortium Quality Framework and the Five Pillars." *The Sloan Consortium,* 2005. ww2.olc.edu/~cdelong/dl401/qualityframework.pdf.

Pew Research Center. "Emerging Nations Embrace Internet, Mobile Technology: Cell Phones Nearly Ubiquitious in Many Countries." *Global Attitudes and Trends*, 2014. http://www.pewglobal.org/2014/02/13/emerging-nations-embrace -internet-mobile-technology/.

Pieratt, Jennifer Ray. 2011. Teacher-student relationships in project based learning: A case study of High Tech Middle North County. PhD diss., Claremont Graduate University, Claremont, CA. In CGU Theses & Dissertations, Paper 13. http:// scholarship.claremont.edu/cgu_etd/13.

Sevillano-García, Ma Luisa, and Esteban Vázquez-Cano. "The Impact of Digital Mobile Devices in Higher Education." *Journal of Educational Technology & Society* 18, no. 1 (2015): 106-18.

Shepherd, Gregory. "Teaching Pre-Service Teachers to Repurpose and Innovate Using Online and Mobile Technology Applications." *Promoting Global Literacy Skills through Technology-Infused Teaching and Learning* (2014): 46-62.

Zimmerman, Heather Toomey, and Susan M. Land. "Facilitating Place-Based Learning in Outdoor Informal Environments With Mobile Computers." *TechTrends* 58, no. 1 (2014): 77-83.

Appendix: Abbreviations

AAC	augmentative and alternative communication
AACTE	American Association of Colleges for Teacher Education
ACM	Association for Computing Machinery
ACTFL	American Council for the Teaching of Foreign Languages
ADA	Americans with Disabilities Act
ADE	Apple distinguished educator
AEM	accessible educational materials
AERA	American Educational Research Association
AP	advanced placement
ASCD	Association for Supervision and Curriculum Development
AT	assistive technology
CAP	content acquisition podcast
CAP-S	content acquisition podcasts for students
CAP-T	content acquisition podcasts for teachers
CAST	Center for Applied Special Technology
CCSS	common core state standards
CDC	Centers for Disease Control and Prevention
CEC	Council for Exceptional Children
CoI	community of inquiry
COLSD	Center on Online Learning and Students with Disabilities
CoSN	Consortium for School Networking
CTML	cognitive theory of multimedia learning
CTV	course tour video
DESI	Dalton Education Services International
DOL	daily oral language
EBP	evidence-based practice
ESL	English as a second language
f2f	face-to-face
FERPA	Family Educational Rights and Privacy Act
FLVS	Florida Virtual School
GCT	Google certified teacher
HPL	how people learn
IASE	International Association for Special Education

ICT	information and communications technology
IDEA	Individuals with Disabilities Education Improvement Act
IEP	individualized education program
ILA	International Literacy Association
iNACOL	International Association for K–12 Online Learning
IPA	integrated performance assessment
ISTE	International Society for Technology in Education
ITP	individual transition plan
LEA	local education agency
LMS	learning management system
LO	learning object
LRE	least restrictive environment
LTI	Learning Tools Interoperability
M-learning	mobile learning
MOOC	massive open online course
NACOL	North American Council for Online Learning
NAGC	National Association for Gifted Children
NCLD	National Center for Learning Disabilities
NCTQ	National Council on Teacher Quality
NEA	National Education Association
NGSS	next generation science standards
NIMAS	National Instructional Materials Accessibility Standard
NLA	Nevada Learning Academy
NLS	National Library Service for the Blind and Physically Handicapped
NSC	Nevada State College
OCR	optical character recognition
ODU	Old Dominion University
OER	open educational resource
OLC	Online Learning Consortium
OSEP	Office of Special Education Programs
P21	partnership for 21st century skills
PBL	project-based learning
PCK	pedagogical content knowledge
PECS	picture exchange communication systems
PI	practical inquiry
PLE	personal learning environment
PSEO	postsecondary enrollment options
QM	Quality Matters
QR	quick response
RSS	really simple syndication
SAMR	substitution, augmentation, modification, and redefinition

SDE	Staff Development for Educators
SETT	student, environment, task and tools
SGD	speech generation device
SIG	special interest group
SIGAdmin	special interest group for administrators
SIOP	sheltered instruction observation protocol
SLD	specific learning disability
SMILE	Stanford mobile inquiry-based learning environment
SOOC	small-short-supported-social open online course
TCK	technological content knowledge
TK	technology knowledge
TPACK	technological, pedagogical content knowledge
TPK	technological pedagogical knowledge
UD	universal design
UDL	universal design for learning
UDL-IRN	Universal Design for Learning Implementation and Research Network
USF	University of San Francisco
VOCA	voice output communication aids

About the Editors

Sarah Bryans-Bongey, EdD is an assistant professor of education at Nevada State College (NSC). She received her doctorate in teaching and learning from the University of Minnesota. She also holds a master's degree in educational media and technology and undergraduate degrees in English and film studies from The College of St. Scholastica and Syracuse University, respectively. She is a licensed 7–12 English language arts teacher and has taught English classes to 10th and 11th grade high school students in NSC's TRIO Upward Bound program. She is a certified K–12 library media specialist and was a teacher-librarian in Minnesota public schools. She also worked for 10 years at The College of St. Scholastica in Duluth, Minnesota, where she was academic technology coordinator and taught online graduate courses relating to research, instructional design, and educational technology.

Dr. Bryans-Bongey's research interests include online and M-learning, educational technology integration, student engagement, and schools for the future. Her research on universal design for learning (UDL) and teaching with technology has led to various publications and presentations, including a chapter in the book, *Dancing With Digital Natives: Staying in Step With the Generation That's Transforming the Way Business is Done.*

Kevin J. Graziano, EdD is a professor of Education at Nevada State College (NSC). He received his doctorate in international and multicultural education with a minor in educational technology from the University of San Francisco. His teaching and research interests include teacher education, educational technology, and teaching English as a second language. Dr. Graziano received the 2012 Nevada System of Higher Education Board of Regents' Teaching Award, the 2006 Nevada State College iTeach Teaching Excellence Award, the 2006 City of Henderson and Henderson Chamber of Commerce Outstanding Teaching Award, and the 2005 American Education Research Association (AERA) Scholar-Activist Award.

Dr. Graziano taught English as a second language at Charles University in Prague, Czech Republic and completed his master's thesis and doctoral dissertation in South Africa. He has published numerous journal articles on teacher education and continues to present at national and international education conferences.

In 2012, Dr. Graziano completed two international teacher-training fellowships and later received a Fulbright Specialist grant to Sakhnin College in Sakhnin, Israel. In all three projects, he trained faculty and students on educational technology and photovoice, the use of documentary photography and storytelling. He is former chair of the Innovation and Technology Committee for the American Association of Colleges for Teacher Education (AACTE) and is the current co-chair of the Mobile Learning Special Interest Group for the Society for Information Technology and Teacher Education (SITE).

About the Contributors

Kat D. Alves is a doctoral student in the Curry School of Education at the University of Virginia. Before beginning her doctoral program, Ms. Alves spent 7 years as an elementary school special education teacher in the Charlottesville area. Ms. Alves has a master's degree in special education and a bachelor's degree in psychology, both from the University of Virginia. Ms. Alves's research interests include improving literacy outcomes for students with high incidence disabilities. Specifically, she is interested in reading comprehension and vocabulary at the upper elementary and middle school levels. Ms. Alves's primary program of research at the University of Virginia focuses on training preservice and in-service teachers to use evidence-based practice (EBP) for vocabulary and reading comprehension.

James D. Basham, PhD is an Associate Professor in the Department of Special Education at the University of Kansas. He earned his doctorate at the University of Illinois Urbana-Champaign. Dr. Basham's research foci include the implementation of universal design for learning (UDL), learner-centered design, innovation, and technology as it relates to cognition, learning, and behavior. Individually and as part of a team, he has been awarded more than $12 million in research funding. Currently, he is a co–principal investigator at the Center on Online Learning and Students with Disabilities (COLSD). Dr. Basham has consulted several school districts, universities, state agencies, foundations, and corporate entities regarding educational technological innovation. Finally, Dr. Basham is the co-founder and executive director of the Universal Design for Learning Implementation and Research Network (UDL-IRN), an organization that promotes research into UDL practices across the range of educational settings.

Richard Allen Carter Jr. is a doctoral student in the Department of Special Education at the University of Kansas. Prior to initiating his doctoral work, Mr. Carter worked with learners with disabilities in elementary school settings in Kansas and his home state of North Carolina. His current research focuses on the implementation of self-regulation practices for students with disabilities in both fully online and blended learning environments. He has also conducted work that looks at disability accommodation and individualized education program (IEP) development and implementation in online schools. In addition, Mr. Carter assists with studies that examine a broad range of effects of online instruction for students with disabilities for the Center on Online Learning and Students with Disabilities (COLSD). He is currently part of a research team that is implementing technology-enabled personalization for students with disabilities in public elementary schools.

Diane Carver, PhD is the director of career and college readiness for the Bethel School District in western Washington. She previously taught business education at the high school and postsecondary levels and served as the state supervisor for business and marketing education in the Office of Superintendent of Public Instruction for the state of Washington. She has worked extensively with career and technical educators providing professional development in curriculum integration, instructional techniques, and student engagement strategies. Dr. Carver has published articles in journals such as *Business Education Forum*, *Techniques*, and *the International Review of Research in Open and Distributed Learning*. Her research interests include career and technical education, online learning, and alternative learning experiences.

Lesley Casarez, PhD is an assistant professor in the Department of Curriculum and Instruction at Angelo State University and also manages the online Master of Education in Guidance and Counseling program. She earned her doctorate in educational psychology from Texas Tech University, a master of education in counseling from Sul Ross State University, a Master of Education in elementary education from Texas State University, and a bachelor of journalism from the University of Texas at Austin. She has numerous professional presentations in online learning and distance education.

Elizabeth Dalton, PhD is adjunct professor at the University of Rhode Island, Communication Disorders Dept., senior consultant for Dalton Education Services International (DESI), and director emeritus of development and research for TechACCESS of Rhode Island. She holds a PhD in Education from University of Rhode Island and was postdoctoral fellow in universal design for learning (UDL) leadership at Boston College and the Center for Applied Special Technology (CAST), Inc. Dr. Dalton has spent many years teaching in K–12 special education as well as teaching teachers at the Community College of Rhode Island and Rhode Island College. She consults in areas of curriculum and program development, assessment, diversity, and technology implementation, including ALL ACCESS in the Libraries, a recent IMLS project allaccessri.org/. Dr. Dalton presents on UDL and technology nationally and internationally, is past president of the Inclusive Learning Network of the International Society for Technology in Education (ISTE), and currently serves as co-editor for the *Journal of the International Association for Special Education* (IASE).

Lori Feher, MS earned her MS in Education and BA in Physical Education and Health from the University of Nevada, Las Vegas. Ms. Feher has worked as a teacher, learning strategist, coordinator of student teaching, and curriculum developer over the past 30 years. Ms. Feher spends a great deal of time researching information to keep current in what she is teaching and is familiar with the best techniques for presenting information and engaging audiences. Ms. Feher has always believed that the key to happiness and success in life is rooted in mental, physical, social, and intellectual well-being. Her personal well-being is strengthened by spending time with her family and friends, exercising, eating right, acquiring knowledge, and devoting time each day to being grateful.

Xavier Gomez, MEd has been an instructional designer for over 10 years. Though he dabbled in corporate training, he has worked in higher education for the majority of his career. He was a member of the core group responsible for expanding instructional design for online delivery at University of California Berkeley Extension, the group that now functions as Berkeley Resource Center for Online Education. At the University of San Francisco (USF), he was chosen by the director of online education as the first instructional designer to help build an instructional design team and to establish a culture of online education at USF. Now as senior instructional designer, he provides guidance to the instructional design team in matters of pedagogy, technology, and best practices.

Kendra Grant, MET is an educational consultant working with a variety of companies and institutions on the design and delivery of eLearning, as well as product and business development. Prior to this, she was co-founder and chief education officer of a professional learning company delivering large-scale technology implementation across North America. Prior to that, Ms. Grant was a teacher, district SpEd coordinator and assistive technology (AT) specialist in a large school district. Her ongoing interest in universal design for learning (UDL) began as a teacher in 2004 when she integrated UDL principles and technology into her library-media program. Ms. Grant recently completed her masters of educational technology at the University of British Columbia with a focus on professional learning, eLearning (K–20), and the application of UDL to both. Ms. Grant is also an EdTech start-up advisor at the MaRS Discovery District in Toronto and at the Genesis Centre in Newfoundland, Canada. She is the president (2015–2016) of the Inclusive Learning Network of the International Society for Technology in Education (ISTE) and recently codesigned (with her two esteemed writing partners) a small-short-supported-social open online course (SOOC) on UDL and Apps.

Michael J. Kennedy, PhD is an assistant professor of Special Education at the University of Virginia's Curry School of Education. Dr. Kennedy's research interests include the use of multimedia to support teaching and learning for preservice and in-service teachers as well as students with disabilities enrolled in content area courses.

Jacqueline Knight, MA received her bachelor's degree from the University of California, Santa Cruz. After living abroad, she returned to the United States to work on her master's degree and Education Specialist Teaching Credential at Pacific Oaks College. In 2011, Ms. Knight received a postgraduate Assistive Technology Applications Certificate from Cal State Northridge's Center on Disabilities. Currently, Ms. Knight is an assistive technology (AT) specialist and individualized education program (IEP) coordinator for a small school dedicated to students with learning differences. Additionally, she teaches as an adjunct faculty member at a liberal arts college, specifically with undergraduate and graduate level students working on their teaching credentials. She has presented at a variety of special education conferences and co-authored a recent article in *Preventing School Failure: Alternative Education for Children and Youth.*

Michael Kosloski, PhD is an assistant professor at Old Dominion University (ODU) in the Department of STEM Education and Professional

Studies. Dr. Kosloski holds a PhD in education with an emphasis in career in technical education, leads the career and technical education teacher preparation program at ODU, and has prepared numerous high school teachers throughout his 15 years in teacher preparation. As a former Virginia DECA state advisor, he also works closely with career and technical education teachers throughout the state. He developed the first internet marketing course for the State of Virginia's public schools along with similar courses at ODU. He has numerous publications, including a textbook entitled *Retailing and E-tailing* that focuses on how businesses utilize the web in industry. His research interests include career and technical education curriculum and technology, online learning, student organizations, and teacher recruitment and retention.

Kim Livengood, PhD is an associate professor in the Department of Curriculum and Instruction at Angelo State University. She earned her doctorate in curriculum and instruction with an emphasis on multicultural education from Texas A&M University, a master of science in secondary education from Texas A&M-Corpus Christi, and a bachelor of science in chemistry from Texas Tech University. She developed and now manages the online MA program in curriculum & instruction. She was honored with the 2011 Texas Tech University System Chancellor's Award for Excellence in Teaching, and her online course has earned the Blackboard Exemplary Course Award for 2014. Additionally, she earned an Advanced Online Teaching Certificate through the Online Learning Consortium.

Andrew Miller, MAT is a former teacher and currently an educational consultant. He has taught in traditional secondary schools as well as innovative project-based learning (PBL) schools. He has implemented PBL in online and blended learning environments in the courses of English, social studies, computer literacy, and game design. Mr. Miller has presented his work and ideas at many conferences including the International Association for K–12 Online Learning (iNACOL) Virtual School Symposium, the Association for Supervision and Curriculum Development's (ASCD) conference, the International Society for Technology in Education (ISTE's) conference, and the Internal Literacy Association's (formerly IRA) conference. He is affiliated with the Buck Institute for Education, a nonprofit with a focus on PBL, and with ASCD, which publishes work and provides professional development to educators around the world. He was worked with teachers throughout the United States, Canada, Australia, Mexico, China, India, and the Dominican

Republic. Mr. Miller is a regular writer for Edutopia and ASCD, and he is also the author of the book *Freedom to Fail,* published with ASCD.

Rolin Moe, EdD is an assistant professor and the director of educational technology and media at Seattle Pacific University. His research interests focus on the relationships between theory, media, and society. In addition to practical work on professional development initiatives, Dr. Moe currently researches the sociocultural impact of EdTech phenomena such as massive open online courses (MOOCs) and critical issues in how technology is defined and appropriated in educational contexts (such as open education). Dr. Moe consults with formal, nonformal, and informal learning organizations to develop platforms and strategies for engagement and interaction. He is a member of the Online Learning Consortium (OLC), the American Association of Museums, and the Society for Cinematic Studies. Dr. Moe enjoys travel, reading, hiking, and sports.

Steven C. Moskowitz, EdD has more than 30 years of experience in education as a teacher, teacher trainer, and assistant superintendent. He serves as an adjunct professor at several colleges and higher education institutions, teaching courses in instructional design and online pedagogy. He completed his doctorate degree in educational administration, researching how instructors transition from traditional instructional environments to online environments. He has published in numerous national technology publications and has presented at many technology conferences. He was also a semi-finalist for Technology and Learning's Tech Leader of the Year Program and has served as the vice president of the International Society for Technology in Education (ISTE's) special interest group (SIG) for administrators (SIGAdmin).

Luis Pérez, PhD is an inclusive learning consultant based in St. Petersburg, Florida. He has more than a decade of experience working with educators to help them integrate technology in ways that empower all learners, including his work as project manager of the Tech Ease for All collection of assistive technology and web accessibility resources for teachers developed at the Florida Center for Instructional Technology (FCIT). Dr. Pérez holds a doctorate in special education and a master's degree in instructional technology from the University of South Florida, and he is the author of *Mobile Learning for All: Supporting Accessibility with the iPad,* from Corwin Press. Dr. Pérez was selected as an Apple distinguished educator (ADE) in 2009, as a Google in Education Certified Innovator (formerly Google certified teacher) in 2014, and currently serves as the professional learning chair of the Inclusive Learning Network of the International Society for Technology in Education (ISTE).

Linda Polin, PhD is the Davidson Professor of education and technology in the Education Division of the Graduate School of Education and Psychology. Currently, she teaches courses in innovation and change, qualitative research methods, knowledge creation and collaboration, and the imagining futures capstone course. In 2011, she received the Howard White Teaching Award. Her research interests focus on learning and knowledge sharing in networked formal and informal communities, currently focusing on massively multiplayer online game players and large hobby communities. She is also working with the development and measurement of *computational thinking* in noncompsci students through Arduino/Lilypad construction and in the Minecraft virtual world. She is a member of the Association for Computing Machinery (ACM) and faculty sponsor of the Pepperdine GSEP student chapter of ACM. Dr. Polin is a member of the American Educational Research Association (AERA), Division C Learning and Instruction, and G, Social Context of Education. She enjoys gardening, networked gaming, constructing with Legos and Arduino, and all things Studio Ghibli.

Mary Frances Rice is a doctoral student in the Department of Curriculum and Teaching at the University of Kansas. Prior to initiating her doctoral work, Ms. Rice taught language arts, reading support, and English as a second language (ESL) at the secondary level. She has also taught ESL endorsement courses at Brigham Young University and manages the yearly preparation of new adjuncts and professional developers for these ESL endorsement courses. Her current research focuses on how teachers intersect their personal histories and professional identities as they take up technologically-based instructional practices. Her 2011 book, *Adolescent Boys' Literate Identity* (Emerald Press) was named Publication of the Year in the Narrative SIG of the American Educational Association. She is also the editor of *Exploring Pedagogies for Diverse Learners Online* (Emerald Press), which was published in 2015.

Wendy J. Rodgers is a doctoral student at the University of Virginia pursuing a PhD in special education. Prior to beginning her program at University of Virginia, Ms. Rodgers taught high school special education for

11 years. Her research interests include secondary coteaching and effective instructional practices for students with high-incidence disabilities.

John Elwood Romig is a doctoral student in the Curry School of Education at the University of Virginia pursuing a PhD in special education. Before beginning his doctoral program, Mr. Romig taught for three years as a special education teacher in Spartanburg, South Carolina. Mr. Romig has a master's degree and bachelor's degree in special education. His research interests include writing instruction for struggling writers, writing assessment, teacher preparation and development, and teacher observation. His primary research projects at University of Virginia include using technology to supplement classroom instruction for both K–12 students and preservice teachers along with developing innovative ways to observe classroom teachers.

Christopher Rozitis, PhD holds a doctorate in instructional design for online learning from Capella University and has been a teacher at the high school level with the Vancouver Board of Education for the past 20 years. He transferred to the virtual world of education 10 years ago and currently teaches high school sciences and computer classes online at the Vancouver Learning Network. An Apple distinguished educator, Adobe campus leader, CK12 champion, and a PBWiki certified educator, Dr. Rozitis has a passion for teaching and he seeks to find what motivates students and incorporate that into their course work.

Gregory Shepherd, PhD earned his doctorate from Georgetown University and teaches instructional methodologies, implementation of pedagogy-driven technologies, Latin American literature, and Spanish language at Kean University. Dr. Shepherd has taught educators at the university level for 20 years in several countries—the United States, Ecuador, Puerto Rico, and Cuba. He has designed and directed English as a second language (ESL) and Spanish language immersion programs and workshops globally—most recently leading and participating in teacher education initiatives for instructors from China, South Korea, and Spain. In addition, he researches and deploys disruptive pedagogies in areas as diverse as mobile technology, hybrid and online learning environments, and gaming. His current research focuses on technology integration in teacher education models, the use of gaming and mobile applications in language learning, and the construction of hybrid identities in Latin America. He recently received the Presidential Award for Excellence in Teaching at Kean University.

Chery Takkunen-Lucarelli, PhD is an associate professor and chair of graduate education programs in the School of Education at The College of St. Scholastica in Duluth, Minnesota. She administers the online Master of Education, Graduate Certificates, and the Graduate Teaching Licensure programs. Dr. Takkunen-Lucarelli is a former elementary school teacher and licensed K–12 Minnesota principal. She has served on the Minnesota Digital Learning Plan Committee, Minnesota Innovations Council, and the Minnesota Academic Standards Committee for Mathematics. She is currently the co–principal investigator for the National Science Foundation grant project, TeachIT—Scaling Mobile CSP Professional Development Online. Her research and teaching interests include innovation and leadership, online learning, computer science education, educational technology, and teacher education.

Dianne L. Tetreault, MET has been in the field of education for 28 years. Ms. Tetreault has taught both reading and language arts at the middle school and high school levels. She currently works for the School District of Palm Beach County where she teaches online learners in grades K–12. In addition to teaching online, she has developed online courses in both reading and creative writing. She holds a bachelor's degree in education and a master's degree in educational technology from Central Michigan University and is currently pursuing a doctorate. Ms. Tetreault is also an adjunct professor for Barry University where she instructs students pursuing their master's degree in reading education. Ms. Tetreault is a strong proponent for online learning, reaching today's students, anywhere, anyplace, and anytime.

Norman Vaughan, PhD is a professor in the Department of Education at Mount Royal University in Calgary, Alberta, Canada. His teaching background includes graduate and undergraduate courses in educational technology, K–12 education in northern Canada, technical training in the petroleum industry, and English as a second language (ESL) in Japan. In addition, he has been involved in several consulting projects with book publishers and higher education institutions to develop online courses and resources. He has coauthored the books *Teaching in Blended Learning Environments: Creating and Sustaining Communities of Inquiry* (2013) and *Blended Learning in Higher Education* (2008), and he has published a series of articles on blended learning and faculty development. Dr. Vaughan is the co-founder of the Blended Online Design Network (BOLD), a member of the Community of Inquiry Research Group, the associate editor of the *International Journal of Mobile and Blended Learning,* and he is on the editorial boards of numerous national and international journals.

Heidi Weber, MA holds an MA in curriculum and instruction as well as a gifted endorsement. As a National Board Certified Teacher with 16 years elementary experience, Ms. Weber has taught self-contained first and second grades and third grade language arts. She is currently teaching third and fourth grade gifted reading. Recently selected as a 2015 PBS Digital Innovator, she is also the proud recipient of the 2015 OCTELA Special Distinction Award for English Language Arts (ELA) Education and the 2013 National Council of Teachers of English (NCTE) Donald H. Graves Award for Excellence in the Teaching of Writing. Ms. Weber continues to facilitate professional technology presentations at local, state, and county levels, and has presented for Staff Development for Educators (SDE) and the National Association for Gifted Children (NAGC). She presented at the 2015 International Literacy Association (ILA) Conference, the 2015 International Society for Technology in Education (ISTE) Conference, and the 2015 NCTE conference.

Index